Beyond Aesthetics

Beyond Aesthetics

Investigations into the nature of visual art

General Editor
Don Brothwell
with a Preface by
Professor
C. H. Waddington
C.B.E., Sc.D., D.Sc. LL.D. F.R.S.

Thames and Hudson
London

Printed in Great Britain by
Latimer Trend & Company Ltd Plymouth

Contents

Preface   7
C. H. WADDINGTON
Institute of Animal Genetics, Edinburgh

1   Towards a working definition of visual art   10
DON BROTHWELL
Institute of Archaeology, University of London

2   Primate perception and aesthetics   18
ANDREW WHITEN
Department of Experimental Psychology, University of Oxford

3   Visual art, evolution and environment   41
DON BROTHWELL
Institute of Archaeology, University of London

4   The development of visual perception in children   64
M. D. VERNON
University of Reading

5   Visual education for young children   88
J. M. PICKERING
Crewe and Alsager College of Higher Education

6   Visual art: some perspectives from cross-cultural psychology   98
MARSHALL H. SEGALL
Psychology Department, Syracuse University, New York

7   Trompe l'œil to rompe l'œil: vision and art   115
R. A. WEALE
Institute of Ophthalmology, University of London

8   Defective vision and art   129
    R. W. PICKFORD
    Department of Psychology, University of Glasgow

9   The artist in the population statistics   139
    PETER COX
    Government Actuary's Department

10 Psychology, culture and visual art   151
    R. W. PICKFORD
    Department of Psychology, University of Glasgow

11 The artist and education in art and design in the sixties
    and the seventies   165
    JEAN CREEDY
    Hastings College of Further Education

12 Art, morals and Western society   179
    H. R. ROOKMAAKER
    Faculty of Letters, Free University of Amsterdam

    Bibliographical References   198

    Sources of Illustrations and Acknowledgments   208

    Index   209

Preface

A stupendous number of words has been devoted already to the discussion of the nature of visual art. Nevertheless there seem to me very definite reasons why we should welcome this book which has been edited by Don Brothwell. By far the greater part of the literature about the visual arts has been written by 'insiders': by art historians, by art critics, even by artists themselves, all people who spend a great part of their lives thinking about or doing visual art. They have usually undergone a more or less prolonged period of preparation for such activities, by training in a course of Art History or Aesthetic Criticism, or by practice in an art school. Reading them – though, of course, I could not claim to have read more than a minute fraction – one often gets the impression that they have absorbed a sympathy for, which may even tend towards an understanding of, the visual arts, more by a process of apprenticeship or looking at and emphasizing with pictures, sculptures, and expressions of opinion, rather than by rational processes of logical thought. However that may be, whatever the nature of their relations with things recognized as being art objects, most of these writers can be legitimately considered to belong to the art world; to be, as I called them, insiders.

The extraordinary fact is, however, that everyone is to some extent an 'insider' of the art world, even if he has never undergone any training or apprenticeship, or even thought very much about it. The production of things which have to be considered as, at least in some way, related to art, is an extraordinarily primitive and general type of activity. Very early in the history of the human race, in the Old Stone Age, we find productions which are undeniably to be classed as art, indeed visual art of a very high standard. This is well before we have unequivocal evidence of human language, although of course it is difficult to see how such evidence could be preserved. Even earlier in human history, many of the most primitive human artefacts have not only utilitarian functions as tools, but often possess qualities of balance, or perhaps of symmetry, which give them something of the quality of art objects. The distinction between utility and aesthetic quality in tools is always difficult to draw, and perhaps for very simple tools it is senseless to try to do so.

Art, or something like art, can be recognizable even in biological systems less highly evolved than the human. Certain primates, offered some of the materials used by human artists, which are obviously exceedingly unnatural and exotic in relation to a normal primate life, produce paintings and drawings in which some aesthetic qualities may perhaps be discernible. Qualities which appeal more easily to normal human aesthetic sensibility appear among many of the natural productions of animals living their normal lives. I refer to such things as spiders' webs, birds' nests, and so on. Spiders will repair damage made to their webs, and it is debatable whether this repair is governed solely by utilitarian consideration. Certainly drunken or drugged spiders have been found to spin very unaesthetic webs. Birds that build elaborate nests, such as weaver birds, have been found to build 'better' nests in their second season, after having had a bit of practice; and here 'better' means tidier, neater, better finished, rather than merely more useful; is it then or is it not an aesthetic 'better'? Again, those primitive mammals we know most intimately – our own children – begin at a very early age to exhibit qualities which must certainly be considered as belonging to the field of art. In fact they very often develop these to a high level of achievement while still definitely within their childhood, and may suffer a regression of artistic ability as education in other types of human activity takes hold of them.

This pervasiveness of an 'art quality' throughout parts of life which have only very tenuous connections with the official art world renders one not easily satisfied with discussions of art which originate wholly from within that world. Some scholars from within the art world have, of course, argued that art is a much more fundamental aspect of human perception and behaviour than most sophisticated theories of aesthetics imply. Herbert Read, for instance, in his *Art and the Evolution of Man*, advanced the thesis that it is always by the use of his artistic faculties that man makes important new discoveries, or perceives new types of entity or relationship. Susanne Langer, whose involvement with the art world is more with the fields of music and dance than with visual art, would, as far as I understand her, claim that the primitive form of any direct experience of reality is an art experience, which is only later dissected into rational categories of time, place, and definable characteristics, when the analytical functions of the intellect have time to catch up with it. The merit of this book is that, without in any way committing its authors, either individually or collectively, to such far-reaching assertions about the importance of what I have referred to as 'art quality', it does study the involvement of that quality in many aspects of human and near-human life which are of broader relevance than the rather narrow professional art world. In such a composite work one should not, I think, expect to find any very comprehensive consensus arising from the views of scholars from many disciplines. They agree, perhaps, only on the points that art is very widespread, and very important. Their studies will convey these points to the reader in many contexts of which he was previously unaware or ill-instructed. No one who has any interest at all in the field of art can fail to be both interested and instructed.

C. H. WADDINGTON

Nothing is positive about art except that it is a concept.

RICHARD WOLLHEIM

Art is a great matter. Art is an organ of human life transmitting man's reasonable perception into feeling.

LEO TOLSTOY

The Fine Arts which no longer fulfil their original functions, and which, for this reason, are becoming degenerate, should disappear like prehistoric animals.

JEAN GIMPEL

The visual arts are one of the manifestations of quality by which a nation is judged, and no society can afford to dispense with their humanising influence.

DARTINGTON HALL TRUSTEES

I have come to see that the arranging of artists in a hierarchy of merit is an idle and essentially dilettante process. What matters are the needs which art answers.

JOHN BERGER

Painting has become – all art has become – a game by which man distracts himself.

FRANCIS BACON

The function of art and aesthetic experience as a therapeutic activity in the education of the developing child, in the production of responsive and creative individuals and as a means of communication and source of social knowledge, can be utilized only with a full understanding of the mechanisms involved.

DOUGLAS SANDLE

You choose a good, straight dwarf willow and out of the thickest part of the trunk you carve a doll which you fasten inside the hood of your boy's anorak. Willows which grow straight have more strength than the ones that straggle along the ground, and this charm will not only make a boy grow fast, but will also give him a strong back so that he can walk through life erect and fearless.

EAST GREENLAND ESKIMO

Chapter One

Towards a working definition of visual art

DON BROTHWELL

Discussion of the nature of visual art extends over many centuries, but it is not my concern here to attempt a potted history of this subject. Those wishing to read and consider the earlier views of philosophers such as Hegel, Kant and Croce can pursue these sources independently. I am not trying to dismiss philosophical questions of beauty (Carritt 1962) or the complex subject of philosophical aesthetics in general (Wollheim 1968), but want here to discuss the possibility of a more basic and simple working definition of visual art, seen from the point of view of scientists which might be regarded as sufficient to introduce some of the topics and problems which will be further considered in later chapters.

In its broadest sense, 'art' is concerned simply with human skill and ability. In the Western world the term has come to be distorted to mean non-utilitarian activities such as painting, music, poetry and so forth. In order to embrace all societies, however – and it seems to me that definitions cannot neglect the extremely variable peoples of the past and the present – aspects of art must be defined and left as broadly based as possible. In the case of the visual arts, there seems to me to be little gained, and perhaps considerable bias maintained, if we continue to talk of 'Primitive Art' or 'Fine Arts' or 'Folk Art'. Depending upon the society, its traditions, economy, religions and even politics, there can be infinite gradations between these rather rough-and-ready divisions. Anthropologists, at least, are at last settling down to believing that the best premise is simply that 'art is art is art'!

Perhaps visual art need not even be related to any material phenomenon – except perhaps a neurophysiological reaction. Advanced society thinks of artists as 'specialists' who select materials and compose and synthesize creatively from these – each resulting 'art object' being unique. But surely visual art can remain in the mind, a creative vision? Can one discard as visual art a colourful hallucination achieved by a Central American Indian eating mescal or the psilocybe mushroom?

In the case of visual and manipulative activities which give rise to art objects, they can be infinitely variable – as different as the human culture complexes that have been in existence for well over a million years. It may be simply in the form of minor carving on the outer surface of an ostrich shell water container – as a relief perhaps to the monotony of the smooth surface, or in strict traditional accord, or as a means of identification. On the other hand it may be as complex as a Maori carving, or have the disarming imaginative simplicity of a Henry Moore. The artist may have considerable social freedom to interpret the world about him or may be hidebound in his artistry by his role in, and the specific needs of, society. For all the effort and time expended on early Egyptian art work, and its long history, innovations tantamount to the appearance of a Van Gogh, Picasso or Kandinsky did not appear.

Plate 2

Plate 1
Plate 3

If we exclude the work of the majority of preliterate peoples, as well as craft or folk work, then we are left mainly with the 'specialist' artistry of more advanced society. But is this bias justified? Why define art by reference to one section only of a stratified, or at least fairly heterogeneous, society? Why can't utilitarian art work be pleasurable, creative and even 'spiritually satisfying', just as much as for instance in the creation of an elaborate Gentili candlestick? We are surely at a crossroads in visual art where in fact *all* societies and every pos- sible *art* object deserves to be considered in one perspective, if further under- standing of visual art is to be made.

Is visual art work necessarily 'tasteful', and must it always have been con- sidered – by the artist or someone relevant – as 'beautiful' or 'ugly'? Need it display 'perfection of workmanship', and if so who judges – the artist, society or a particular recipient of the work? Why, as Bahm (1972) believes, should art objects have been made 'for the purpose of producing experiences of beauty'? This may be satisfactory in philosophical aesthetics, but against studies in the human sciences in general it doesn't seem satisfactory. Abercrombie (1926) states that 'Art requires the public, just as certainly as the public requires art', but are either of these points valid on a world basis? Jean Cocteau may well be right in referring to Western society as in an age of 'monstrous vulgarity', and it is very important to question the need for a better relationship between visual art and the populace at large, but art need not be related to more than the artist, and it may well be possible (if only at a theoretical and laboratory level) to visualize a community quite devoid of intentional art work. As Jelly (1963) has pointed out, art work really has no absolute obligation to transmit or arouse feelings at all, and even if it does, what concern is this of the artist? And why should particular art work please us? It may be good, for instance, because of the intensity of the expression of conflicts, or alternatively because of the effect- iveness of the resolution of conflict (Pickford 1970). It may appear ugly and of no aesthetic interest, although some ugly art may have artistic quality (Hender- son 1966) and be very acceptable. As psychological testing has shown (Barron 1963) our approval of certain art may be as much a socially-determined approval of good breeding, or religion or authority, as a true reflection on the art work (or conversely, of course, an approval of radical, sensual, irreligious and socialis- tic works).

Can one also rely on any one to give us correct advice in these matters? Should the art critic have the last word on the qualities of art work? Lucie- Smith (1968) writes: 'What should interest the professional art critic is not just a single answer, but all the possible answers, all the possible reactions. But having explored them, he must choose.' Why? If some stratification must be attempted, however, has the present-day art critic the right training and experience to undertake such classifying? Read (1967) is not impressed by these assessors, and writes: 'But art criticism, even as an academic activity, has shown little consciousness of human psychology, and has remained a hazardous combination of subjective judgment and formal analysis.'

Advanced societies are coming upon hard times, as far as assuring spiritual, as opposed to material, contentment is concerned. Visual art is clearly a field which might carry a considerable social responsibility in the future, and if so, it is time to consider far more carefully and critically the nature of this art in relation to human communities. And this is not the time for closed-shop tactics. The artist and the art critic are only two among the many groups who are concerned with the phenomenon of visual art in societies. This field, although concerned with the intangible subject of aesthetics, deserves to be researched soberly. The careful statement on visual art in relation to society published by the Dartington Hall Trustees (1946) is a type of precise comment on art which is still all too rare. Gobbledygook in various forms is all too common. It may be patronizing and superior, as in Ballo's (1969) *The Critical Eye*, or imprecise writing excused as 'highly theoretical speculation' as in Ehrenzweig's (1967) *The Hidden Order of Art*.

I myself am in no doubt that science has an important role to play in exploring and identifying the true fabric of visual art, and it is to be hoped that a combined study of the various chapters of this book will give the reader a clearer idea of how certain of the sciences are being applied to this end. As Getzels and Csikszentmihalyi (1967) have said, there is really no great incompatibility between 'art' and 'science', and it is time this artificially sustained division was eliminated. Artistry is a 'product of human action' (Sandle 1967) and as such can be approached scientifically, and to some extent with reference to experi-
Fig. 1   mental work. For instance, colour preference can be investigated precisely and in relation to different socio-cultural groups. Differences can be considered carefully in relation to both cultural and neuro-physiological variables. Similarly,

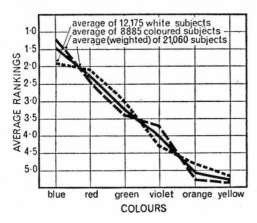

Fig. 1   *Colour preference experiments reveal a consistent average order of preference, blue being the most popular colour. This graph is a summary made by Professor H. J. Eysenck of results from many different cultural and social groups; the average order of preference is: blue, red, green, violet, orange and yellow*

preference judgments in response to patterns or combinations of colours can be precisely investigated – differences again being relatable to personality, socio-economic factors and so forth. So that visual art aesthetics can be lifted out of philosophy or art criticism and made a far more important interdisciplinary subject.

Science, of course, is having an impact on art in other ways. As Waddington (1969) says, some aspects of scientific discovery caught the imagination of artists, in particular 'a whole complex of ideas deriving from quantum physics'. This coming together of widely varying disciplines can in fact do nothing but good in the long run. Wilson (1963) also sees 'the imageries of science' as being 'startlingly interesting as aesthetic objects'. New scientific technology means perhaps further dimensions for the artist to explore (Preusser 1973). High-speed computers might even assist creativity, but it is important to remember that computer art is man-programmed art and will never go beyond this into an independent state of 'computer as artist'. Electron microscopy has similarly opened up a new world, and the latest development, stereoscan microscopy, provides a new minute world of three-dimensional shape. Plates 4–6

Of the sciences, it is the biological and social disciplines which will perhaps make the most significant contributions to the definition of visual art and artistic creativity. By this, I don't mean that visual art can or will ever be reduced to a set of equations, and Chaguiboff (1974) is right to caution those of us who get over-confident in this respect. There are still very fundamental questions to answer, which clearly have relevance to art interpretation. Why does visual memory vary in a group, and why are a few individuals in any group eidetic, i.e. endowed with a photographic memory (La Brecque 1972)? Is there, as some believe, a sub-cortical part of the brain specifically concerned with aesthetic satisfaction (Molnar 1974)? Studies on vision itself (Weale 1968) are basic to an understanding of the artist's technical performance. Differences in vision in relation to art can perhaps be checked out more certainly than most things (Hodge 1969; Pickford 1967, 1969, 1972; Trevor-Roper 1970). So far, psychology and psychiatry have produced the largest volume of work on artists and visual art, the quality of these studies varying as much as the art itself! Considerable numbers of studies are concerned with experiments in visual perception (Vernon 1970; Arnheim 1972; Haber 1970). Broader and more ambitious works include Arnheim's (1966) study *Towards a Psychology of Art*, Pickford's (1972) *Psychology and Visual Aesthetics* and Valentine's (1962) *The Experimental Psychology of Beauty*. Psychoanalytic studies of artists noticeably vary in quality, that by Schneider (1962) being more careful and readable than some.

A noticeable amount of attention has been given to the psychological aspects of the art of mentally abnormal people – that is, psychotic art, psychiatric art or psychopathological art. Visual art work derived from mentally disturbed individuals has interest not only as a possible indicator of the state of mind of these individuals, and for its possible therapeutic value, but also in terms of what it might tell us generally about the mechanisms of artistic performance (Pickford 1967, 1972; Jakab 1968). The study of drug-induced states, at times simulating mental abnormality and at others producing heightened states of perception, has also begun (Anon 1961; Hollister and Hartman 1962). The mental stability of particular artists is an interesting topic, worthy of further investigation. Pickford (1971) reports on a 'normal' artist who lived through a lengthy depressive phase and changed her art style noticeably (a so-called *stilwandel*). Slater (1970) considers the evidence for the emotional stability of 'artists' versus 'scientists' and notes that the artists are more likely to be schizophrenic and to develop 'unclear endogenous psychosis'. Considering the population as a whole, the incidence of psychopathy was between 10 per cent and 12 per cent, whereas 27 per cent of the artists were thus diagnosed. This is not to say that creative work is the result of abnormality, but perhaps one can question whether phases of psychopathy might at times provide an extra dimension of experience of some relevance to creativity.

At one extreme of psychotic art is of course the individual who may turn to art only following a phase of mental disorder, or who may show a radical transformation as a result of this mental trauma. It could be that the Swedish painter Carl Fredrik Hill (1849–1911) only really produced work of great merit following mental ill health. Schmidt, Steck and Bader (1961) discuss in detail some psychotic patients and their 'art'. Some of this work is weird visual poetry indeed, which I certainly find very appealing and which surely merits the term 'art', even though we are dealing here with individuals who are not artists, have no art experience, and can not even be considered of sound mind.

Plates I, II

So far, I have been considering the more physical and biological sciences in relation to visual art, and have suggested that they have an important part to play in redefining visual art. At the same time, I have tried to point to the need to consider art in relation to groups and populations, whether advanced societies or preliterate communities. But this question of art and society deserves further consideration.

During the past five thousand years in particular, since the emergence of farming communities which have increased their population densities and developed cultural specializations as never before, there has been a general meander upwards towards increasingly complex technological societies. We now live in a plastic-influenced runaway world where perhaps, as Hofstadter (1973) suggests, we have reached a peak in our need for more freedom from the social environments which have evolved. It is certainly to be expected that visual art will reflect something of the environment which has influenced the artist during and after development. The relationship between ethology generally and development is a field still in its infancy (Barnett 1972) but there is no doubt as to its importance – among other things in the assessment of the artist. The interaction of the visual arts and 'society' is of course complex (as illustrated by the essays in Creedy 1970), and this is especially confusing for the public at large (Phillips 1973). Visual art may reflect feelings of revolution against one or other social 'establishment' (Berger 1969; Rothschild 1972). Art work may similarly be considered to be intimately related to aspects of morality and social 'decadence' (Bahm 1968; Rookmaaker 1970). 'Man today is in revolt against the world in which he lives, against its dehumanizing tendencies, against slavery under the bosses of the new Galbraith élite, under a computerized bureaucracy, against alienation and the loneliness of the mass man. He searches frantically for a new world.' (Rookmaaker p. 196.)

Responses in visual art to the social and ethical problems of our age range from nihilism in art style to socialistic optimism. There is clearly a real danger that, just as in the art of the film wealth may be more geared to the production of 'decadent' film art than progressive and financially less rewarding films (Stephenson and Debrix 1970), so our values may be debased where the other arts are concerned. That visual art is reflecting the chaos of our age is good proof that, for all the traditional independence and bloody-mindedness of the artist, he is sensitive to the human environment about him. Might we then presume that, although some art work can be expected to go its own creative way related to the idiosyncrasies of some proportion of those who undertake this art, a further proportion might respond to the general needs of the community as a whole? And it is clear that the needs of society are considerable, if we are to remain a viable socialized species. The insensitivity to the arts in modern societies (Read 1967) must be modified as a part of further social adaptation. At a practical level, Fischer (1964) has this to say of art in the socialist society he believes in: 'The boundary between entertainment and serious art can not be clearly drawn, nor is it unalterable, least of all in a society that deliberately sets out to educate the entire people towards knowledge and culture. Entertainment should not mean silliness any more than serious art should mean boredom; both the public's education and the artists' social consciousness should prevent this.' (P. 211.) Rothschild (1972) is his conception of a better society says: 'Much will have to be done to reconstruct artistic attitudes and techniques able to serve such a culture. Indeed, a largely new type of artist may have to be recruited for the task and a new means of distributing their work will certainly be needed to bring them into contact with the public, which despite its natural appetite, has long rejected the fine arts as failing seriously to reflect common realities.' (P. 328.)

Whatever seems best in the way of a policy for relating art to society, the backbone of any changes must come through education. The seemingly 'biased' attitudes to works of art which can be found in cities today (Willett 1967) surely *Fig. 2* deserves to be modified by better art education? The public in general should also be the ultimate arbiters of architectural taste in their particular community (Edwards 1968), but it is most doubtful whether they could be so at this point in history. Design in industry and our everyday lives must be carefully thought out and managed (Farr 1966), which all too frequently does not happen – so that advanced society is full of a visual pollution. We must be visually educated, then, from the home and school to the factory and art gallery.

The principal aim of art education is stimulation, not production (Steveni 1968). To begin to cope with the great variety of art styles which have evolved or are still being created also means education in human tolerance towards others 'doing their own thing'! Incidentally, child art is not only an indication of the extent to which the child is sensitive to the visual world and can produce art work to reflect this degree of perception; the art itself may have special aesthetic qualities because it is frank and unsophisticated (Tomlinson 1947).

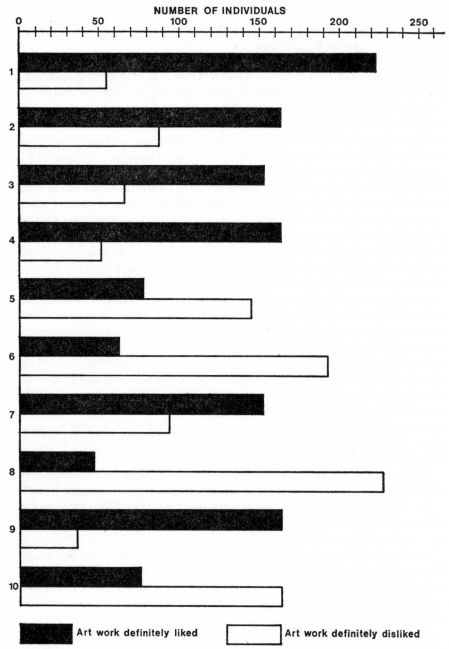

NUMBER OF INDIVIDUALS

■ Art work definitely liked   ☐ Art work definitely disliked

Fig. 2   *Variation in positive responses to visual art work on the part of a group of individuals from Liverpool. (From data in Willett 1967.) The 'Don't care' category is here omitted. The artists represented are: 1 Peter Scott; 2 Laura Knight; 3 Oskar Kokoschka; 4 Alfred Munnings; 5 Ben Nicholson; 6 Victor Pasmore; 7 Antoine Pevsner; 8 Germaine Richier; 9 L. S. Lowry; 10 Henry Moore*

. Our education must cope of course, not only with the classic aspects of visual art such as painting and sculpture, but also with such newer arts as photography, cinema and television. Indeed, Gimpel (1969) even urges that these should have greater priority as visual art media in our technological age! Drama, another human activity combining aspects of vision and sound, certainly has a place in moulding progress in future society. As Brook (1968) puts it: 'In everyday life, "if" is an evasion, in the theatre "if" is the truth. When we are persuaded to believe in this truth, then the theatre and life are one.' Edwards (1968) sees the cinema as a natural extension of drama, whereas ballet to him 'affords the highest development of the dance . . . and is a necessary supplement to the art of sculpture'. The visual arts certainly merge into other aesthetic dimensions, and in particular, combinations of sound and vision perhaps offer the best avenues for approaching maximum numbers of individuals in communities.

But to return to the beginning. My task here has been to introduce the various studies by providing a 'background' on the question of visual art. My intention has been to demonstrate that the question of the nature of visual art is a complex one, and that the artist himself and the art critic are by no means the only ones who have a contribution to make to this subject. A scientific attitude to art is by no means incompatible with the nature of art, and the subject must be viewed at both the individual level, and in relation to the population at large – whether this is a preliterate community or an advanced technological one. We must see art both as an expression of some inner mechanisms of one individual in relation to his biology and environment, and at the same time as an aesthetic matter which deserves to have wide repercussions in any society. We all have some responsibility for the art within our own community, which means that at an individual, educational and group level, particularly in this chaotic world, we neglect art at our own peril.

Chapter Two

Primate perception
and aesthetics

ANDREW WHITEN

INTRODUCTION. WHY SHOULD WE BE INTERESTED IN PRIMATE AESTHETICS?

There are several reasons for an inquiry into those responses of monkeys and apes which seem to indicate some sense of aesthetics. My own interest, as an ethologist trying to understand why I am also a painter, centres on the expectation that it may throw some light on a question so basic that it is seldom asked: why does this thing 'visual art' (or indeed any art at all) exist, an apparently universal product of man's nature?

The motivation behind, and even some of the overt expression of, most of man's behaviour does make sense in evolutionary terms. Feeding, sexual behaviour, social and family bonds, tool-use, status-seeking, aggression, and even the play of infants; all are displayed both by humans and chimpanzees, and their existence can be understood in terms of their contribution to the survival of individuals of both species as they passed their genes from generation to generation over the past several million years. But what drove man to start painting? Is the urge to create perhaps a functionless (in terms of survival value) side-effect of functional characteristics of the higher primates? If so it may perhaps be elicited in apes, and a study of their responses may lead to a better understanding of the nature of visual art.

Desmond Morris, in his book *The Biology of Art* (1962), pointed out that the traditional sources of an understanding of the origins of art – prehistoric cave paintings, the art of primitive peoples, the creations of infants and the mentally handicapped – are all highly differentiated art forms in their own right. In contrast the responses of monkeys and apes provide simple material, more amenable to analysis. But before describing this I should say a little about the way primates see the world.

PRIMATE VISION

The apes and the monkeys of the Old World have vision which appears to be essentially similar to ours. Those species which have been studied have colour vision similar to normal human trichomats; not enough have been investigated to know if there are monkey equivalents of the several variant types of colour vision – colour 'blindness' – to be found in the single species of man (DeValois and Jacobs 1968). The ability to discriminate hues has been shown to be similar in chimpanzee and human (Grether 1940). Fewer studies have been made of the less closely related New-World monkeys and lower primates, but their colour vision appears to be generally less well developed, and indeed many of the prosimians are nocturnal and have little use for colour vision. We may guess, then, that our present way of seeing colour has a history dating back to around 45 million years ago, when the Old-World monkeys evolved away from the primitive primate stock.

Little attention has been paid to reasons for the evolution of colour vision; it may have helped in spotting ripe fruits and other specific food items, and in differentiating branches and foliage, which could have been important to an animal which depended for its survival on rapid movement through the trees. This latter factor must also have been responsible for the development, early in primate evolution, of binocular vision. Fossils show that primates of 70 million years ago had their eyes on the side of the head, as does a rat. The two eyes would thus see different things. By 60 million years ago the eyes had moved round to the front of the head, so their views overlapped, permitting precise estimation of the distances of objects. Clearly such a system was very valuable to an arboreal animal which had to jump from branch to branch.

Thus two important features which have made possible coloured paintings and three-dimensional sculpture (colour vision and depth perception) we owe to our arboreal ancestors. However our sensory characteristics also impose biological constraints on our art forms; our range of colour is limited to our visible spectrum for example – unlike bees we cannot see ultraviolet. Our acuity of vision cannot match that of a hawk, to whom a miniature would seem merely impressionist, and we are also able to fixate only a small area at any one time. These points may seem petty, but I think that when we are tempted into haughtily thinking that there are no limits to human art, it is worthwhile remembering that the forms it can take are indeed limited by that fraction of the known animal senses with which we have been endowed through the processes of mutation and natural selection. Whether or not there are biological principles which actually govern the nature of ape and human visual art within these sensory limits is dealt with later.

APE PICTURE-MAKING

We sometimes think of a piece of human art as a communication between artist and observer; certainly each is aware of the other in the aesthetic event. In the analysis of primate aesthetics, however, the two halves of the process are split. The ape artist does not consider (we imagine) the likely responses of his viewing public, and his *creations* are studied in isolation. It seems equally likely that a monkey's visual preferences for pictures are independent of the means by which these were produced, and so aesthetic *responses* to works of art are also studied separately. In this section we shall be concerned only with the creative act. The human visual art of today is possible only through the lucky combination in our species of the visual abilities already discussed together with the beautifully flexible hand, and a high degree of intelligence and curiosity. Each of these qualities evolved because they performed functions advantageous to survival, and they are all present in the great apes – less well developed than in humans but more so than in lower primates. It is therefore not surprising that the great apes – the chimp, the gorilla and the orang-utan, appear to make the best subhuman artists.

Wolfgang Köhler, in his *Mentality of Apes* (1925), gave one of the first accounts of spontaneous 'painting' in captive chimpanzees. When first given lumps of clay the animals merely licked and chewed them, but quite soon 'the painting of beams, iron bars and walls grew to be quite a game on its own'. What is important here is that the activity seemed to be an end in itself.

Similar spontaneous behaviour was observed by W. N. Kellogg and his wife (1933) in a young chimpanzee, Gua, which they kept in their home; when Gua's breath condensed on the window-pane, she would make marks in the misted area using either the nail or tip of her index finger. The Kelloggs were attempting to compare Gua's development with that of their infant son, and this behaviour struck them as being comparable to the scribblings of the child.

Several such anecdotal reports of ape creativity exist, and they are listed by Morris (1962). However only two serious studies (Schiller 1951; Morris 1962) have focused specifically on such responses, and these must be described in detail.

Unfortunately Paul Schiller died before publishing the results of his experiments, but he left more than 200 drawings made by an eighteen-year-old female chimpanzee, Alpha. K. S. Lashley, who had been closely involved with the study, took it upon himself to publish the work, basing the text on his recollections of Schiller's interpretations. Alpha had shown an interest in drawing for a number of years, begging for any pencil and notebook she saw, and if given them, retiring to a corner of her cage to scribble with great concentration. It was noted that she tended to mark the corners of the paper, and this suggested the application of formal tests with papers already marked in some way. To do this, each test sheet was clipped to a board which could be presented for some period (10–80 sec.) and then withdrawn from the cage before Alpha could make her usual final response of tearing the paper up. She was provided with one or two coloured pencils.

Plate 7   Desmond Morris was more fortunate in his choice of a very young chimpanzee, Congo, because no cage was required and the animal's efforts could be supervised directly. Alpha was allowed to sit in a high chair, provided with a pencil, and presented with one sheet of paper at a time. Since Congo was only the second ape artist to be studied, he was given tests similar to those which Schiller had used, and his responses may be compared to those of Alpha.

1 Drawing on blank paper

Alpha typically made short strokes in the corners of the sheet, then the margins, finishing by filling in the centre with coarse lines. On only two or three occasions did she ever mark the frame in which the paper was held. Similarly Congo always kept his drawing within the space of the paper. This may seem trivial, but as Morris points out, 'simple as this achievement may sound from a human standpoint, it is nevertheless the whole basis of visual composition and its existence in the chimpanzee forms the foundation on which all other compositional tendencies are built'.

During the course of these experiments the drawings changed considerably. Alpha's early ones were uncomplicated, but there was a gradual tendency to introduce rambling lines and zigzags, and towards the end of the six-month study her drawings consisted principally of heavy strokes in the middle of the paper. A similar stylistic change had been noted between early and later drawings of a young chimp called Joni, which was kept by Nadie Kohts and later compared with her child (1935). The simple lines of Joni's early work gave rise to a more varied style, with long bold lines being criss-crossed by shorter marks.

Fig. 1
Fig. 2

Fig. 3

Fig. 1 (Far left) *Early drawing by Alpha. White ground, blue and red crayons, 3 min. (After Schiller 1951)* Fig. 2 (Left) One *of Alpha's later drawings, showing her change in style. White ground, black and blue crayons. (After Schiller 1951)*

Fig. 3 *Four drawings from the Russian study by Kohts showing: a, early scribble by chimpanzee Joni; b, early scribble by the experimenter's son Roody; c, later drawing by Joni showing greater complexity but no imagery; d, later drawing by Roody showing development of recognizable image. (After Kohts 1935, from Morris 1962)*

(a)   (b)   (c)

(d)

Figs 4, 5

Plate 3,
Figs 6, 7
Plate 8

Congo showed a similar change over the two years of the study; his early drawings were simple compared to the later bold work, which is again different from that of Joni. Morris also notes the development of a characteristic 'fan pattern', which occurred in 15 of Congo's 40 drawings, and in over 70 further cases of painting. Each line of the fan was started at the top of the page and drawn towards the animal, producing a rhythmical radiating design which appeared both in isolation and with other markings in pencil drawings, pastels, brush and finger paintings. One's first impression is that this could be simply the result of the animal using the easiest mechanical arm movements to fill the space. However, Morris described some behavioural details which in his opinion support the view that the ape may have developed some sort of 'fan image' in his mind, and it is this which became the prime source of the image expressed on the paper. The first point was that if Congo was distracted from drawing, he sometimes returned to complete the pattern using his other hand. Secondly Congo always drew the lines towards him, until suddenly one day 'a strange intensity seemed to overtake him and with soft, almost inaudible grunts he began laboriously to make a fan, starting each line at or near a central point and spreading it away from him. As each line was marked out, he could be seen carefully studying its

Fig. 4 *Early drawing by Congo. (After Morris 1962)*

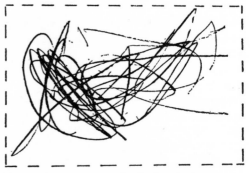

Fig. 5 *Later, more complex drawing by Congo.*
(After Morris 1962)

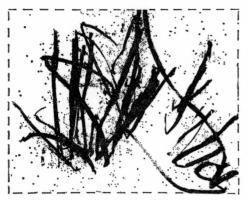

Fig. 6 *A 'fan' drawn 'in reverse' by Congo.*
(After Morris 1962)

Fig. 7 *A 'looped fan' by Congo.*
(After Morris 1962)

course, so that it radiated away in a fresh direction from those already made. The fan was therefore similar in appearance to any normally produced one, but had been drawn completely in reverse.' The third observation suggesting a fan image was that in one painting a small but well-formed black fan was drawn off-centre, using a new set of arm movements.   Plate III

As time passed the fan evolved into several related forms, such as a fan split into two halves, sometimes together with a central blob and a 'looped fan' in which lines were drawn out and in again in one movement. This elaboration of a 'theme' with subsequent minor variations is also to be observed in the chimpanzee's play and also, of course, in human art.   Plate IV

2 Influence of a single figure

In order to understand Alpha's preferences for marking corners, Schiller made tests with marks already on the paper. The results were quite striking. If a figure more than about an inch in diameter was placed on the paper, Alpha marked within it. Only in three out of 25 tests did she make a significant number of marks outside the figure.   *Figs 8, 9*

However if the figure was less than one inch across, it was rare for Alpha to keep her marks within it, although only once in 21 tests did she respond as if to a blank sheet by corner-scribbling; in the other cases this response was inhibited and her scribbling seemed to be affected by the position of the figure. If the figure was close to the middle of the sheet, it was used as a starting point for scribbling, but more interesting was the response to a figure presented off-centre, for this seemed to evoke a tendency to 'balance' the drawing.   *Fig. 10*

Fig. 11

A rudimentary sense of composition in apes was thus implied, and Morris investigated this further with Congo, who had already shown that tendency to mark on central figures which was characteristic of Alpha (although unlike Alpha he did not confine his scribbles within figures more than two inches across). Morris presented 33 test sheets with two-inch offset squares, and in only three of these did the presence of the figures appear to have no effect. In only a further three was the figure itself marked with no attempt at balancing. Where the remainder were concerned, about half produced both marking of the figure and balancing of the picture and half balancing only. The frequency of marking figures which were offset was in fact only 58 per cent, as opposed to 92 per cent for centrally placed figures.   *Fig. 12*

Fig. 13

Morris pointed out that we must make a distinction between two possible strategies which could have been used by the chimp in making these responses. One is 'space-filling'; that is, an attempt to mark in the middle of the space between the figure and the furthest side of the sheet. The other is 'true balance', in which the (perhaps more sophisticated) aim would be to mark at a point equally offset from the centre. In sixteen of the tests Congo had scribbled in a concentrated patch which made it possible to make measurements and thus to attempt a distinction between the two strategies. The results indicated that when the figure was displaced as much as 3 or 4 inches from the centre of the sheet, Congo tended towards 'space-filling', for in six of the ten cases the scribble patches were within ½ inch, and in three cases within 1 inch, of the space centre.   *Fig. 14*

Fig. 14

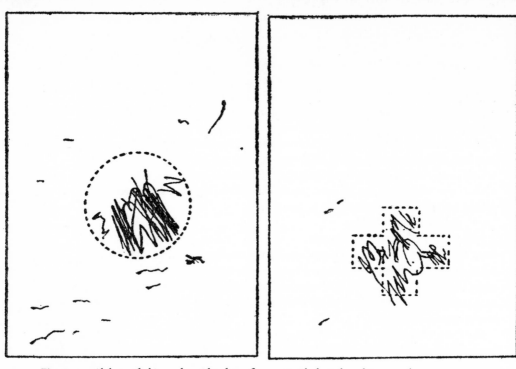

Figs 8, 9 *Alpha made his marks within large figures. 8, Black circle, white ground, green crayon, 3 min.; 9, white cross, black ground, yellow crayon, 1 min. (After Schiller 1951)*

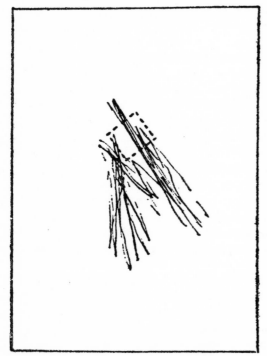

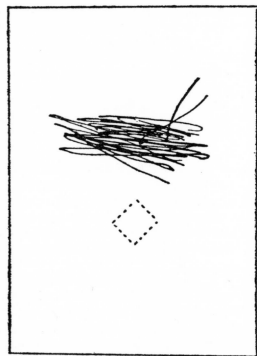

Fig. 10 *A small figure placed near the centre was used as a starting point for scribbling. Green square, white ground, green and blue crayons, 10 sec. (After Schiller 1951)*

Fig. 11 *An example of Alpha's 'balancing' an offset figure. Green square, black ground, green and blue crayons. (After Schiller 1951)*

Fig. 12 *Marking of central figure by Congo. (After Morris 1962)*

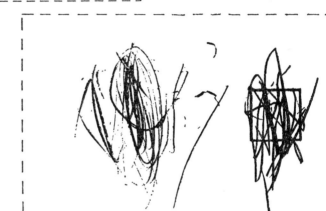

Fig. 13 *Marking of offset figure, together with balancing. (After Morris 1962)*

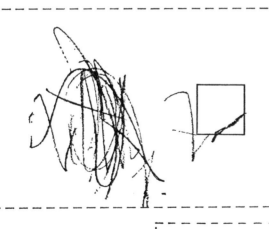

Fig. 14 *Balancing by space-filling. (After Morris 1962)*

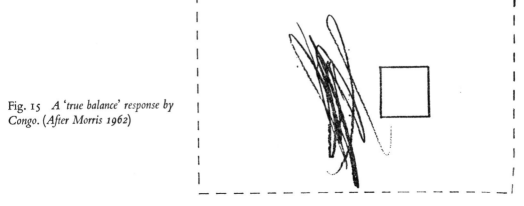

Fig. 15 *A 'true balance' response by Congo. (After Morris 1962)*

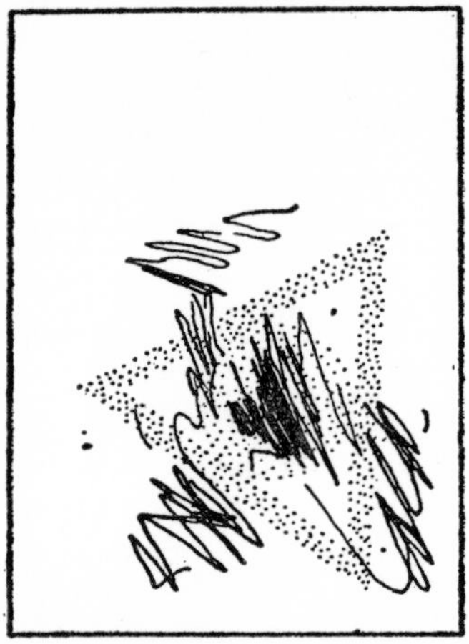

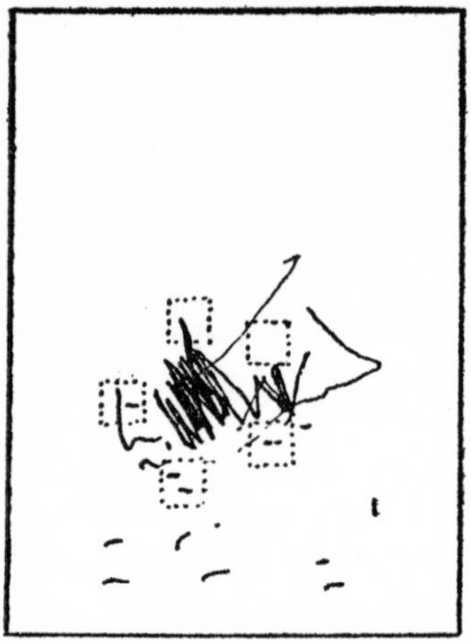

If the figure was displaced only 1 or 2 inches from the centre there was evidence of true balance, four of the six patches being within ½ inch, and two within 1 inch, of the true balance point. Bearing in mind the difficulties of estimating the centres of such scribbles, the small number of tests made, and the proximity of the space centre and true balance points (especially for the two-inch displacements) we must admire Morris's perceptive analysis but at the same time be wary of regarding his conclusion – that there was a real dichotomy – as proven. Nevertheless the tendency to balance a picture, whether by space-filling or true balance, was clearly evidenced as a chimpanzee compositional ability held in common with Alpha, and these tests did strongly suggest that two factors were at work.

Fig. 15

Schiller tackled responses to asymmetry in a further way, by presenting unbalanced figures of various designs, and in about half of these scribbling was concentrated in the unbalanced portion. More impressive were Alpha's responses to triangular figures, in most of which she scribbled symmetrically along the sides. Lashley notes: 'The proportion of symmetrically spaced scribbles in the total collection is so great as to argue strongly that Alpha has some feeling for a balance of masses on the page.'

Fig. 16

3 Influence of multiple figures

Alpha's response to multiple spots depended on their patterning. If they enclosed some fairly regular polygon, the response was as to a single large figure of this type. This response was variable when only three or four spots were used, but in all of eight tests with five or more spots, scribblings were confined within the figure. However if a central spot was added the response could be markedly different, consisting of little more than random scribblings.

Fig. 17

Fig. 18

Morris found that Congo appeared fascinated when several figures were presented on the sheet, and in six out of eight tests he gently marked each figure in turn. Lashley also remarked of Alpha that she would put check marks on each of several small figures, behaviour never seen when only one such figure was present.

These tests, then, gave no indication of an attempt to relate one object to another; the objects were treated separately, or if close to each other, as one object. In contrast, when Congo was presented with three vertical figures he *linked* them by using long vertical lines. This, of course, could have resulted

Fig. 19

Fig. 16 (Opposite, left) *Symmetrical marking of a triangle by Alpha. Green circle, green outline, white ground, blue crayon, 30 sec. (After Schiller 1951)*

Fig. 17 (Opposite, right) *Alpha responded to closely spaced spots as if to a large figure (cf. figs 8 and 9). White squares, black ground, green crayon, 90 sec. (After Schiller 1951)*

Fig. 18 *A central spot destroyed the tendency to mark only within the figure. White squares, violet ground, yellow crayon, 3 min. (After Schiller 1951)*

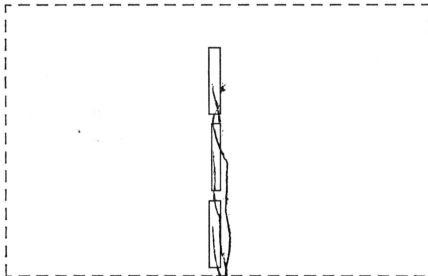

Fig. 19 *Congo drew only vertical lines over vertically placed bars. (After Morris 1962)*

Fig. 20 *Congo's joining of two vertically separated figures was particularly striking. (After Morris 1962)*

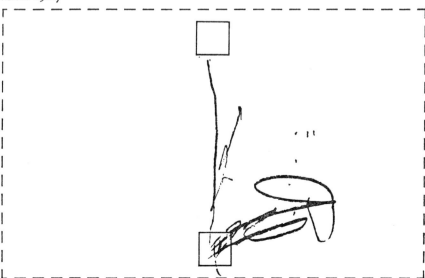

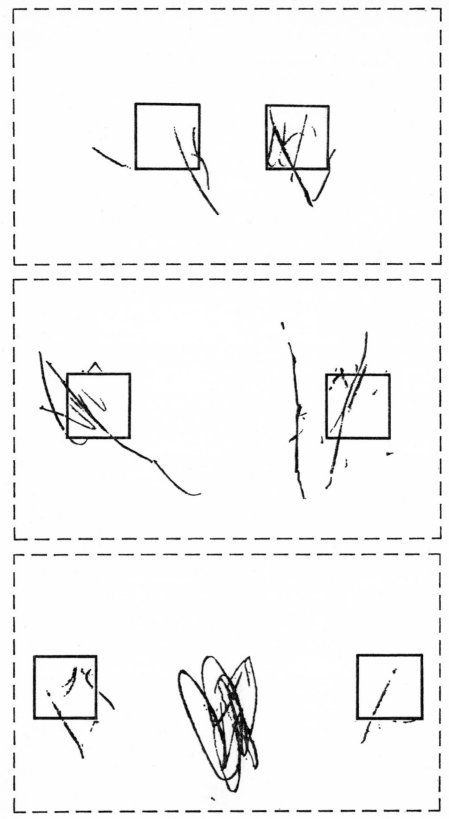

Fig. 21 *Three tests showing how the tendency to mark figures gave way to space-filling as the space was made larger.* (*After Morris 1962*)

from simply marking over the figures as one unit; more remarkable was the
drawing of a long line linking two widely spaced figures. Unfortunately   *Fig. 20*
Morris did no more tests of this kind, and does not state if the test with the two
squares followed immediately on that with the three bars.

A different response was obtained when the figures were separated horizontally, and was studied by presenting a series of three sheets in which the distance
between figures was progressively increased. When the figures were placed
centrally, they were marked in the usual way; but in the intermediate separation
the marks began to stray into the central space; the third and final picture was
balanced by bold scribbling in the central space. These responses seemed to be   *Fig. 21*
guided by two desires – one to mark the figures, and another, to mark in the
central space, which was fully operational only when the space was of sufficient
size. Clearly two such desires can conflict at any one moment, although they can
both be expressed in the same picture, and it would be interesting to study
further the sequences of behaviour, or strategies, by which apes resolve such
problems.

4 Figure completion

The question of whether the chimpanzee has some sense of composition was
asked in another way by presenting incomplete figures. Would the ape recognize the deficiency and attempt to rectify it?

Schiller made several such tests. In the first type of test outlines of triangles,
squares and various polygons were presented with one side missing. There was
no attempt to complete the figure. In the second type a solid figure was presented, but with a segment missing. In four out of six tests the figure was
marked in the usual way, but Lashley considered that in two the space had indeed
been carefully filled.   *Fig. 22*

In contrast to these rather ambiguous results, tests with dots omitted from a
pattern gave consistent completion. In all of six tests, the space left by removal of
one unit from a circle of dots was filled in. Likewise, the space was filled in eight   *Fig. 23*
out of eight tests using a 3 ×3 inch square with one of the nine units missing.

Fig. 22 *A 'figure-
completion' response
by Alpha. Blue
circle, white ground,
blue crayon, 1 min.
(After Schiller 1951)*

Fig. 23 *Comple-
tion of an incomplete
pattern. Blue squares,
white ground, blue
crayon, 1 min.
(After Schiller 1951)*

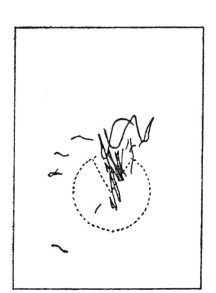
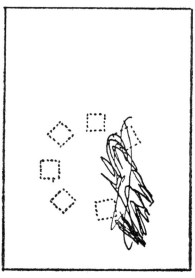

Congo was presented with tests of only the first two types, and he showed no interest in completing them; he marked in the figures as usual.

5 Use of colour

Many of Schiller's tests were interrupted after 5–30 seconds, and Alpha was given a crayon of a different colour. Lashley could find no evidence that this event had any effect on the location of the scribbling; nor did the degree of colour contrast appear to affect the response. When presented with test sheets containing two colours she would mark both, but put more marks on the lighter colour. She also appeared to have a preference for marking red and yellow, but this may have been because the red colours were simply brighter than the blue ones.

Congo was given the opportunity of *painting* in colour, a step which promised fascinating rewards. However when provided with a brush and a free choice from six pots of paint, he proceeded to mix all the paint until it was uniformly brown! It was therefore decided to offer him only one loaded brush, to be exchanged for another when the paint was used up. In this way six colours were presented in a random order. This method of constantly changing the colour seemed to have a 'boosting effect' on Congo's painting drive, and he appeared, like Alpha, to have a preference for reds and oranges, for he would sometimes continue to work with these colours, having refused blue. The paintings so produced are very fine, but this is obviously due in large part to the method of colour presentation. The study of colour painting therefore seems to have made little progress; perhaps a free colour choice could be more successfully provided by the use of the recently developed felt-tipped pens.

Plates III,
IV

6 Motivation

Alpha's spontaneous desire to scribble was responsible for initiating this whole field of investigation; Lashley notes that she would work 'with complete pre-occupation .... The motivation is intense.'

Congo's creative urge fluctuated, and Morris reported that sometimes he would lose interest after only a few paintings, while at other times 'he was insatiable and on one occasion worked non-stop for practically an hour, pro-ducing the huge total of thirty-three drawings and paintings'. On one occasion an attempt was made to film Congo's ability to balance a test-figure. He was evidently distracted by the novel situation, and although he did actually paint and draw, the balancing response was absent; he merely marked the offset figures.

Here we must also mention two other ape artists. Hermann Goja (1959) described how a male chimpanzee, Jonny (apparently sexually mature) exhibited a sexual excitation which increased with the intensity of his drawing and painting. Unfortunately Jonny seems to be the only adult male artist on record, so we do not know if he was unusual in this respect.

Another chimpanzee, Bella, showed remarkable concentration; 'the most striking thing about Bella, when she was in a good drawing mood, was her high level of motivation. Miss Hylkema (her caretaker) once made the mistake of interfering when Bella was in the middle of a drawing, with the result that she was bitten by the animal. Bella would never bite when Miss Hylkema interfered with any other activity, not even when taking attractive food away from her.' (Kortlandt 1959.)

BIOLOGICAL PRINCIPLES OF PICTURE MAKING

The fact that painting can be such a rewarding activity in itself is one of the six 'Biological Principles of Picture Making' which Morris elaborated. Clearly this is not the only motivation behind many examples of human art, but it is certainly bound up with our notions of 'high' art.

Morris's second principle is that of compositional control, the biological (as opposed to cultural) reality of which has already been illustrated by the responses of Congo and Alpha. The third principle, that of calligraphic differentiation, is perhaps less strikingly exhibited by apes. In children calligraphy rapidly evolves through formless scribbles to circles and thence human representation; Congo progressed along this course to the stage of drawing circles and marking inside them, but no further. Clearly the child possesses potential which the ape does not, but it seems reasonable to suppose that this potential is realized through that same tendency which produced a development in the style of Congo's and Alpha's drawings. The fourth principle, thematic variation, has already been illustrated by the elaboration and subsequent differentiation of Congo's fan motif. It is clearly a principle which also underlies the work of the modern professional artist.

Morris puts forward these principles only as a working theory, and certainly his last two rules are of dubious status. He suggests that the composition and point of completion of each picture is governed by a principle of optimum heterogeneity. Now, it seems to me unjustified to conclude that because Congo would frequently stop painting, he considered the painting to be of optimum heterogeneity. In addition, he sometimes covered the whole sheet with scribble, which was also Alpha's usual response if the paper was not removed. In the human case we must also ask if a picture has a universal 'absolute' optimum heterogeneity, or whether the optimum depends on the individual (artist or observer), his mood at any one time, and his culture.

Morris gives as his final principle that of universal imagery, yet strangely takes his examples from child art rather than ape art. It seems that unless we regard the scribble as an image, this principle has yet to be demonstrated in primates. The only likely candidate so far is the fan image, which occurred many times in Congo's work, and can also be discerned in one of Bella's drawings and in a photograph of a capuchin monkey scrawling on the wall of his cage. It would not be surprising if the fan did appear as a universal image, simply because of the common arm movements used by primate artists, but it seems rather premature to conclude that this is what has happened on the basis of subjective interpretation of so few examples.

THE VISUAL PREFERENCES OF PRIMATES

We now move from problems of artistic creation to those of aesthetic appreciation. Unfortunately, perhaps, this has been better studied in monkeys than in chimpanzees.

The first serious approach to this problem was made by Bernhard Rensch (1957, 1958), who tested the preferences of individuals of several species, including monkeys, for regular patterns over irregular ones. This was done by simply introducing the animal into a situation with several cards, half of which were marked with one of several regular designs, and the other half with an irregular version of this design (e.g. straight lines versus crooked lines, regular circle versus wavy circle). The monkey's 'preference' was taken to be the first card he picked up. Rensch found that 'the monkeys preferred geometrical, i.e. more regular patterns, to irregular cues. It is very probable that the course of a line, the radial or bilateral symmetry and the repetition of equal components in a pattern (rhythm) were decisive for the preference.' Rensch found his two bird subjects to have similar preferences, whereas fishes always showed preference for irregular patterns. One wonders to what extent these preferences were conditioned by the environment – perhaps the birds and monkeys lived in straight-sided cages whereas the fish were surrounded by irregular weeds. In this case it might be revealing to compare the preferences of wild and captive-reared primates.

Nicholas Humphrey has more recently (1971, 1973) designed a means of better controlling the types of visual array presented, and of measuring the degree of a monkey's preference for one view over another. The monkey was allowed to sit in a small dark compartment, which was provided with a push-button. For as long as the push-button was held down, a stimulus was back-projected on to a screen which the monkey could view through the bars on one side of the compartment, and after the button had been held for a total of 100 seconds a reward of banana pellets was given. However, the button was rarely held for more than six seconds at a time, and two different stimuli were alternately presented at each pressing. To indulge a preference the monkey had simply to hold the button down longer when viewing the preferred stimulus, so the ratio of total time spent with one stimulus to total time spent with the other provided an index of how much one stimulus was preferred to the other.

The first experiments were designed simply to see if monkeys had favourite colours and preferences for certain brightnesses. To test for the former, a series of 100-second sessions was given in which the choice was between a standard white slide and one of five plain coloured slides. All four monkeys gave remarkably similar results; the order of preference in each case was blue, green, yellow, orange and red. The percentage of time spent with the coloured slide as opposed to the white slide was in fact monotonically related to the wavelength of the light from the coloured slide. Further, the percentage preference was above 50 per cent for blue and green, below 50 per cent for yellow and orange and red; the monkeys were thus responding positively towards the former, and negatively to the latter.

1 Carved wooden door lintel. Maori, New Zealand. Chapter 1

2 Decorated ostrich egg shell drinking vessel used by Bushmen at Luderitz Bay, Namibia (south-west Africa). Chapter 1

3 HENRY MOORE *Two-piece carving interlocking*. Chapter 1

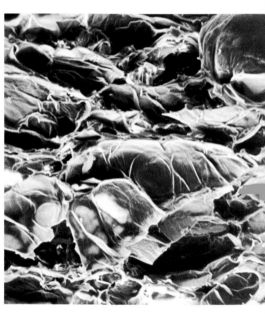

4–6 Minute shape variation as revealed by a stereoscan electron microscope Chapter 1

7   The chimpanzee, Congo, making a standardized experimental drawing. Chapter 2

8   Fan pattern drawn by the chimpanzee, Bella. Chapter 2

9 Masked dancers with striped body paint. Ingaladdi, Australia. Chapter 3

10 *Ghost Gum at Palm Padd* Painting by the Austral aboriginal artist, Albert Namatj Chapte

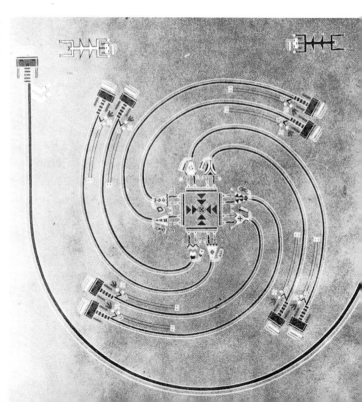

11 Navaho Amerindian sand painting, 'Whirling Rainbow'. Chapter 3

Brightness preference was determined by pairing the standard white slide with white slides of differing brightnesses, and the results were similar in that percentage preference was monotonically related to brightness over the range used (0·2–2·2 log-foot-lamberts). The colour and brightness results were also similar in that the average degree of preference for a stimulus changed little over many sessions, whereas *within* each 100-second session there was a change towards greater expression of the preference, which Humphrey called 'sensitisation'. For example, a monkey might start by showing 60 per cent preference for white over red, but by the end of the session be choosing the white slide 80 per cent of the time. When the monkey was tested again later, this change in preference would have been 'reset' – in this example the monkey would start off again with a preference of 60 per cent.

When Humphrey moved on to test preferences for pictures, the time-course of the response was found to be quite different. The stimuli used were thirty coloured photographs, which could be classified as either 'men' (e.g. a portrait of the keeper), 'monkeys' (two infants playing), 'other animals' (cow), 'foods' (banana), 'flowers' (daisy) or 'abstract painting' (Mondrian: *Composition*, 1920). Each was paired with a plain white slide in a series of 100-second choice sessions. The first few sessions revealed negative preferences, the monkeys preferring to watch the plain slide, and it was clear from watching them that this was simply the result of fear of novel stimuli. However, testing was continued with two of the monkeys, and by the fourth or fifth session the pattern of response changed to one of initial positive preference which quite rapidly waned towards indifference. This pattern was observed with each class of photograph, but there were differences in the absolute percentage preferences and the rates of decline. Judging from the preferences in the first 100 seconds of testing, the order of preference was: other animals/monkeys/men/flowers/paintings/food.

It seems likely that the decline in preference with time was a result of increasing familiarity with the picture, and indeed Humphrey found that 200 seconds of pre-exposure to the picture before the choice session very much reduced the initial preference, although it was still significantly above 50 per cent. Tests with cartoon films showed that constantly changing pictures would maintain the preference at a high level indefinitely.

One may well ask whether such preferences have anything at all to do with aesthetics. Humphrey answers this question by distinguishing between the pattern of response to fields of light (steady positive or negative preferences with 'resetting' and 'sensitisation') and the response to pictures (initial positive preferences turning to indifference unless the novelty factor was somehow maintained). These two different patterns seem to reflect the dichotomy in the ways both we and monkeys may exploit our senses; that is, we may look at a stimulus 'purely for pleasure' or 'purely for interest'. The pleasure dimension – which we might regard as 'purely aesthetic' – can be either positive or negative, and is little affected by novelty (e.g. the responses to blue and red) whereas the interest or curiosity dimension is positive and changes only towards indifference as the novelty of the stimulus wanes (e.g. the response to photographs).

The two types of response may operate quite independently, although if they operate at the same time – as clearly they often will – their effects will be combined in the final expression of preference. In order to study this interaction, Humphrey presented various combinations of stimuli, such as 'red' photographs and 'bright' film loops. The results showed that the effects were not simply additive, for with red continuous films the preference for the changing pictures was hardly affected by the negative preference for red, and with the red film loops the red only had a negative effect once the novelty had worn off.

Humphrey has incorporated this finding, that interest overrides distaste, into the five simple principles which, he suggests, govern these monkeys' preferences:

'1   Two independent kinds of relationship obtain between the monkey and the stimulus, called "interest" and "pleasure/unpleasure".

2   When there is a choice between two stimuli, the monkey ranks them according to their relative interestingness and relative pleasantness.

3   If one stimulus is "appreciably more interesting" than the other, the probability that the monkey will prefer it is 1.

4   If one stimulus is "appreciably more pleasant" than the other, the probability that he will prefer it is 1 unless the other stimulus is appreciably more interesting.

5   If neither stimulus is either appreciably more interesting or pleasant, the probability that he will prefer each is $\frac{1}{2}$.'

The monkeys showed remarkably little individual variation in their preferences, and from the quantitative model Humphrey was able to *predict* with a high degree of accuracy the preference which a monkey would show for a stimulus which combined elements of both interest and pleasure/unpleasure. This was possible because the separate elements were simple and already defined (e.g. redness versus pictorial content) and it is a problem for the future to be able to tease apart these elements in an already constituted work of art.

With these principles in mind we may return to consider the creative act. We do not yet know the preferences of apes for ape pictures, but we may guess that visual feedback is an important part of painting for apes – that is they would not do it if it did not produce marks on the paper. It seems likely then, that creative responses may be affected by this feedback in the same way – by interest and pleasure/unpleasure.

Interest or curiosity may well be the prime motivation behind early ape (and child) drawing; thus Morris (1958) on Congo's initiation: 'I held out the pencil. His curiosity led him towards it. Gently I placed his fingers around it and rested the point on the card. Then I let go. As I did so, he moved his arm a little and then stopped. He stared at the card. Something odd was coming out of the pencil. It was Congo's first line. Would it happen again? Yes it did, and again and again.' Curiosity, so characteristic of primates, and one of the reasons for their evolutionary success, must similarly have been at the root of the evolution of human visual art. Clearly the desire to create visual art is latent in apes but it seems that only in captivity does it ever surface, either spontaneously or under provocation. One group of wild chimpanzees has been intensely studied for over ten years, but although they make and use simple tools (Lawick-Goodall 1971) they have shown no behaviour which might be construed as comparable to the efforts of, for example, Alpha, or Köhler's chimps (Lawick-Goodall 1973). The simplest interpretation of this difference would be that captive apes are freed from the chores necessary to everyday survival, and their curiosity thus leads them to exploit the greater range of creative tools available. Yet this cannot be the whole story, for wild chimps appear to have a fair measure of leisure time which they spend in play and grooming, and they have access to, for example, mud, as Köhler's chimps had access to clay.

Turning to the pleasure/unpleasure dimension of feedback – the aesthetic sense – we may point at those creative acts which imply some sort of compositional control. But why has nature equipped the chimp and the human with such ability? The interest or curiosity dimension of art can be seen as an offshoot, functionless in terms of survival value, of the functional exploratory tendency which has made primates so good at adapting to the capricious conditions of life in the wild. But if a pure aesthetic sense is a functionless offshoot of some other functional attribute, what is this? This is a difficult question which nobody so far has been able to answer, though N. Humphrey (1974) has attempted to do so. Perhaps it should not be regarded as a single question – the origin of each aesthetic response might be explained independently, and so far we have to deal with three which have been demonstrated in primates; the preferences for blue/green colours, bright light and the ability to compose pictures. We may perhaps have a clue to the colour preference in the behaviour of frogs which, when frightened, will instinctively jump towards blue colours, and away from green ones (Muntz 1962). This behaviour guides them away from grass and into water, a tendency which has obvious survival value. The equivalent for monkeys would be a preference for blue/green (foliage) over red/orange (earth colours). Blue and green slides may thus be relaxing to monkeys, and in this context, we should note that a human subject placed in a blue-coloured room does become more relaxed; blood pressure, heart rate and breathing are all reduced.

The preference for bright light may be interpreted simply as a desire, which has obvious survival value, to see things – even the inside of the testing chamber – as well as possible. Such a desire would be fulfilled by increasing light intensity, but presumably only up to a point which was not reached in Humphrey's experiment, after which preference would decrease again because of the pain produced by very bright light.

A sense of composition, almost synonymous with general visual aesthetic sensibility in humans, is the most difficult attribute to explain. I can only suggest that its existence may have something to do with the development, in the brain of an arboreal animal, of a capacity to handle notions about complex spatial relationships, but this does not explain exactly why a chimp should derive pleasure from balancing a picture.

We may note here that Humphrey's pleasure principle coincides with Morris's principle of composition and consider the other relationships between the two sets of principles. Firstly then, either or both types of preference – pleasure or interest – could contribute to self-rewarding activation. Secondly, compositional control seems more likely to be motivated by pleasure than curiosity, whereas the opposite is so for calligraphic differentiation and thematic variation. Finally, although both types of preference will be involved to some extent in all of those principles, they could actually conflict yet reach some compromise in a principle of optimum heterogeneity.

Primate aesthetics, then, may be subjected to this sort of simple analysis which is difficult if not impossible with more complex human art. The relevance of the former to the latter is that it provides a unique background against which we may try to understand the origins and fundamental nature of visual art in our species and in the individual.

Chapter Three

Visual art, evolution and environment

DON BROTHWELL

During the past four or five million years the hominids, a line giving rise to *Homo* perhaps over a million years ago, were able to evolve because of the complex interaction between their biology and their mental processes. Their cultural development was a survival measure, part of the adaptive process of the group, determined by the 'pressures' of their environment and their variability (including mental traits – general intelligence, perception, innovatory ability). Once behaviour changed and the early stages of material culture emerged, there was a 'feedback', a reciprocal influence on the biology of the population – which could be in terms of survival, fertility and so on. In man, then, the Darwinian rule also embraced the 'survival of the *culturally* fittest'. We assume that the earliest stages of cultural development were perhaps mainly concerned with modifications in social interaction, the beginnings of collective hunting, the production of basic rather all-purpose artifacts. As yet there is little evidence to the contrary, although the assumption might be wrong. One of the early hominid (australopithecine) sites has produced a stone which appears to have found its way from the deposits from which it was derived – presumably by being carried – and it is of considerable interest that the stone is 'face'-shaped. *Fig. 1*

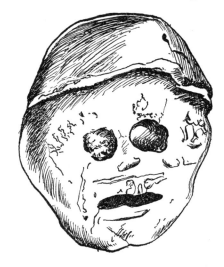

Fig. 1 *A rounded pebble, from an early hominid site at Makapansgat, Transvaal. The markings forming a 'face' are natural, but the stone does not seem to occur 'naturally' in the local deposits*

Although it owed its shape and markings to natural causes, one can reasonably question the appearance of this 'face' made of 'foreign' stone at the site, and ask whether some early hominid had been sufficiently perceptive to see and be attracted by the apparent face object, and carry it back to his habitation area (Oakley, personal communication). The major problem is, of course, that although we see the 'beginnings' of advanced primate aesthetics in the studies of great apes (Morris 1961; Schiller 1951), without much good material evidence, it is impossible to even guess usefully about the perceptive and 'artistic' capacity of the very early hominids.

Before entering too deeply into this subject of visual art in relation to the great range of human societies, past and present, perhaps I should make some brief comment about terminology. Claerhout (1965) and others have discussed the concept of 'primitive' applied to art, and there is clearly growing feeling that the less we try to label forms and varieties of art, the better. A variety of names, some alternatives, have been used to refer to the art of various populations, including 'primitive', 'tribal', 'pre-civilized', 'ethnic', 'ethnological', 'preliterate', as well as more culture-oriented terms 'Palaeolithic', 'Bushman', 'Pre-Columbian' and so on. One might similarly classify aspects of visual art in relation to peoples. Obviously, to some extent we must refer to painting, rock art, sculpture, tattooing, dance, and even body deformation. But these can be complexly interwoven together and need not be simply and precisely correlated with items of belief, ritual or symbolism. The field of art must be regarded as a whole, even though one can see themes – art as a mode of communication, art as styles, similar communication by different objects, art as aesthetic response, perceptive innovation versus formalized design, and so forth.

The problems of considering the nature of art and art objects in populations of ancient times is of course far greater than in the study of recent peoples. There are considerably more difficulties in asking such questions as: Why was the art object made and what does it represent? Why is there variation in style or between regional samples? When and by whom was it made? Has it practical value of a material kind or is it involved with aspects of religion, mythology or other beliefs and social roles? Does it tell us much about the skill and perception of the particular artist or group of artists? Was the production of the art object technically easy or complex and difficult? How 'original' is the work or is it in a well defined already established style? Willett (1971) states that, in the case of recent African art, we can't hope to understand the intention of the artist purely by examining the work – but rather there is a great need for field-work, in which the artist is seen in relation to his particular life and to society in general. Clearly there are great difficulties therefore in producing more than tentative generalizations in the case of past peoples, but nevertheless some progress is being made.

Fraser (1962) separates 'primitive art' (the 'high art of low cultures') from crafts, folk art ('the subordinate art of high cultures'), and the art of advanced society; my concern in this brief review is to look for broad patterns of change, basic 'rules' linking art with society and environment, and reasons for change and variation. Clearly some division of visual art forms could be made, and because of the indisputable variation in human aptitudes and capabilities there must clearly be a gradation in the technical perfection and creative distinctiveness of works of art in any society. But the primary need of all comparative art studies, where varying cultures are considered, is to see visual art in relation to the society and its environment. This approach seems to be used all too infrequently as the starting-off point for art studies. Forge (1965) in his excellent study of some aspects of art in New Guinea (Sepik river basin) correctly emphasizes that the art, myths, and rituals appear to be completely interlocked and interdependent. Moreover, he feels that all visual symbols present in such a community are 'statements' about the people and their culture in relation to their environment. These 'statements', he says, 'may not be totally conscious in either the creators or the beholders of the art – who do these things because they are correct – but which are relevant to and essential for the existing social structure.' Moreover, in the particular communities he is concerned with, he further concludes that 'these statements are not usually made, and possibly even cannot be made, by other means of communication' (p. 30). Wolfe (1969) has similarly been concerned with the nature of art in relation to society – in particular the variation between communities in the apparent quality and quantity of art work. One possible answer, he suggests, is the alienation of males from local lineage centres, as a result of matriliny, and in the resulting emotional response which encourages aesthetic expression in the men. Yet again, Fischer (1961) is interested in the connections between art forms and sociocultural conditions, and realizes that further, more penetrating questions must be asked beyond simply 'how do art, society and natural environment' interact. As he says, it may be especially significant to ask rather why there is a differential selection of materials within the environment, and why are some potentially useful items ignored?

Visual art, of course, should be considered not only in relation to the complex social status quo in a community at one time, but when possible through time. For social change, whatever the reason, must ultimately lead to changes in the art of the group; although the degree and nature of the changes will vary according to such factors as population size and social complexity, 'level' of material culture attained, as well as chance phenomena linked with 'emotional' climate and creative potential. And not only has change gone on over many thousands of years in human societies, but it is still occurring even in the most advanced cultures. The repercussions on art of world changes in advanced societies over the past half century, might be seen as a rather depressing massive pandemic climax to a cycle of events which has occurred in miniature many times before. But there is much difference of course between a simpler non-literate society and an advanced Western culture. Charlotte Otten (1971) in her introduction to *Anthropology and Art* sums up the situation well when she says 'Our Western art only partially and sporadically carries this freight of prescribed symbolic meaning functioning simultaneously on many levels, reinforcing cultural values and at once enlarging, sensitizing, and unifying our perceptions. Accordingly we are experiencing along with the fragmentation of our value system, the disintegration of symbolic unity and coherence in art. This is, of course, why art invariably deteriorates and becomes peripheral when internal cultural integrity is disturbed and dislocated by new elements in acculturation and the breakdown of a former system of values.' (P. xv.)

BIOLOGICAL VARIATION, EVOLUTION AND VISUAL ART

The basis of all our evolution, both physical and cultural, is the potential variation in any human community – especially that controlled at a gene and chromosome level. Our capacity to adapt to, to survive, varying environmental situations was initially intimately bound up with this physical variation. The earlier hominids, our ancestors, were lucky in having sufficient genetically-determined variation to permit significant increases in brain size to take place during the past million years. Hand in hand with this cerebral increase has been the elaboration of material culture – at first very humbly in the lower Pleistocene hunters and tool-makers but eventually resulting in the magnificence of Upper Palaeolithic cave art and later still in the first early civilizations. So the elaboration of visual art could not have happened had the increase in brain size not been of special value to the hominids.

Inherited variation is of course not only related to time, but also to space. What I mean is that at any point in time, human populations will show gene frequency differences for particular characteristics. Genetically-controlled differences in brain size or skin colour could be seen on a geographical basis in 500,000 BC as in AD 1974 (the patterns of variation at these two dates by no means being the same). Unfortunately, most of the interesting differences between people, including I.Q., creativity potential or artistic output, are a combination of multifactorial (many gene) inheritance and environmental influence – not an easy complex to disentangle. Indeed, there are still considerable problems in analysing differences in mental abilities, and as Bodmer (1972) has said, although there may well be a genetic component to signify intelligence differences between groups, we lack sufficient data to resolve this question.

In the earlier stages of our cultural evolution, and perhaps especially during the Pleistocene period, any slight improvement in our mental capabilities had selective (and thus survival) advantage. But with the increasing populations and cultural complexities of the earlier civilizations, artistic potential may have been wasted (or diverted to menial tasks) more and more. As regards the difficult-to-define phenomenon of genius, Eric Newton (1967) rightly points out that its recognition and contribution is just as relative to the period and society: 'the stature of genius depends as much on the existence of opportunity as on the power to seize it. In the sixteenth century Renoir would probably have been as big a man as Titian because Venice would have used him to better purpose than Paris did.' So that 'In an age in which the artist is no longer a major ingredient in the social fabric it is difficult for him to attain to full stature.' Looking at modern society as the final point so far in the long sequence of cultural elaboration, it seems more than likely that the inherent artistic potential of the world population is suffocated by the ultra-mechanized and over-specialized communities so many live in. At the other, temporally distant, end of the scale, the time consuming basic needs of the earlier Palaeolithic hunter-gatherer were similarly not conducive to a full expression of any inherited creative and artistic potential. So inherent artistic potential need not be highly correlated with the actual art objects of a society, a fact which does not make any attempt to assess the art and artists of non-literate or ancient cultures any easier. The Australian aboriginal artist Albert Namatjira adapted completely to an advanced European style of painting (Hall 1962), although genetically he and other living aborigines may be the result of some 30,000 years of independent adaptive biological and cultural evolution on that island, where indigenous art styles remain simple.

Plate 10
Plates 9,
11

Progressing beyond genetics to a neurophysiological level, there appears to be further variation pertinent to a consideration of changes in visual art in societies. In the case of colour preference, Sandle (1967) suggests that this may be some basic built-in adaptive response, originally bound up with man's evolution and varying ecology. Studies both of reactions to basic colours, and of preferences for colour combinations, suggest that aesthetic preference is by no means a haphazard matter, but that 'Variables relating to personality, socio-economic status and the physical properties of the stimulus reveal regularities in their relationships with one another.' Somewhat in contrast to this type of study has been that of Shortess (1974), who has been interested in some of the physiological limitations on aesthetic experience in the visual arts. As he points out, nervous system activity is at least part of the response to art objects, so that particular impulses it sends out will filter and accentuate sensory information and thus place constraints on, and partially define the aesthetic response. Hominid evolution has been intimately bound up with changes in the brain and nervous system, and the variation which has occurred must not be underestimated in considering the evolution of aesthetic responses. Averbal concepts of three-dimensional space (visual and tactile space fusing to form a homogeneous experience) and the occurrence of aesthetic factors in pre-hominid primates have interested Bernard Rensch (1972), who feels that experimental evidence even suggests that the brains of higher primates 'are able to accomplish more than their life in a natural state requires'. So in evolutionary terms, aesthetic potential for a hominid population may have tended to develop beyond that generally needed for the survival of the group as a whole.

It seems more than likely that the physical evolution we see represented in the incomplete fragments of various fossil hominids may be relatively insignificant compared with the evolutionary changes which have occurred at a biosocial and cultural level. Because they have left few traces it would be rash to ignore these 'unknowns', and one of the dangers of dealing with what remains as osteological or limited cultural material is that it may well provide us only with evolutionary minutiae of secondary importance, and yet divert our attention from more major – if resolvable – issues. There can be no denying that somewhere in time, perhaps five or ten million years ago, hominid innovations began, and that there was eventually a mosaic of trends aimed at the accumulation and transference of experience to successive generations, the elaboration of language to cope with this first 'cultural revolution', and perhaps later still the symbolization and sanctification of types of experience. These early cultural processes and modifications must have been intimately linked with the genetic variation present in the early hominid groups, with brain size and complexity, personality traits and so forth. Survival in relation to the environment had gone beyond simple questions of who could run from danger the fastest, and involved more and more such characteristics as sociability, educability and creativity. In their bio-cultural complexity, the hominids had pulled away from all other primates.

Regarding the use of tools, the genius of the hominids has been that they alone have continuously sought to adapt natural materials to a variety of ends – initially perhaps only economic and purely technological, but later aesthetic and ritualistic. Alcock (1972), in reviewing the evolution of the use of tools by animals when feeding concludes that 'The selective advantage enjoyed by the original tool-users in any population may be great enough to set in motion a chain of evolutionary events which can reflect the frequency of the trait in a population and a complex of factors underlying the behaviour.' (P. 469.) Moreover, as he points out, selection may favour the development of specific kinds of manipulatory play and exploratory behaviour; or tool-using may be related to types of conflict behaviour. Also, there may well be a selection differential in favour of especial attentiveness to parents or companions – a 'plagiarism' factor! A final matter which may have been of critical importance in hominid evolution, is the ease with which tool-using and other cultural knowledge could be learned. With increasing cultural information to assimilate was there a survival differential in favour of delayed maturation – producing an extended learning period? The hominids have certainly slowed down their maturation; is it on this account? It would at the same time mean a longer period for perceptive and creative development in an extended childhood.

If, as the fossil evidence at present suggests, the early erect-walking hominids were at first tropical species, by the emergence of *Homo erectus* over a million years ago he had started to move into wider and more variable environments. It was at this evolutionary level that man progressed beyond the production of crude chopping tools and a bone-tooth-horn (osteodontokeratic) culture. Fire became a part of his equipment for survival. In these respects man repeats, in a more elaborate way, a trend seen in every major tool-using species, for they have all invaded niches that are uncharacteristic of their phylogenetic groups. By later Middle Pleistocene times, between 250,000 and 100,000 years ago, wood was certainly being utilized, and stone tools were becoming very skilfully and symmetrically worked – to the extent that an appreciation of shape and proportions is evident, and one suspects that a certain aesthetic satisfaction may have been derived from the manufacture of some of these artifacts. This might be viewed as early 'applied' or 'utilitarian' art, but the reasons for manufacturing these 'tools' is by no means known and it is thus still conceivable that they may not all have had purely utilitarian value. Similarly, the absence of pigment which might have been used in body painting or of any form of musical instrument, does not preclude the possibility that dancing, singing and body ornamentation did not occur. Considering brain size (which was by then well within the range for modern man), it could be that Occam's razor might in fact be used to misrepresent and render less developed, a cultural situation which was in fact far more elaborate than we think.

Plate 12

46

By Upper Pleistocene times (*c.* 100,000–10,000 BC) we see a great elaboration of material culture. From the evidence of burials, death was clearly a pheno- menon of emotional significance; at the same time artifacts became more and more refined until highly 'sensitive' leaf points were achieved in the Solutrean period. Some burials show evidence of red ochre (?placed on the dead, or was it in fact body paint?). Then during the final thirty thousand years of the Pleisto- cene, in Europe in particular, there was the emergence of cave and rock-shelter art – some of it clearly of ritual significance.

Bannatyne (1966) sees this period of transformation from *Homo erectus* through to the skilled cave artist, who was advanced *Homo sapiens sapiens* (like modern man), as critical to the emergence of men with considerable visuo-spatial ability. The hunter who had poor spatial ability and could not dispatch an arrow or spear well was a hungry hunter, and so was his family! Thus visuo-spatial ability – the capacity to manipulate objects and their interrelationships intelligently in three-dimensional space – was at a considerable premium in the evolving hunter- gatherer species of *Homo*. And in its wake – in fact a combination of brain development and manipulative skill – was the capacity to produce advanced art work. Indeed, the sensitivity and technical expertise needed to produce advanced art work could have been latent in the hominids for two hundred thousand years or more. Only when the artistic potential had relevance at a social level – and the general cultural threshold had first to be reached – did 'Palaeolithic Art' make significant advances. Plates 13, 14

We know all too little of population density in relation to environment in Late Pleistocene times. In some areas where game was relatively plentiful, increased population numbers may have occurred, as well as periodic sedentary living. Indeed, it seems worthy of debate whether even in a prehistoric hunter community, population is the primary factor which triggers off certain aspects of further cultural development. There is, of course, a considerable literature which refers to 'Palaeolithic' or later prehistoric art – much of it from the point of view of its aesthetic appeal, or what it looks like or where it is to be found. Some of the writing is rather romantic and a lot is really quite sterile; but some publications are critical or put forward ideas which are worth further considera- tion. Koppers (1950) is suspicious of all too easy magical explanations for Palaeo- lithic art, and prefers to see the artist engaged in a 'fundamentally rational kind of artistic activity'. Morris (1966) points out that the art of Lascaux and Altamira Plates 15, 16 can't be regarded as first fumbling attempts, but clearly represents the 'mature expressions of an advanced picture-making culture, the origins of which appear to be lost forever'. He questions whether the earliest stages of art may have occurred as a self-rewarding activity, consequent on the relaxation of survival pressures. Whether referring to primate 'art', cave painting or more recent visual art, Morris considers that there are six basic principles applying to picture making: the principles of self-rewarding activation, compositional control, calligraphic differentiation, thematic variation, optimum heterogeneity, and universal imagery.

Others have similarly been interested in constructing a new perspective by which to view Palaeolithic art. Wilson (1963) refers to cave art as 'relatively

Fig. 2

recent art', suggesting that the reason why earlier art work has not survived is because it consisted of perishable materials. Rieser (1972) points out that a range of patterns and shapes was commonly available to the prehistoric artist in the form of phosphenes, the common experience of 'seeing stars'. These pattern categories originate in the visual pathway as a result of pressure on the eyes, and might at least have influenced some of the images seen in some later prehistoric art. Marshack (1972) has a very different type of comment to make regarding the few thousand engraved and carved mobiliary artifacts of bone and stone from Upper Palaeolithic sites in Europe. These diverse bodies of evidence, he says, 'document a complex use of manufacture art and symbol among regionally scattered and culturally and genetically diverse groups of modern *Homo sapiens* from the period of the typical Aurignacian, *c.* 32,000 BC to the terminal Magdalenian, *c.* 10,000 BC' (p. 445). He notes, however, that there may be some evidence from scattered Mousterian sites for a use of symbol. From a detailed study of this data, he argues for a tradition of notation in general use in Upper Palaeolithic Europe, and rightly points out that if this is indeed correct, it raises important questions as regards the evolution of man's cognitive-intellectual capacity and the level of symbolic development in these earlier cultures. If nothing else, he is against the older simplistic explanations of such engraved materials in terms of 'magic', 'religion', 'decoration', 'sexual symbolism' and so forth.

Fig. 2 (Upper) *Geometric designs similar to phosphenes which appeared in different art forms from earliest times: 1, prehistoric rock painting from the Niaux cave, France; 2, aboriginal Churuga design from Western Australia; 3, eye motif from a pottery vessel from the cemetery at Los Millares, Spain. Possibly fourth millennium* BC; *4, megalithic passage-grave art from County Cork, Eire.* (Lower) *Electrically induced phosphenes grouped by Dr Max Knoll into 15 recurring categories.* (From Scientific American)

Young (1971) is also of the opinion that aesthetic endeavour may have begun much earlier than the Upper Palaeolithic – in the improvement of the symmetry of tools and perhaps (he thinks) in carvings of wood or in the production of ornaments. It is interesting that Young, with long experience in neuro-anatomy, feels that there is a reasonable case for believing that the creation of new aesthetic forms 'has been the most fundamentally productive of all forms of human activity', for new artistic conventions, he thinks, may provide a route to new interchange and communication between people – and this capacity is the basis of human history. Ucko and Rosenfeld (1967) have reviewed at length and in detail the problems of analysing and interpreting Palaeolithic cave art. They see no easy answers in explaining the complex of art work in early Europe, and perhaps all the variety of alternative explanations – art for art's sake, sympathetic magic and totemism, fertility magic, doodling, pictorial history, story telling, and so on – have all been determinants at times. An important associated question as regards European cave art is what exactly were these Upper Palaeolithic people using the caves for? In some cases, the art is deep in dark recesses, which rather excludes certain explanations. On the other hand some were clearly intended to be viewed, so that Ucko and Rosenfeld even question whether 'theatre' may have been behind some of the representations. They conclude by emphasizing the considerable variety to be seen just in European Palaeolithic art alone, a fact which again points to the need to view these 'artistic' endeavours as evolving out of much earlier aesthetic experimentation.

With the emergence of early agricultural societies, and eventually of advanced civilizations both in the Old World and the Americas, there was a proliferation of artistic work as never before. Populations increased in overall size, and in regional density. Social stratifications occurred which could not have been achieved in the earlier Palaeolithic cultures. There was an elaboration of 'craft' work, basketry, pottery and of artifacts for combat. Ornaments, luxury articles, tomb decorations, religious art, even the art of the theatre indicated the rapid proliferation of more and more variety with the evolution of increasingly advanced society, with stratification, complex social organization, and the differential apportioning of wealth. At a biological level, these socio-economic changes of the last ten thousand years probably heralded little beyond demographic changes. The physical skills, powers of observation and thought, variation in perception and creativity from one individual to another, were characteristics already well established many millennia before. The only profound physical changes were in the patterns of disease, and of these, only one inherited abnormality has relevance to artistic performance. This is the sex-linked deficiency of colour blindness (red and green). Post (1965) has argued that with the growth of advanced cultures, there have been changes in the rates of natural selection for particular characteristics. In the case of these colour vision defects, he argues that there was a strong differential against the survival of such individuals in Palaeolithic communities – so that frequencies as low as 2 per cent were maintained. In advanced urban societies, this defect was no longer such a disadvantage, the result being relaxed selection and a marked increase in individuals with these vision defects.

Plate 24

So what can be concluded about Palaeolithic art? First, it seems likely that the ability to produce art work greatly predates the high standard of painting, engraving and fashioning figurines achieved in Late Pleistocene times. Mean brain size comparable with living populations was probably achieved 200,000 years earlier, and there is no reason to believe that they were lacking in sufficient perceptiveness and creativity. It may be that considerable body ornamentation or art objects made from perishable materials represents the first stage – and it is interesting that much of recent 'primitive' or 'ethnographic' art is on this type of material and would not have survived burial for long. Considering animal 'decoration' generally, it would surely be a very reasonable hypothesis to put personal body decoration as the first step in artistic (but socially functional) development beyond tool-making. The most 'vulnerable' art – if one can think of it as an extension of the artist – is the art work placed well away from his normal place of work and leisure. But are there any other basic factors behind the production of at least much of the Upper Palaeolithic art? Could it, for example, be related to some form of social threshold that was only attained in certain late Pleistocene communities? Mendelssohn (1974) has recently suggested that Egyptian pyramids were not only funerary monuments, but were also socially oriented labour-demanding procedures geared to encouraging political unity. Could a basic reason for some Upper Palaeolithic art also be linked with population factors – tribal identity, the need to emphasize group cohesion through ritual, or ceremonial associations involved with age changes or the different sexes? If population numbers were indeed on the increase by late Palaeolithic times, it could well be that patterns of group conflict were changing – a further reason to ritually emphasize group unity. There is no doubt at all that future progress on the reasons for the appearance of advanced artistic standards in late prehistoric times will have to carefully take into account factors connected with the biology, social status and general environmental background of such groups.

VARIETY, STYLE AND SOCIETY

Although variety in art work clearly occurred in the Upper Palaeolithic, and noticeable stylistic differences can be seen even in one type of art object such as the figurine, nevertheless it seems likely that only with the emergence of the far more variable societies of post-Pleistocene times, especially during the past five thousand years, do we see something of the full artistic potential of man expressed. The objects show a very great variety, and as far as recent examples from preliterate communities are concerned one might list, say, a highly stylized wooden figure, a decorated 'thumb piano', an initiation trough with decorative designs, an initiation ceremony mask, a decorated harp, a fetish figure, a helmet mask, a carved wooden door, a ritual altar, a decorative lock device, an ornamental bowl, a bronze plaque with elaborate design work, a portrait of a 'king', an elaborately carved lintel, the figure of an ancestor, a head-hunting horn, a decorated fish-hook, a carved head rest, a killer whale mask, a carved feasting spoon, a carved and painted shadow puppet, an ivory game score, a totem pipe,

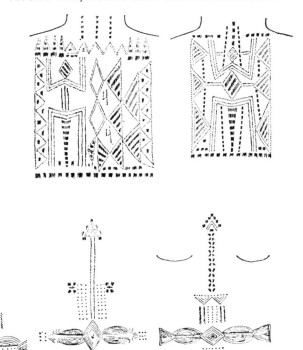

Fig. 3 *Body decoration (scarification) among the Tiv of Nigeria. (Upper) Women's back scars; (lower) women's belly scars. (From Man, September 1956)*

a shaman's rattle, a woven shirt with complex design, a decorated pottery bowl and a cotton doll. The list could of course be extended for pages, and if one plotted the frequency of the different items, they would vary according to the society, the natural environment and locality, and time. My purpose is not any sort of world review, but it is pertinent to refer to various communities and art objects as a means of exemplifying some general principles.

Africa, even south of the Sahara, provides vast contrasts in the material culture of negro societies. The nomadic Hadza are a hunting and gathering tribe of Tanzania with little inclination for material possessions beyond those that made food collecting easier. In contrast, the Nigerian state of Benin in the 17th century produced a wealth of sensitive skilled art work in bronze, ivory, wood and iron. Much of the work appears to be related to upholding the divine status of the king. Faris's (1973) study of the personal art of the Southeastern Nuba of the Sudan examines in detail the traditions of body painting, the purpose of which is to celebrate and enhance the strength and health of the human body. He points out that some body designs in fact require movement if the full aesthetic effect is to be achieved. In his studies of the Tiv of West Africa, Bohannan (1961) interested himself both in the views of the artist and those who made critical comment on particular art objects. He noted that the Tiv did not always aim for symmetry in their art work, but could find pleasure in some art which displayed noticeable asymmetry. Their views on making themselves personally

Plate 25

51

Fig. 3

beautiful include not only dressing up but also chipping the teeth in an attractive way and scarification of the skin (Bohannan 1956). Although such ornamental scarring may not be regarded by some as 'art', there is no doubt at all that it can form part of the 'aesthetic of body decoration' in some communities. Changes in the content of the art work of a group can be by 'internal' evolution within the group or by outside influence. The Ibo of Nigeria, for instance, are great borrowers of ideas, and their carvings show the influence of neighbouring peoples (Murray 1948). Wolfe (1955) has discussed a particular artist Bosokuma, living in the Belgian Congo. He was known to have introduced figurine carving into his group – to whom the tradition was foreign. The figurines show a range of style from fairly human-like to highly 'surrealist'. The carvings are used as part of a hunting magic complex, and because they are generally believed to have powerful properties, their introduction has been extremely successful. Here we see art related to wizardry which is in turn concerned with basic problems of hunting. Associations with magic are rather different in the case of the masked and colourfully clothed dancers of the *gelede* society of Meko in western Yorubaland. Here, the dances are intended to placate the witches in their society by entertaining them (Willett 1971). Somewhat divergent from the variety of art in Negro and Bushman communities is that of northern Africa (including Egypt); its traditions are linked with the cultures of southern Europe and western Asia. Little remains of the art of pomp, which reached a climax in some of the objects buried in Egyptian royal tombs, but there is today still much skill and aesthetic taste to be seen for example in the elaborate and colourful 'folk' jewellery of Algeria (Camps-Fabrer 1970).

The artistic work produced by peoples in other parts of the world show yet more variety, though perhaps possessing the same aesthetic 'common denominators'. Differences in morphology can for instance be related partly to differences in function. The wood and ivory figures from western Polynesia (Barrow 1956) show interesting shape differences depending upon their use (e.g. oil dish, food hangers, necklace). Adams (1949) points out that among the Amerindians of the northwest coast of the U.S.A., there appears to have been a proliferation of artists in pre-European times. Talented sculptors were found in the Haida, Tlingit, Tsimshian and Kwakiutl tribes. This area provides a good example of cooperation between sculptors in producing massive totem poles. Another case of group cooperation is seen in the construction of certain highly decorated ceremonial houses in New Guinea.

Plate 26

Simplicity of design need not be equated with simplicity of meaning, although could it be. Peterson (1972) shows that simple-looking clan designs among some Australian aborigines are in fact full of ritual meaning. Such designs may reenact a piece of clan history, and thus what may appear to be disjointed marking may have a complex background. The art work of the Eskimo has a varying history in different areas. The economy and environment of the Angmassalik Eskimo has not been conducive to much artistic elaboration, and it is interesting that the art work which is produced has a strong aesthetic basis – 'art for beauty's sake', as it were. In the case of the Canadian Eskimo sculptors (Meldgaard 1959) their works have mainly been produced during the past forty years, as a result

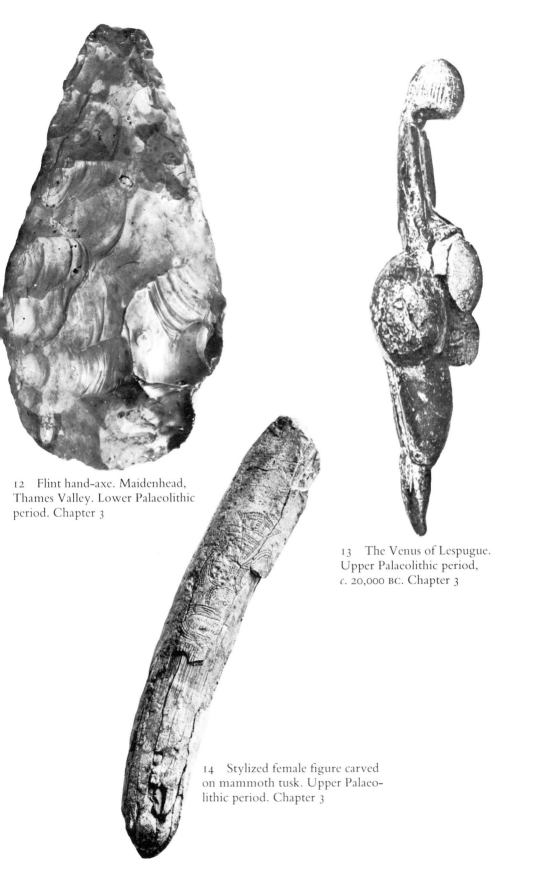

12 Flint hand–axe. Maidenhead,
Thames Valley. Lower Palaeolithic
period. Chapter 3

13   The Venus of Lespugue.
Upper Palaeolithic period,
c. 20,000 BC. Chapter 3

14   Stylized female figure carved
on mammoth tusk. Upper Palaeolithic period. Chapter 3

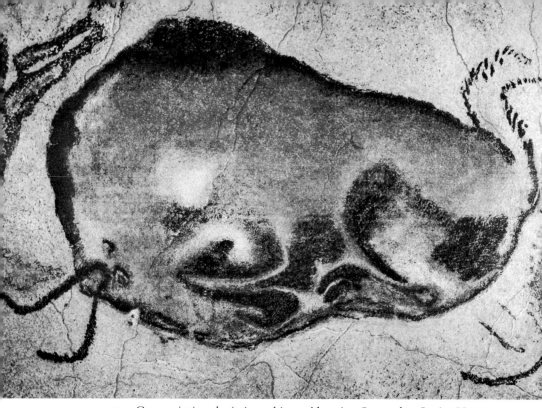

15 Cave painting depicting a bison. Altamira, Santander, Spain. Upper Palaeolithic period. Chapter 3

16 Cave painting of wild ox and horses. Lascaux, Dordogne, France. Upper Palaeolithic period. Chapter 3

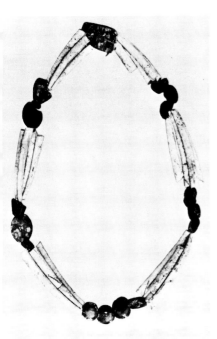

17 Necklace of carnelian beads and tusk-shaped shells, used in Pre–pottery Neolithic burial. Khirokitia, Cyprus. Chapter 3

18 Beaker decorated with a stag. Siyalk III, Iran. *c.* 4000 BC. Chapter 3

19 Plaster skull with cowrie-shell eyes. Neolithic period. Jericho, Jordan. Chapter 3

20 The Throne Room of the 'Palace of Minos', Knossos, Crete. *c.* 1450 BC. Chapter 3

22 Electrum helmet from a burial at Ur, Mesopotamia. Chapter 3

21 Statue of a ram in gold, silver, lapis lazuli, shell and red limestone from Ur, Mesopotamia. *c.* 2500 BC. Chapter 3

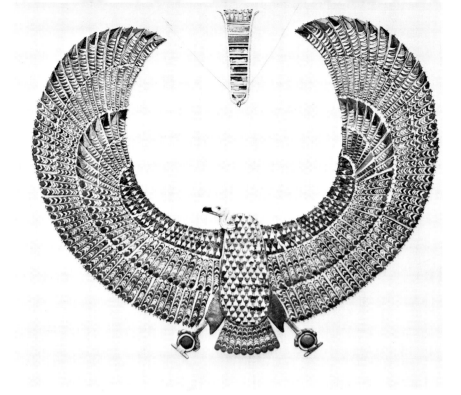

23 Nekhebet collar of Tutankhamun, Thebes. Mid-4th century BC. Chapter 3

24 Painted Greek Black-Figure vase showing actors dressed as birds. The costume perpetuates the traditional use of animal disguises in early religious ceremonies. *c.* 500 BC. Chapter 3

26 Blanket braided by Amerindian women of the Chilkit tribe, showing a school of stylized killer whales. Dried cedar fibres and mountain goat hair. Early historical period. Chapter 3

< 25 Bronze head of a queen-mother of Benin. South-west Nigeria. *c*. 17th century. Chapter 3

27 Bird-shaped bowl, Pellew Islands, Micronesia. Chapter 3

28　Wooden three-horned helmet. Batelela tribe. Zaïre (Congo). Chapter 3

29   Set of bronze sacrificial vessels found at Feng-Hsiang, Shensi Province, China. Chou/Shang dynasty, 12th–11th century BC. Chapter 3

30   Bronze ceremonial vessel of 'ho' type with face on cover. Shang dynasty. 12th–11th century BC. Chapter 3

of encouragement from various authorities, traders and missionaries. They now have a considerable output of work of a high standard, showing that contact between two widely contrasting cultures needn't necessarily depress and reduce artistic activity in the less developed of the two communities. Although there has been considerable contact between European settlers and the Navaho Amerindians, the dry paintings of the indigenous community are very much a reflection of their past culture. In particular, their art is intimately bound up with the maintenance of health and of corporate organization. Memory of traditional designs is more important than originality.

Plate 11

So it will be seen that there is a vast range of art objects, whatever the concepts of art work might be for a particular culture. The object may be developed to the limits of its material or social function. It may or may not have considerable aesthetic value to the artist or to the community. Here it is a question of considering the whole range of art work in more recent world cultures. It is essential of course, in undertaking field studies on art objects, whatever the community, to detail the differences and similarities as precisely as possible. Haselberger (1961) has discussed this question of recording and analysing 'ethnographic' art in some detail, and it is a most important step in trying to unravel the complexities of art in relation to social and economic differences. What might similar style and content mean? A somewhat exotic example of the problem is seen in similar facial deformities from two very different areas. In the case of Efik-Ibibio masks (Simmons 1957) there is a frequent portrayal of a face with marked disease at the nose. In such cases, the masks are supposed to frighten the beholder. Perhaps it might also be a reflection of the fear the community have of this disfiguring condition, which in fact is clearly damage caused by the tertiary stage of yaws. A similar kind of facial destruction is depicted in some Chimu pottery from Peru, but in this case it is the disease *uta*, the result of infection with the parasite *Leishmania braziliensis*. Price (1970) provides a further warning as regards the danger of reading too much into apparent similarities. He concludes from his detailed study of woodcarving in the Bush-Negro tribes of Surinam that the 'dynamic aspect of Bush-Negro cultures, the importance of fads and fashions, should serve as a caution to the researcher seeking African survivals. And it might encourage scepticism towards any African attributions based on formal rather than specifically historical evidence.' Fischer (1961) is similarly suspicious of using general features of art style to establish historical connections, or on the use of known historical connections alone to explain the similarities of art styles of two distinct cultures.

Plates
27–30

I have been discussing at some length art differences – varieties, styles, fashions – and it will be seen that even for less 'advanced' or preliterate cultures there are many problems of interpretation. The challenge for the future is to elaborate precise methods of identifying and assessing the reasons for the 'layering' of factors which so often contribute to the production of a work of art. Kroeber (1963), who has done much to reduce the study of style to a laboratory exercise, gives the example of changes in clothing styles or fashions. These differences are perhaps now regarded as a distinctive feature of recent advanced society, yet similar but slower changes were no less in evidence in Ancient

Greece and Rome and in the early societies of China and Japan. Basic to clothing design are utilitarian needs, for protection and warmth. Added to this is usually the factor of allurement and the common interest in self-beautification (but why?). In addition, there is the social effect of the style of dress, as an expression of rank, power and wealth. There is also, as Kroeber points out, the factor of 'novelty', really an individual expression of creativity, which is perhaps the most hominid feature of such 'displaying'. In dress fashions as in all forms of art, any attempt to understand the complex of factors involved not only demands a consideration of spatial differences but also those through time. As Kroeber says, predecessors must influence successors, even if their effect is in the form of a negative stimulant. The visual arts then, are 'cultural processes resulting in cultural products', often to be seen as complex patterns of variation between societies or trends through time. This can be seen just as clearly in the various schools and styles of art in China from the Han Dynasty through to recent times

Figs 4, 5   (Lin Yutang 1967). Newton (1967) has similarly tried to show in diagram form the same complex situation as regards the chief schools of European painting from Giotto to the present day.

In considering the art of advanced civilizations we have come a long way from the Pleistocene beginnings, and in the course of millennia the attitude towards art – what it is about and why it was produced – will have undergone many changes. What I have attempted in this brief review is to emphasize that the visual arts at whatever point in time and space, are socio-cultural phenomena, at first 'permitted' by the extent of our biological evolution and our adaptations to different world environments, but eventually caught up in the processes of demographic change and the elaboration of cultures following the agricultural and urban revolutions. As Molnar (1974) says, it is now time for all of us to view the science of art as a part of the science of human behaviour.

Fig. 4   *Changes in Chinese art styles. (After Lin Yutang)*

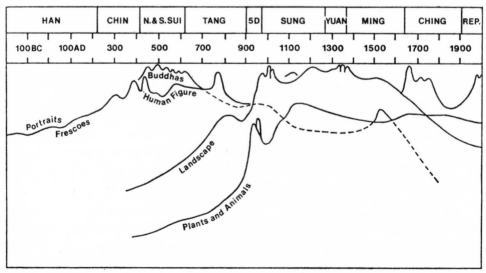

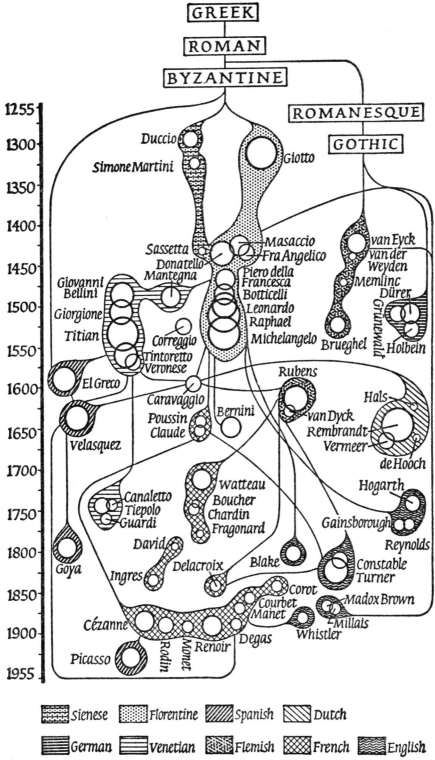

Fig. 5 *Chief schools of European painting from the twelfth century to the present day.*
(After Newton)

Chapter Four

The development of visual perception in children

M. D. VERNON

INTRODUCTION

During the first year of life children develop the capacity to perceive their immediate surroundings and to recognize many of the objects which they encounter daily. Not only does the appearance of these become familiar, but also how they can be manipulated and what is their use. Most important of all, the children begin to understand that these objects have a permanent existence. Though their appearance may vary in certain regular ways as, for instance, when they are turned round in space, nevertheless they possess a continuing and recognizable identity. Thus children develop expectations that when objects reappear after a temporary removal from sight, they will have the same nature and properties as heretofore. The physical environment is therefore expected to possess stability, despite changing circumstances. Even the human environment is stable up to a point, though considerably more variable than the physical environment. The speed and accuracy of perception depend to a great extent on these expectations.

However, it must not be supposed that the young child's perceptions of the environment are identical with those of older children and adults. These perceptions are frequently fragmented and unintegrated, in the sense that a form or picture may be perceived in one way on one occasion and differently at a later view; the figure perceived may be irrelevant to what has preceded it or to the existing setting. Thus there is no coherent view of the environment as a whole. Moreover, fundamental characteristics may not be accurately perceived. Again, in some situations the young child may not be fully aware of the exact nature of objects themselves as independent of his own viewpoint and his actions on them. Indeed, in some cases the tendency to display egocentric perception remains strong until a considerable age. Furthermore, Piaget (1955) demonstrated that children of two to three years of age expected to encounter familiar objects in their most frequent settings, and were surprised if they appeared elsewhere. It is true that adults perceive objects more readily when these appear in familiar rather than unfamiliar surroundings, because perception is facilitated by expectation; they know what to look out for. But young children may even be doubtful as to the identity of objects in unfamiliar surroundings.

It is impossible for anyone to perceive all the features in the surrounding environment, and inevitably there must be some selection. Even when the adult is not deliberately searching his surroundings, his attention is nevertheless pre-set through expectations based mainly on past experience, and he tends therefore to perceive certain features which are important or interesting to him, and to ignore others which concern him little. One of the most important characteristics of the development of perception is the gradual improvement in the capacity to attend to and to perceive what is relevant, both in undirected gazing, and even more in deliberate search. This capacity, termed by Piaget (1969) 'perceptual activity', does not become fully operative until about the age of 5 to 6 years, when children develop the ability to think intelligently in practical situations, at Piaget's stage of 'concrete operations' (Piaget 1952).

At this stage also the child ceases to depend entirely on his immediate direct perceptions, but controls and integrates them through the use of intelligence. He is then able to employ his knowledge of the environment to correct erroneous impressions which may arise in immediate perception. Thus we shall see that, as perception develops, so it becomes more precise, more relevant and more conducive to understanding the veridical nature of the environment.

THE PERCEPTION OF FORM

Although children during the first year of life develop the capacity to identify objects, they do not perceive every detail of the appearance of these. Objects possess a number of different characteristics which are 'redundant', corroborating each other; and a general and global perception of some of these is sufficient for identification. The same is probably true of patterns, which are also discriminated by children during their first year. This global perception was demonstrated by asking children of 2 to 10 years what they saw in the Rorschach ink-blots (Ames et al. 1953). The younger children responded to the general form of the blots, which they perceived vaguely and inexactly. Only children of four years and upwards noted the details, though it is probable that visual acuity is good enough in younger children to see such details. But they do not perceive them until later; and then the amount of redundancy or proliferation of detail required for identification diminishes.

It must be noted however that it is difficult to judge exactly what it is that young children perceive in ordinary everyday life circumstances, which may differ from those studied in experimental conditions. Many experiments have been carried out to investigate discrimination, distinguishing between two simultaneously presented objects or patterns. Gibson (1969) considered that development in perceptual ability depended largely on the increasing accuracy with which children discriminate, and in particular on their ability to discriminate between the invariant characteristics of objects, those which remain unchanged despite changes in setting, position, distance, etc.; and the minor variable features which might differ on different occasions. Discrimination between two simultaneously presented objects or patterns, which may occur comparatively rarely in everyday life situations, may be performed by directly

Standard   Topological   Geometrical
                                      match

Fig. 1 *Matching a standard figure against one which is topologically similar, or one which is geometrically similar. (After Cousins and Abranavel)*

comparing certain of their aspects; whereas the extraction of invariant characteristics requires the perception that objects or patterns are the same as or different from those previously perceived. This usually involves identification, a common feature of everyday life perception; and it clearly depends on memory as well as immediate perception. Thus although discrimination of salient characteristics may be a necessary antecedent to identification, it does not necessarily lead to identification.

There is undoubtedly a gradual development with age in the capacity to discriminate between meaningless forms or patterns, as shown for instance by matching a form against one among a number of variations. Under four years of age discrimination may be performed principally in terms of certain very general, or 'topological', characteristics such as open or closed outlines, inclusion in or exclusion from another figure, and curved or straight lines (Piaget and Inhelder 1956; Laurendeau and Pinard 1970). However, when children of 4 to *Fig. 1* 5 years were required to match a shape against one which was topologically similar or one which was geometrically similar, the majority chose the latter when the shapes were regular and familiar. But only half of them chose the geometrical match when the shapes were irregular and quite unfamiliar (Cousins and Abranavel 1971). It was also found that at five years irregular shapes might be matched mainly by their relative elongation and jaggedness (Owen 1971).

It might be supposed also that many geometric shapes would be easy to discriminate and match because of their symmetry and regularity. It has indeed been found that they can be matched with fair accuracy at four years (Terman and Merrill 1937). But matching which involves exact discrimination of size of angles and slope of lines cannot be performed until a later age. Again, in the matching of irregular figures resembling letters against one of a number of variations, certain topological characteristics such as openness and closure were accurately discriminated at four years (Gibson et al. 1962). But straight and curved lines and differences in orientation were not discriminated until later. Moreover, identification of these forms from memory, as tested by recognition of the previously seen form from among variations, continued to show frequent errors until 7 to 9 years (Trieschmann 1968).

But discrimination and even identification do not appear to necessitate accurate perception of every detail. Copying of shapes requires more detailed perception. Thus the age at which children are able to copy shapes correctly is usually greater than the age at which they can discriminate them. Children of 3 to 5 years who could discriminate between a circle and a triangle could not copy them with even approximate correctness (Maccoby and Bee 1965). Most simple geometrical shapes were not copied correctly till 5 to 6 years (Piaget and Inhelder 1956); the diamond not until 7 years, because of its sloping lines and the difficulty of estimating its angles. It might be supposed that inability to copy is due at least in part to lack of skill in drawing; and indeed it was found that straight-line figures could be copied correctly by making matchstick constructions at an earlier age than by drawing (Lovell 1959). But this is not the whole explanation; indeed it does not explain the frequent tendency in children to reproduce straight-line figures as circles, which may be regarded as topologically the simplest of all figures (Piaget and Inhelder 1956). Thus when the characteristics of figures cannot be precisely perceived and copied, the figures are simplified to a circular form.

Complex forms made up of parts and containing interior detail are not perceived correctly until a later age than applies to simple geometrical shapes. Whereas at first children perceive the total shapes globally, at 5 to 6 years they may perceive the parts rather than the wholes, or parts and wholes in alternation (Elkind et al. 1964). This depends to some extent on the relative prominence of parts and wholes. But it is not until about eight years that both can be perceived, and the manner in which they are related to each other. Constructing a whole pattern from its parts is more difficult than analysing this whole into parts (Greenberg 1972). Presumably again the former requires more precise perception of detail than the latter. But analysis is exceptionally difficult if the outlines of the parts are continuous with those of the whole, as shown in tests in which children are required to extract a simple figure embedded in a more complex one. When the contours of the former are shared with those of the latter, chil- *Fig. 2* dren even of 8 years may not be able to perform the task correctly (Ghent 1956). But performance varies considerably with the complexity of the form, and the number of contours shared by the simple and complex forms (Reed and Angaran 1972).

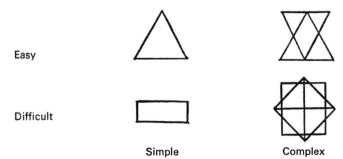

Fig. 2   *Tracing simple figures which are embedded in complex figures. (After Reed and Angaran)*

(a)

Fig. 3 *The Müller-Lyer illusion and the Oppel illusion*

(b)

Fig. 3a

Fig. 3b

Difficulty in perceiving the parts of which a figure is made up independently of the whole figure would seem to be one factor operating in some of the visual illusions; though many other factors may be involved (see for instance Robinson 1972). The Müller-Lyer illusion, in which the horizontal line with outward-pointing arrowheads tends to appear longer than the line with inward-pointing arrowheads, has usually been found to be greater in young children than in adults (Vurpillot 1963). On the other hand, the Oppel illusion of filled and unfilled space was less in young children than in adults. In the former, the children failed to perceive the horizontal lines independently of the whole patterns; whereas in the latter the children perceived the cross-hatched line as a whole without breaking it up into parts, the source of the illusion.

A particular characteristic of forms which young children seem in some cases to perceive less readily and correctly than do adults is their orientation. Now, young children in the first year of life learn to recognize familiar objects in any orientation, and to disregard changes in the images they project caused by inversion, slanting or tilting. But forms and pictures presented on the printed page are different; indeed inverted forms may appear to be quite different figures. Even three-year-old children found them easier to recognize in the upright position than if they were inverted (Ghent and Bernstein 1961). Children of 4 years readily discriminated between a form when upright or inverted (Wohlwill and Wiener 1964). The difference is less when forms are tilted than when they are inverted, and children may fail to discriminate tilted from untilted forms, especially in memory (Bryant 1966). Shapes reversed from left to right like mirror images are even more difficult to distinguish from each other, and children under 5 years are seldom able to do this (Rudel and Teuber 1963).

In view of the relatively slow development in perception of complex forms, it is at first sight surprising that the ability to perceive and identify objects in pictures arises at an early age; though usually redundancy of detail is operative. Up to a year of age children respond little to most pictures, but they do appear to be attracted towards and pleased by pictures of faces, and can discriminate these from pictures of scrambled facial features. It cannot of course be assumed that at this age they recognize them as representing people, though this may be possible during the second year of life. Indeed, a child of 19 months was able to name a number of pictured objects, although he had not been shown any pictures previously (Hochberg and Brooks 1962). By 3 to 4 years most children can recognize familiar objects depicted in their normal positions by simple outline drawings (Terman and Merrill 1937). This indicates that they can understand the correspondence between these outlines and the contours of solid objects. However, objects depicted in unusual positions may be recognized only by older children (Keir 1970). More detail may be necessary for the identification of unfamiliar than of familiar objects. Again, when parts of pictured objects were obscured, children under 8 years were less able than older children to identify them (Spitz and Borland 1971); the younger children required greater redundancy of detail. The same occurred if the pictures were very blurred (Draguns and Multari 1961). Younger children were not only slower to identify such pictures correctly, but also made many incorrect and mutually incompatible guesses before they did so (Potter 1966).

Young children who can identify single objects in pictures may nevertheless be incapable of understanding complex pictures depicting scenes and people in various activities. Thus at 5 to 6 years perception of these was fragmented; children tended to pick out objects one after another without relating them together (Terman and Merrill 1937). Some description of the picture as a whole occurred at about 7 years (Vernon 1940). But the meaning of the pictures and of the activities depicted was usually not understood until 9 to 10 years; though naturally this depended on the clarity of the meaning and the familiarity of the activities.

Understanding also depends on the experience of seeing pictures. Thus uneducated people living in uncultured societies may fail to understand any but the simplest pictures of familiar objects, realistically depicted (Holmes 1963). Indeed, Zambian women were found to experience difficulty in matching pictures against the objects they represented (Deregowski 1971). The conventional ways of depicting distance were found to be little understood by 6-year-old children and also by uneducated adults (Hudson 1960). But cues to distance provided by superimposition of near on far objects appeared to be utilized more readily than those supplied by perspective (Kilbride et al. 1968). *Fig. 4*

Fig. 4 *Representation of distance pictorially. (After Hudson)*

Not unnaturally the capacity to recognize objects in pictures develops before the ability to draw them. Scribbling begins as early as 13 months, and it is clear that the child enjoys making marks on paper and seeing what he has produced (Gibson 1970). At about 3 years circles appear among the scribbled lines, and the drawings are named as representing objects, though these may be unrecognizable by adults (Di Leo 1971). The most frequent of these is the human figure, which is shown as a single circle representing the head, and

Fig. 5a   containing smaller circles for the eyes and sometimes for the mouth. Later, straight lines are appended for the arms and legs, which are directly attached to

Fig. 5b   the head. At 4 to 5 years an oval or rectangular shape indicating the body is

Fig. 5c   drawn beneath the head, to which the arms and legs are attached. As age increases, more detail is added.

Now, it would seem that children of these ages try to represent what are to them the salient and important characteristics in their global percepts of human figures: first the head and eyes; then the limbs; and then the body. But they do not reproduce direct perceptions of the human figure until at about 6 to 7 years they attempt actually to copy it by drawing it in profile; the profile being easier to copy than the full face. Sometimes there is a transitional stage in which the

Fig. 5d   profile and full face are combined. But Arnheim (1956) considered that young children utilize in their representations certain universal concepts of form, of which the circle is the earliest. (We noted that it might be used to copy other

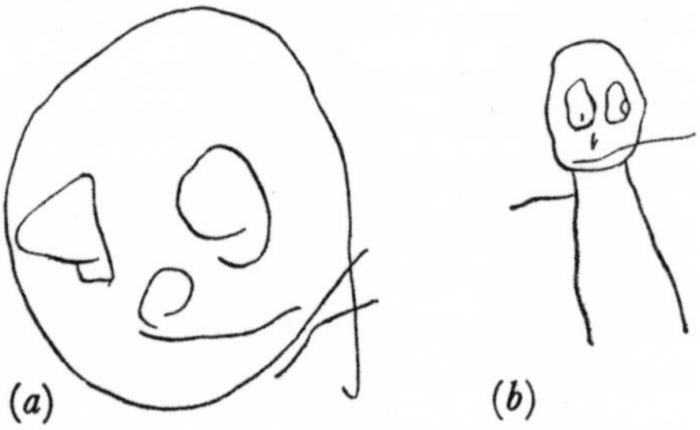

Fig. 5   *Development in children's drawings of the human figure. (After Di Leo)*

Fig. 6 *'Sunbursts'. (After Arnheim)*

geometrical shapes.) There then emerges the 'sunburst', in which a circle is   *Fig. 6*
combined with straight lines; and this is used not only for the human figure but
also for many other objects, the sun, a flower, a tree with leaves. It seems that
these early drawings occur in many different cultures. But even if their forms
originate in some general tendency to produce certain fundamental forms, they
may nevertheless be employed to represent those characteristics of familiar and
interesting objects which are striking and important to children. Moreover, the
later developments in figure drawing may well be affected by experience in
seeing pictures.

ATTENTION

Global perception and the inability to perceive details and their relationships
are due at least in part to the failure of young children to direct their attention
towards these; to look for characteristics which it is essential to extract; and to
disregard what is unimportant. This appears to be due to incapacity for concentrated attention, it being focused upon that part of the field of view which is
fixated by the eyes. But also the direction of attention may be faulty in what
has been called 'ambient' vision: the observation, sometimes in peripheral vision,
of aspects of the field not directly fixated, and the subsequent focusing of central
vision upon them. Here attention must cover a wide field, yet be successively
directed to different environmental features which are then perceived as 'figure'
standing out from the surroundings, the 'ground'. Finally these salient features
must be integrated together to produce an overall impression of the environmental surroundings as a whole.

   Now the differentiation between 'figure' and 'ground' is an innate capacity
exhibited even in early infancy; but the ability to select what is properly figural
develops later. Although infants gaze about the field of view, they do not
voluntarily direct their attention towards its principal features; still less can they
integrate their percepts into a consistent overall impression. Gazing is thus undirected; but from time to time attention is caught and held by something which
attracts it. This may be something striking, such as a bright light or a brightly
coloured or moving object, which stands out clearly from its surroundings.

Or it may be something which appeals to the child's needs or interests. In infancy, the principal object of attraction is the child's mother. He looks for her and at her, and gazes fixedly at her face whenever it is in view. Hence perhaps the salience of the head and eyes in his early drawings. But other types of object may attract his attention and hold it at least momentarily. These are in the main objects which are novel and unexpected; and objects which are complex in structure. Attention is maintained by changing and variable events, for instance moving objects, but quickly declines in a homogeneous and unchanging field and where objects are shown repeatedly. Again, attention is quickly attracted by anything incongruous and unexpected. Thus two-year-old children looked longer at pictures of a man with three heads or with his head upside down than at an ordinary picture of a man (Lewis et al. 1971). Indeed, the incongruous and unexpected may be more likely to attract attention than the completely novel, which is sometimes disregarded because it cannot be understood.

Again, complex stimuli may be viewed for longer than simple ones – a picture of three men rather than of one man (Lewis et al. 1971); they are explored until they are fully grasped. Children as a rule take longer to do this than do adults; therefore they look longer, or more frequently, at complex forms. Moreover, they cannot integrate different views and aspects into a single impression. Children under 5 years were unable to identify a cross and an 'E' when the parts of these were shown sequentially (Gilgus and Hochberg 1970).

It can be shown by recording eye movements and fixations that children do not explore in a systematic manner the figures which are shown them. Thus at 3 to 4 years children did not follow the contours of figures with their eyes (Yendovitskaya et al. 1971), but looked at certain parts only, or even wandered quite outside them. At 4 to 5 years of age the eyes began to be directed towards the salient features of the figures, though not in a systematic manner; and even at 5 to 6 years certain features were neglected. Recognition of the figures was correspondingly inaccurate. It was not until about 7 years that the adult pattern of viewing developed: general orienting movements in ambient vision until significant features were selected, followed by a small number of fixations on these, in focal vision. The more familiar the figures presented, the less extensive the exploration.

These patterns of viewing were demonstrated by recording eye movements in six-year-old children and adults when shown blurred pictures which were difficult to perceive (Mackworth and Bruner 1970). The children gazed about, not knowing what to look for, and then made a large number of fixations on small areas often of no great significance. The adults, after long orienting movements followed by a few fixations on relevant features, often made further long movements in order to relate together widely separated details which were mutually relevant. Thus the adults were able to integrate together the significant aspects of the field until its whole meaning was understood. Children's eye movements are more irregular owing to their inability both to select what is significant, because they do not know what to look for in order to comprehend the picture; and also to interrelate features and integrate them together through successive deployment of attention. Thus in viewing complex pictures, irrelevant

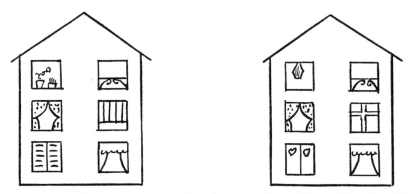

Fig. 7   *A pair of houses with some windows the same and some different. (After Vurpillot)*

but perceptually striking details are often noticed which catch the children's attention though they may not be related to the meaning of the picture as a whole. But younger children may also be distracted by such details from discovering what is significant. Thus children of 3½ years of age were slower to select from a number of differently shaped hooks the one which would extract a sweet from a container when the hooks were of different colours than when they were the same colour (Zhukova cited by Berlyne 1970). Attention was distracted from shape by colour, the children being unable to inhibit the attraction of the striking colour characteristics.

The inability to judge what is relevant and what irrelevant, and to direct attention to the former while disregarding the latter, was also displayed in experiments in which children of 4 to 6½ years were shown pairs of pictures of houses, and asked to say whether the two members of the pair were the same or different (Vurpillot 1969). Each house had six windows of different patterns; *Fig. 7* varying numbers of windows were the same or different as between one house and the other. Almost all the children judged correctly when all the windows in the pair of houses were identical. But the younger children often judged a pair of houses to be the same when some of the windows were different because they ceased scanning after observing that some of the windows were the same, and therefore did not notice that some were different. This happened even when the children were asked to look carefully, especially in the later stages of the task when they were beginning to lose interest. Indeed, it has been shown that young children may be unable to observe significant aspects even when instructed what to look for. But the older children scanned systematically until they had covered all or nearly all the windows. The same behaviour occurred when the children were shown pairs of identical or slightly dissimilar drawings of familiar objects; the younger children failed to observe small differences of detail.

Inability to scan systematically is also exhibited by children of about 6 years when viewing a wide field with objects scattered about it. When asked to name pictures of objects scattered over the field, these children scanned in a random manner, often omitting or repeating objects (Elkind and Weiss 1967). Even pictures arranged in rows and columns were not reported in systematic order

(Gottschalk et al. 1964). The failure of young children to perceive sequential order may be associated with this inability to direct attention systematically. The order of beads on a string was not grasped by children aged under 6 to 7 years (Piaget and Inhelder 1956).

Piaget (1969) considered that children do not develop until 6 to 7 years of age the capacity for 'perceptual activity', that is to say, the systematic direction of attention to significant aspects of figures and their orderly perception. Younger children wander about or centre on certain features, neglecting the remainder. But older children direct their gaze intelligently; they understand what to look for, searching systematically until they have observed and related significant aspects but disregarding or passing quickly over unimportant details. The close relation between intelligent understanding and direction of attention was displayed in the performance of 'conservation' tasks. In these children are required, for instance, to judge whether the number of objects remains the same when they are widely scattered as when they are close together; or whether there is the same amount of plasticine in a ball when it is squeezed out into a long cylinder. Children are normally incapable of understanding conservation until 5 to 6 years, when they attain the stage of 'concrete operations' at which they can reason in concrete situations and can thus argue that properties like number and amount of substance remain invariant in spite of perceptual transformation. Before that age their judgments are over-weighted by perceived changes in the area over which the objects are scattered, or in the length of the lump of plasticine. Children who had achieved conservation made relatively few eye fixations located systematically on the features of the objects relevant to conservation, *Fig. 8* which they compared together (O'Bryan and Boersma 1971). Children who had not attained conservation showed many confused eye movements and fixations located at random.

Non-conserver   Conserver

Fig. 8 *Eye movements made in comparing the sizes of plasticine lumps by children who had or had not attained conservation. (After O'Bryan and Boersma)*

IMAGERY, VERBALIZATION AND CONCEPTUALIZATION

We have noted that for the identification of objects, memory of previously perceived objects of the same type is essential. Thus there must be some kind of internal representation in memory. In young children this may take principally the form of imagery; but verbal representation, especially in naming, may occur also, and become increasingly frequent as age increases. However, it was found that even at two years children were enabled to recognize objects which had been shown previously by naming them or their characteristics. For instance, a sweet placed under a red cup was found more quickly when the word 'red' was spoken (Liublinskaya 1957). At 3 to 4 years children themselves named forms and pictures of objects to help them remember them (Babska 1965). However, very young children who are still learning to speak may name incorrectly, partly because they have not learnt the right names, but partly also because they are uncertain which objects belong to a particular class and should be given the class name; e.g. which animals are called 'dogs' and which by some other name.

Thus visual imagery is frequently employed by young children in the identification of objects. Indeed, in matching the memory of a specific object to a present percept, imagery may be more effective than naming (Prentice cited by Bruner 1966). Again, if exact shape characteristics which cannot be named or described verbally are to be remembered, visual imagery may be essential. Moreover, in the perception of simple forms and objects by young children, naming may not be essential, though verbalization may assist differentiation and remembering.

As age increases, imagery is increasingly supplemented and replaced by naming or verbal description in appropriate situations. Thus discrimination of complex irregular shapes by six-year-old children was assisted by giving the shapes arbitrary names (Katz et al. 1970). Familiar shapes and objects are usually named. They are perceived as belonging to a conceptual class of similar objects, for instance, cups, chairs, etc. of different shapes and sizes; and the name of the class concept is commonly used in identifying them. Children with strong visual imagery may have difficulty in classifying specific instances into conceptual categories of object (Kuhlmann cited by Bruner 1966); and in applying names of conceptual categories to new instances (Hollenberg 1970). But in remembering specific instances independently of categorization, those with good visual imagery may be superior to those without. Also, when objects are named they tend to be remembered in a form corresponding to the known characteristics of the conceptual class, rather than as they actually appear. Young children may find it difficult to perceive and recognize the characteristics of objects which are essential for conceptual classification, and indeed may employ just the type of feature which, as we noted above, is liable to attract attention – for instance, colour (Olver and Hornsby 1966). But older and more intelligent children increasingly employ appropriate conceptual classification in the identification of objects which possess familiar and frequently used names (Conrad 1971).

The development of the capacity to conceptualize particular objects as belonging to a class of objects, similar in use and function, for instance, though different in details of appearance, does not depend on verbalization but on increasing intelligence. Nevertheless, giving a class name to individual objects emphasizes that they belong to this class and hence not only facilitates their rapid identification, but also indicates to the child what functions and uses he can expect from them.

Again, the development of more general principles such as those of constancy of number, amount, etc., depends on the emergence of concrete intellectual operations rather than on verbalization. It is possible, however, that the application of these principles to a variety of related situations may be facilitated by their verbal formulation.

INDIVIDUAL DIFFERENCES

The ages given in the preceding discussion are of course approximate, and not every child is capable of performing the various activities described at these ages. Less intelligent children take longer to reach the successive stages of development, although it has been found that even mentally subnormal children eventually attain the stage of concrete operations. Cross-cultural studies have shown that children in less cultured societies than our own (other than in very primitive hunting and food-gathering societies) are as a rule capable of understanding conservation; though the age for this is usually later than for children in our society (Lloyd 1972). This depends partly on the education they have received, and partly on the nature of the conservation tasks and the employment of familiar material and situations. Thus it was found that children of Mexican potters demonstrated conservation of amount, or substance, using plasticine, at a significantly earlier age than did those who were not children of potters (Price-Williams et al. 1969). Again we noted the difficulty of uncultured people in perceiving certain pictures. The absence of schooling may have more effect on the performance of perceptual and memory tasks requiring the use of words than on conservation tasks (Goodnow 1969).

It has frequently been found that children in the lower socio-economic classes exhibit a slower rate of perceptual development than do middle-class children, though the causes of this are not entirely clear. Thus in one experiment, children of $2\frac{1}{2}$ to 3 years of low socio-economic status showed little interest in learning the names of objects; indeed, the latter sometimes seemed to have no meaning for them unless they were in familiar use (Malone 1966). Characteristics of objects such as colour, size, etc. could not be named correctly, and names might be used interchangeably. Perception of form also seemed to be related to socio-economic status. Thus children of 5 to 7 years of low status were inferior to those of higher status in copying simple line patterns with sticks (Wise 1968).

It appeared that poor perceptual performance, as well as verbal inferiority, might be related to the language of the mother and its effectiveness in description and abstraction (Olim 1970). The ability of four-year-old children to perceive and name pictures and to sort objects conceptually was related to the intelligence of the mother, but even more to her language; these relationships were independent of social class. But in another study it was found that lower-class mothers were less capable than middle-class mothers of explaining to their children how to perform an object-sorting task (Hess and Shipman 1965). The lower-class children were correspondingly inferior in performance of the task, in understanding its meaning and in describing verbally how it should be done. It is also possible that the methods of child rearing employed by more intelligent and verbally competent mothers encourage their children to examine and identify objects and understand their use; though ability for abstraction may be even more affected, as it is by education.

31   Perceptual responses occur at a very early age, and this boy of two-and-a-half was exploring the various qualities of an egg. Such natural responses tend to fade in the world of conceptual education. Chapter 5

32   Activities with reflections may aid the understanding of light. Chapter 5

33   Very young children are attracted by light, and play activities involving light and shadow can be a starting point. Chapter 5

34 Children study-
ing the change in
appearance of paper
propellers in the
wind. Chapter 5

35 Movement
changes the
appearance of
objects. Chapter 5

36   Mosaics in the chancel of Cefalù Cathedral, Sicily. Chapter 7

37   Page from the Egbert Codex, showing
a circle in perspective. Chapter 7

38   NANNI BIGIO *Madonna* in the south porch
of the Duomo at Florence. Chapter 7

39   UGOLINO DI NERIO *Resurrection*. Chapter 7

40   Doric pillars of temple at Paestum. Chapter 7

41   LORENZO GHIBERTI *Flagellation of Christ.* Bronze relief on the doors of the Baptistery, Florence. 15th century. Chapter 7

42   Interior of the church of San Spirito, Florence, designed by Brunelleschi. Chapter 7

43   The façade of San Andrea, Mantua, designed by Alberti. Chapter 7

44 *The Fall of the Rebel Angels* by the Master of the Rebel Angels. Siena. 14th century. Chapter 7

45 DONATELLO *Lamentation*. Bronze. 15th century. Chapter 7

46 LUCA SIGNORELLI *Pan*. 1491. Chapter 7

47 LEONARDO DA VINCI *Virgin of the Rocks*. 1506? Chapter 7

48 LEONARDO DA VINCI *Virgin of the Rocks*. 1483. Chapter 7

49 Staircase of the Laurentian Library, Florence, by Michelangelo and Vasari. Chapter 7

50   ADAM ELSHEIMER *St Paul on Malta*. Chapter 7

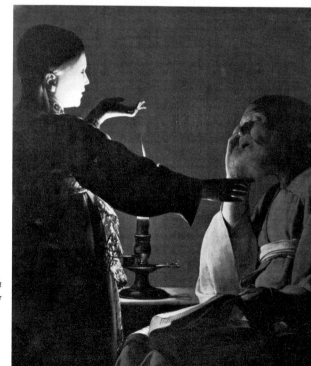

51   GEORGES DE LA TOUR *St Joseph and the Angel*. Chapter 7

It is claimed that perceptual development may be affected by certain personality qualities which may in themselves be related to upbringing and interaction with parents. Thus in one enquiry children were rated at 2½ years for their dependency on adults, as contrasted with their capacity for sustained and directed activity (Pederson and Wender 1968). At 6 years of age the less dependent and more consistently active were superior to others in conceptual classification of objects. The ability to differentiate, analyse and organize the perceptual field objectively and independent of self-reference, as for instance in the embedded figures test (see p. 67), has been related to parental treatment of children, and especially to the mother's encouragement of freedom and independence (Witkin et al. 1962). This hypothesis has been supported by investigations on cross-cultural differences in various types of perceptual performance (Lloyd 1972). For instance, Eskimo children were remarkably proficient in the embedded figures test; and this may be associated with early encouragement of independence, though also with training of perception of detail in the environment (Berry 1966).

It has been suggested that differences in perceptual performance may be associated with consistent tendencies towards global or analytical perception; the more dependent giving global responses and the less dependent, analytical (Kagan and Kogan 1970). In recognizing pictures, in matching shapes and pictures and in naming shapes superimposed on a patterned background, the analytical were more accurate and more able to abstract details. They were also more capable of sustained attention. These differences appeared to be independent of intelligence (Satterley and Brimer 1971).

There seemed to be a relationship between these tendencies and reflectiveness or impulsiveness in behaviour (Kagan et al. 1964). Impulsive children, who were consistently active and restless, showed a poor capacity for sustained attention, reacted quickly and were not anxious about making mistakes. Reflective children responded more slowly; considered the task carefully; produced a number of alternative hypotheses; made fewer errors and were more anxious to be correct. These differences were demonstrated in a variety of tasks. They appeared at 4½ years in matching pictures of familiar objects (Katz 1971); at 6 years in matching letter-like forms and remembering their variations (Odom et al. 1971); and at 8 years in the rapid perception of incongruous pictures (Kagan 1966). At this age also reflective children searched more carefully and made more comparisons of detail in matching familiar figures (Drake cited by Kagan and Kogan 1970). These differences were found to be consistent over a period of two years (Kagan 1966), and during frequent retesting (Yando and Kagan 1970); though reflectiveness increased with age (Kagan and Kogan 1970). It may be associated with tendencies to anxiety and inhibition. But reflectiveness and impulsiveness may also be due in part to temperamental qualities.

It is difficult to judge whether these characteristics of cognitive and other personality differences operate directly on perception, in that children with different characteristics actually perceive differently. It seems possible that they relate rather to direction and control of attention in the selection of significant features of the field. Gardner and his colleagues have postulated the existence of what they termed 'cognitive controls' of attention and perception. The first of these was called 'field articulation', which was the capacity to direct attention appropriately to the significant aspects of the field and to disregard irrelevant aspects, as, for instance, in the embedded figures test (Gardner and Moriarty 1968). A second type of control was of extensiveness of scanning, shown in the tendency to deploy attention widely over a broad field or concentrate it narrowly on a small area. It could be assessed directly from the number and distribution of eye fixations. This control therefore appeared to subserve ambient vision, whereas the first operated in focal vision. These controls were demonstrated in children of 9 to 13 years, as was also a third type, constricted-flexible control, operating in the inhibition of irrelevant responses when there is the possibility of alternative responses. However, this control has been shown to correlate with extensiveness of scanning in children of 6 to 10 years of age (Santostefano and Paley 1964). The first type of control, field articulation, and the tests employed to demonstrate it, resemble those of perceptual differentiation as postulated by Witkin et al. (1964). Extensiveness of scanning seems to cover somewhat the same ground as global versus analytical perception; and the third control to relate to reflection as opposed to impulsivity. Clearly these characteristics have much in common. But the whole problem of individual differences in performing perceptual tasks is obscure, and has not been elucidated by the overlapping of tests and of the factors which the analysis of their results is claimed to demonstrate. Even more confused are the personality characteristics that may be involved. Gardner and his colleagues have formulated some of these in terms of the Freudian 'mechanisms of defence'. But they acknowledge that in children these hypotheses do not receive much support from the experimental evidence (Gardner and Moriarty 1968).

CONCLUSIONS

It would seem that during the first few years of life the child acquires a reasonable understanding of his normal environment and effective perception of the objects he commonly encounters. He is able to identify these readily in terms of their appearance, functions and use; not only through familiarity with particular objects, but also by establishing conceptual categories which can include new but related instances. Moreover, he realizes that these objects are congruent with and fit into certain general settings which his actions have enabled him to understand; thus the familiar environment 'makes sense', and engenders expectations as to what will occur in it.

But in conditions which differ at all markedly from those of the familiar environment, the child's capacity to perceive and understand is much more limited. In real-life situations which are quite unusual and which he has never investigated through his own actions, he may be capable only of observing a few familiar objects, and have no general understanding of the situation as a whole. We noted such an occurrence in the case of pictures; it may well arise in real-life situations also.

Again, the child may only gradually develop the capacity to perceive the structure and interrelationships of parts of the complex material with which he is confronted in many experimental situations, and indeed in school tasks. He has to overcome the confusion caused by a multiplicity of dimly perceived data and adopt a suitable approach to these. He must acquire the ability to select in ambient vision the significant features of the field which suggest its meaning. Then he must fixate these and view them focally, analysing them and extracting and differentiating cues to identity which may be obscured or buried in a mass of irrelevant detail, and comparing and relating these together. In this he will be assisted by an emerging capacity for conceptualization, which even when adequate for familiar objects, only gradually becomes competent to establish the identities and meanings contained in the complex material. His language may be sufficient for ordinary communication some years before it develops as an effective medium for analysing and discriminating such material and formulating hypotheses as to its nature. But it is likely that the naturally reflective child will be more efficient in performing many of these activities than the impulsive child.

Clearly the type of intelligence which emerges at the stage of concrete operations is essential for the fully efficient functioning of the processes of directing attention, analysing out significant form, selecting cues to identity and classifying perceived material appropriately. Wide experience of a varying environment is important in learning to apply these processes in many different but related situations. But it is essential that the child should be enabled to understand them, principally through feedback from the consequences of his actions in these situations; though parental explanation is also valuable. However, it is doubtful if specific training can advance the effective functioning of these processes beyond that which emerges at each successive stage of maturation.

Chapter Five

Visual education for young children

J. M. PICKERING

Art Education has undergone several changes since its emergence in the 19th century. The two most important shaping factors occurred early in its development. In the first place there were the adult-imposed attitudes based on a belief in original sin; this produced a curriculum that was severe and disciplined and paid little attention to the needs of children. It concerned itself more with the industrial needs of the commercially-minded 19th century. The second factor resulted from a complete change of attitude from a belief in original sin to an acceptance of the innate goodness of the child. The duty of the teacher was seen to be one of protecting the child from the evils of the world, whereas previously children were controlled to prevent them from erupting in antisocial behaviour.

The history of Art Education is normally traced through the teacher innovators. These were eclectic people who worked mainly by intuition and experience. They gathered information from many sources to support their ideas, borrowing from philosophy, psychology, the world of Fine Art and other areas of Education. The names most commonly associated with English Art teaching for young children are those of the Austrian Professor Franz Cizek, Marion Richardson, Sir Herbert Read, and from America Viktor Lowenfeld, but the methods used may be traced to a wide range of educators.

Their ideas filtered through the years and when they emerged, often half understood and distorted, they resulted in both good and bad teaching methods. From the work of Franz Cizek came the view that the child was an artist in his own right although Cizek believed that this state rarely continued into adolescence.

Marion Richardson, strongly influenced by Cizek's work with its emphasis on free expression, structured her work, in the grammar school, around the imagination. She placed importance on the use of visual stimuli through verbal descriptions of scenes and activities which she had experienced, and tried to pass these on to children whom she considered visually deprived. She also presented objects and still-life groups in various ways using unusual lighting and settings aimed at a sharpening of the children's visual awareness.

The term self-expression owed much to the influence of the Expressionist painters and came into general use during the 1920s. This influence led to confusion among some teachers who interpreted the self-expression initiated by Cizek in terms of the Expressionist painters, which seemed far removed from the importance of the innate development of the child.

Psychoanalysis, which was evolved by Sigmund Freud in the early part of the 20th century, focused attention on actions previously considered chance or useless behaviour. Freud's theories implied that no behaviour could be considered uncaused. Feeling and emotion basic to Art activities of the New Art and Self-Expression eras, gained support from such thinking. Few coherent explanations of a child's emotional development existed at this time and psychoanalytical thinking provided a framework upon which to build. Although such theories were unsubstantiated they did reinforce in the minds of Cizek, and others like him, the importance of expression of feelings. Cizek stated, 'Everything great has originated from the subconscious, Art more and more dries up because it is surplanted by the intellect.'

The result of such thinking has not always been as encouraging as it appears on the surface. A dazzling array of colour and symbols in children's drawings and paintings such as may be seen in many of our first and middle schools, may delight the eyes of visitors but reveal little of the processes involved which may have been good or bad. The romantic ideas of Cizek placed great emphasis on the Art product, and its production was to be encouraged by the presence of a teacher who, according to Cizek, should hover like an invisible spirit over his pupils ready to encourage but never to press or force his ideas upon the child.

Teachers who have assimilated such thinking find it difficult to know when or how to aid development, and are forced into a position of recognizing all products as good.

The humanistic influence of teachers like Cizek and Marion Richardson cannot be denied; the happy atmosphere which has been found to be necessary in the production of states of readiness for learning and the need to find some good in the self-initiated work of children are obviously necessary.

At present what seems lacking for many teachers is a structure with aims and goals, which appear readily available in other areas of the curriculum. The mystique of Art and the apparent ephemeral nature of the subject frequently result in teachers whose training has been brief in this area, producing with young children either a therapeutic session, or craft activities which are often designed to support other areas of the curriculum. However, there are teachers who have an innate skill in achieving a great deal in other directions from such methods. The extension of perceptual learning, and increasing visual awareness, and of the ability to analyse in visual terms is unlikely to result from such occupation, and a reappraisal of the situation would seem justified.

The importance attached to the Art product has drawn criticism in recent years. Among the critics was Viktor Lowenfeld who saw the necessity of stressing the process as an integrating force in the development of a child. Similarities exist between the work of Lowenfeld and Herbert Read, both being concerned with aesthetics as an organic process of physical and mental integration. The work of Sir Herbert Read in *Education Through Art* (1947), although a hallmark in Art Education literature, has failed to have had the impact of Cizek and Marion

Richardson. The reason may be that the book is not attractive to general teachers whose knowledge of psychology and Art is not specialized. Read, however, puts forward a powerful case for the education of the child through Art. Essentially Read is concerned with three vital activities in Art teaching:

1 Self-expression and communication.

2 Observation and the extension of conceptual knowledge through the involvement of perceptual and practical activities.

3 Appreciation, the response of the individual to the work of others.

The move towards these three elements in Art Education signposted clearly the way to Visual Education and the extension of the concept of Art Education at the present time.

Creativity, which became of great importance during the 'space race' between America and Russia, has tended to become a rather overworked term in English Education. Syllabuses exist on Creative Writing, Creative Dance, Creative Drama, Creative Arts, Creative Activities and so forth, but present social needs have produced new pressures which are beginning to influence curriculum development. Concern with the conservation of the environment is turning the attention of many educationists towards perceptual learning.

There is a growing body of opinion that seeks to relate Art activities to perceptual responses, rather than to an exclusive concern with self-expression, which tends to take place with young children.

The justification for a Visual Education is simple; there is a social need for efficient seeing with a development of aesthetic discrimination. Dedicated exponents of this approach maintain that perceptual learning is a neglected area and that children are visually deprived in the conceptual world of Education.

Such ideas suggesting a more structured approach in Art teaching are by no means new and may be traced to Rousseau, Spencer, Sully and Dewey. Evelyn Gibbs, a lecturer at Goldsmiths College, wrote in 1934, 'The teacher must not teach the child to draw so much as to help him to see.'

Herbert Read in *Education Through Art* proposed that Art Education should more properly be called Visual or Plastic Education and these should form two aspects of a total scheme for Aesthetic Education.

The Bauhaus teacher Moholy-Nagy, who died in 1946, sought and proposed ways of increasing skill in visual analysis as an answer to a social need. His ideas were taken up by his student Gyorges Kepes who emphasized the need for a Visual Education.

There is sufficient evidence of visual illiteracy in terms of urban sprawl, and in the ugliness and vulgarization of the misused environment the utility of vision necessary for living is undeniable, and obviously vision forms a normal part of most Art activities. The aim, however, is not to be concerned with the simple act of seeing but rather to consider visual learning, visual qualities, visual language in terms of communication, and visual thinking, leading to visual efficiency. The perceptual theory that underpins such ideas is that of Gestalt psychology, which the Bauhaus teachers used as a method of aiding the understanding of design.

More recently Gestalt psychology has been used by teachers like June King McFee in America and it has also served in England as a method of handling information in Nuffield, and Schools Council, Science and Mathematics projects. Sorting, grouping, classifying, closure and good organization have all been used effectively.

The book *Preparation for Art* by June King McFee, published 1961, applies the Gestalt Laws in Art-learning situations. She expresses concern about the emphasis on conceptual learning in present Education.

Visual Education, with its emphasis on perceptual learning, may be introduced as an extension rather than as a contraction of present methods. It may be introduced at any age level but would obviously be more beneficial if commenced as early as possible. This attitude towards Visual Education is based on the assumption that perceptual learning is likely to result from a range of experiences which focus attention on perceptual responses.

It has been suggested that the intention is to engage children in problems and activities that may be considered to be visual learning situations; this may be seen not as an end in itself but as a preparation for the time when they will reach perceptual maturity. There is ample psychological evidence that sensory stimulation is necessary for healthy living. Animals and children who have been deprived of a stimulating environment in experimental situations appear to be at a serious disadvantage. It is not sufficient to regard sensory stimulation and sensory learning as either innate or direct, as too much depends on the kind of environment and learning situation in which a child might find himself. Situations and activities therefore, have to be arranged and structured and a curriculum planned. It might be argued that present Art teaching methods engage children in visual activities and that there is no need for particular emphasis on perceptual learning. Lecturers in higher education often find that children coming from secondary schools are visually illiterate even though they have been engaged in Art activities for the whole of their school life. They are often unable to analyse, or even discuss the work of others in terms of visual or aesthetic responses, and are frequently limited to subjective opinions or narrative descriptions. There would appear to be a need to provide teaching which might overcome this apparent deficiency. The importance of words and concepts is not denied, and language aids perceptual learning just as perceptual experience can aid language. The knowledge of words, however, is not essential to perceptual awareness, a baby almost from birth assimilates and accommodates to its environment both through its tactile and visual responses. The colours and textures that we might use in the decoration of the interior and exterior of our homes, do not require specific labels before we can respond to them.

The approach to be considered is one in which conceptual learning with its use of language and perceptual learning with its consideration of visual qualities and relationships need to be balanced.

Methods in Art Education have tended to polarize towards either those that state that Art is a subjective activity concerned with intuition and self-expression, or those that are concerned with a more objective approach which proposes that there are particular areas of information that have to be taught and learnt.

It would be difficult to present a curriculum which does not contain both subjective and objective elements. The scheme proposed here involves both these aspects and is in keeping with emerging trends in English Education.

The essential area in which visual learning can take place is within the real world where children can experience a wide range of perceptual activities. Four main aspects will form the foundation for the work with children:

1 Tactile perception.

2 Perception of light.

3 Spatial perception.

4 Perception of movement.

Using Gestalt psychology as a method of handling information, four ways may be involved in the process:

1 The lowest level of perceptual response is *detection*, that is the critical moment when the child becomes aware of the existence of a touch, a sound, or sees something. To a teacher of educationally subnormal children or of very young children the attainment of this response may be an achievement.

2 The way in which information is organized is a sorting process leading to *discrimination* and may be concerned with similarities or differences.

3 Objects given to children who have not previously known them may be classified and given *identification*.

4 However, when objects are seen or heard or touched and are matched with previous experiences, *recognition* takes place.

There is a tendency for us to recognize things even though they exist in different situations, which might involve different lighting conditions, size relationships, textures and viewpoints. This is normally referred to as *constancy* and although it is useful it tends to generalize our perception, so that we fail to observe what is really there and find it very difficult to overcome generalization through gross abstraction. A teacher may solve some of the problems created by constancies by engaging children in a wide range of particular activities, for example they might be introduced to the variations of size that occur when they stand spread out across a field or study unusual size relationships that take place in the environment.

Perceptual education, through situations and activities which may be considered to be conducive to visual learning, will involve teaching that will be balanced between:

Perceptual Aspects	→	Visual and tactile aspects
Conceptual Aspects	→	Logical Thinking and Meanings
Emotional Aspects	→	Expression, Intuition and Imagination
Techniques	→	Learning skills.

Perceptual education

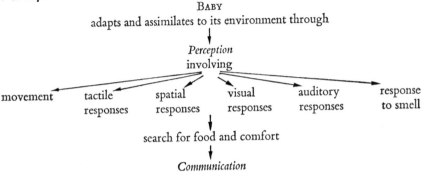

BABY
adapts and assimilates to its environment through

Perception
involving

movement — tactile responses — spatial responses — visual responses — auditory responses — response to smell

search for food and comfort

Communication

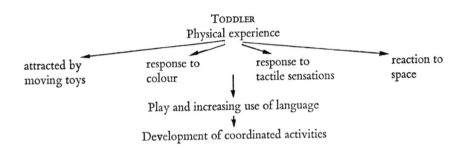

TODDLER
Physical experience

attracted by moving toys — response to colour — response to tactile sensations — reaction to space

Play and increasing use of language

Development of coordinated activities

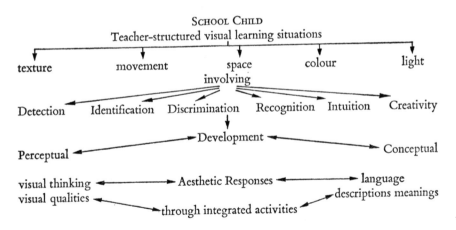

SCHOOL CHILD
Teacher-structured visual learning situations

texture — movement — space — colour — light
involving

Detection — Identification — Discrimination — Recognition — Intuition — Creativity

Development

Perceptual — Conceptual

visual thinking — Aesthetic Responses — language
visual qualities — through integrated activities — descriptions meanings

CURRICULUM DEVELOPMENT

It is generally accepted that the early stages of a baby's life are concerned with physical experiments and experiences through which he comes to terms with his environment. One of the earliest sensations of pleasure and security is provided by touch and there is also psychological evidence of an awareness of light, space and movement. Children come to understand qualities of materials by manipulating them in a variety of ways and there is a strong relationship between the tactile and visual senses.

93

The approaches suggested are for children of any age and should be related to the needs and abilities of individuals but have particular relevance to pre-school, primary and middle school children. The content of the curriculum therefore will consist of particular activities within the areas of space, light and movement, but children may involve all three areas in their activities. However, it may prove beneficial to structure situations, on some occasions, within one of these areas. It is suggested, therefore, that such activities should be started as soon as possible. The following notes suggest some ways in which situations might be developed where visual learning should take place.

The content of the curriculum will depend upon:

1 Readiness of the children to respond.

2 Provision of opportunity of exploration and discovery.

3 Possibilities for developments.

4 Development of the creative potential.

5 Consideration of perceptual, conceptual, and cognitive development.

6 The usefulness of the subject matter in relation to Art and other areas of the curriculum.

7 Its importance to the consideration of the environment.

All or some of these considerations may be necessary in the selection of content.

In the earliest stages of development, children have yet to achieve a command of language and therefore the content at this time will be concerned almost entirely with activity and perceptual responses. Situations which are pleasurable to the child and in which he can use the senses in exploring and discriminating should be provided.

Opportunities within the content selected should seek:

1 To teach children to see different and similar aspects of form, texture and movement in space and light in a wide variety of situations.

2 To teach them to see through the analysis of things observed.

3 To involve the use of both concepts and percepts in the cognitive process.

4 To involve the intuitive and imaginative in problem-solving situations.

5 To attempt to develop a rich perceptual vocabulary of images and objects.

NOTES ON VISUAL LEARNING SITUATIONS

Pre-school

Perceptual responses, often instant and intuitive, related to physical activities in exploring the immediate environment. Importance of self. All senses used. Emphasis on play. Integrated activities. Concentration often spasmodic.

SPACE   Use of bricks, boxes, constructional toys and large apparatus. Wide
variations in size of materials and equipment. Exploration of shape, holes, simple   Plates 5, 6
structures and balance. Surfaces and tactile responses to them. Inside and outside
appearances of fruits and objects.   Plate 31

LIGHT   Awareness of light and shadows. Exploration of a variety of transparent,   Plates
translucent and opaque materials. Observation of reflections in water, mirrors,   32, 33
metals and other reflective surfaces.

MOVEMENT   Observation and activities with a wide variety of things. Toys –
push, pull, mechanical, wind-driven. Interest in enjoyment of movement in the
environment, water, wind, fire, animals, birds, fish and insects. Awareness,   Plate 34
through testing different materials for movement in the wind. Play activities
involving rolling, pushing, pulling, bouncing, blowing bubbles and paint.
Pouring and dropping materials. Painting activities related to finger, hand, arm
and body movements, and to the materials used.

METHODS will aim at stimulating attitudes of interest in visual responses through
detection, observation, collection, sorting, identification and recognition, using   Plate VII
discussion and practical activities. Recording methods may involve rubbings,
printing from surfaces, casting impressions in clay, plasticine and plaster.

First school

Continuation of physical activity and intuitive behaviour with a development of
cognitive activity. According to Piaget, abilities are limited to objects and
materials that can be manipulated concretely, therefore this area is concerned
with the development of thinking through the exploration of actual objects that
have relevance to the child.

SPACE   Recognition and awareness of shapes related to the room, school and
environment, comparison, classification and consideration of aesthetic qualities.
Increase of vocabulary related to shape. Use of work-cards. Shapes found in
pockets – sweets, buttons, keys, etc. Discovery of shapes that fit together, nut
and bolt, egg and cup, hand and glove. Created environments. Shapes and size
relationship.

LIGHT   Increasing discrimination of colour. Observation of how light changes
the appearance of things. Observation of convex and concave reflective surfaces.
Observation of lighting produced by man. Drawings and paintings concerned
with light, by children and artists. Comparison of transparent and translucent
materials and the effects produced by them. Refraction produced by water.
Photography, photograms, photoplay. Projection of slides and films made by
children.

MOVEMENT   Observations of movement in environment, things that move
slowly and quickly. Objects that rise and objects that fall. Rain, snow, wind,
water and fire effects. The influence of time on things leading to change,
erosion, disintegration, rotting, rusting. Changes in plants through growth. Use

of toys and games that involve movement. Display photographs of all things, for example, that rise.

Practical activities such as examining the effects of movement on dots, lines and colour. Use of apparent movement in paintings and drawings. Flick books, zoetropes, mobiles, paper aeroplanes, kites, propellors, puppets.

Plate 35

METHODS would be similar to those proposed for pre-school but with the increased ability in language and writing children will support their visual activities, in some instances, in a written form. Photography should play an increasingly important part as a recording medium.

Middle school

Mental activities becoming more varied and important. Work may be related to more particular areas in Art rather than generalizing on the subject. More abstract thinking possible and the ability to be more analytical in observations. An increased awareness of aesthetic qualities of materials and more ability to relate these. An awareness of objects from different viewpoints with the ensuing understanding of size relationships and the translation of three-dimensional objects into two-dimensional diagrams and symbols.

SHAPE Observation of shapes in the environment leading to a study of buildings. The translation of three-dimensional objects into drawings and paintings, natural objects into clay models. Consideration of clothing and shapes related to human anatomy, e.g. helmets and armour. Problem-solving, for example, creating structures from a limited number of drinking straws or tubed paper, seeking strength and height. Three-dimensional structures in card, clay, wire and wood within the limitation for example of rectangular or circular elements.

The analysis of shapes, e.g. sliced potato or pieces of wood to create sections from which a contour diagram could be built. The study of natural structures, extension of vision through the microscope and the study of the infinite produced by outer-space photography. Collections and study of natural forms, recording through photographs, monoprints, drawings and paintings.

LIGHT Study of colour through pigments and projected light. Increased use of photography, photograms, photoplay and film. Projection of light on to objects to change appearance. Experiments with various materials on the overhead projector. Exploration of dyes, inks, paints. Further considerations of reflections used in two- and three-dimensional structures. Construction of large three-dimensional structures in which shadow plays an important part. Shadow puppets. Study of light in relation to form through drawings using wide range of media.

MOVEMENT Translation of actual movement into apparent movement, e.g. drawings, diagrams, and card bas-relief to describe, say, a spinning lid. Drawings that describe progression or actions in sequence, e.g. how to make a telephone call. Observations of movement in the environment through photography – cars, sport, washing billowing on a line. Use of clues to suggest movement in drawings and paintings which might be symbols or words, e.g. smoke blowing,

multiple images, blurring, words like zoom!! whoosh!! wham!!. Recording of
changes of materials through time and decay, erosion – change through forces Plate VIII
tearing, cutting, twisting, explosions. Mobiles. Optical effects – moiré, corruga-
tions which present different facets. Study of flows of movement, people,
traffic, etc. Appreciation of the kinetic works of painters and sculptors. Study of
the design of objects that move, ergonomics.

METHODS   Greater emphasis on translation from three dimensions to two
dimensions. Consideration of the image and its meanings through discussion.
Use of a wide range of media and skills, e.g. the ability to use a camera, develop
film and print in a variety of ways extending to photographic silk screens. Use
of equipment that will extend human vision. Analytical drawing, important.
Consideration of relationships in design, such as proximity, similarity, linear
expectation, closure, figure/ground relationships. Study of the work of artists,
visits to galleries, use of reference material from many sources. Consideration of
man's ability to effect change in the environment through design.

CONCLUSION

It has not been the intention to propose that children should no longer be engaged
in painting and drawing, and the wide range of crafts offered in many schools;
rather that such experiences play an important part in the methods suggested
and also exist in their own right as forms of expression. However, where picture-
making activities are repeated and rely upon conceptual attitudes, perceptual
learning can only be considered to be at a low level.

The Art Education is a subject that in the past has been noted for its progressive
attitudes. If stereotyped approaches are to be avoided in the future, teachers need
to look critically not only at the content and methods of their curriculum but at
the long-term effects it may have on the children. There is a need for research
in this area to provide evidence upon which to shape curriculum content so
that it has relevance both to Art and life.

The need for a child to find pleasure, excitement and interest in natural and
man-made things as well as an ability to make aesthetic responses should be of
vital concern to all involved in education. The social benefits that such concern
could have upon the environment are extensive.

With technological development methods of communication are changing
rapidly and the need to make sensitive perceptual responses is growing; education therefore must be prepared to meet this challenge in a new visual world.

Chapter Six

Visual art: some perspectives from cross-cultural psychology

MARSHALL H. SEGALL

INTRODUCTION
Art, culture, and behaviour

It is customary to think of art as an aspect of culture; it is less common to think of it as behaviour. Art is, however, both culture and behaviour. Art is also, to complete the circle, behaviour that is culturally influenced.

Art as culture: Once a work of art is done, it occupies a place in culture. Because it is a manmade part of the environment, existing potentially to influence present and future generations who live their lives in that environment, a work of art satisfies both the anthropological and popular definitions of an aspect of culture.

Art as behaviour: For the very same reason – because a work of art is manmade – it is a product of behaviour. Every work of art, because it is fashioned by a human being, can be viewed as a product of human actions or as a tangible record of what someone has done. Each work is an accomplishment, reflecting the perceptions of some actor and expressing his imagination and skill. When a psychologist, whose subject matter is behaviour, considers a work of art, he may therefore properly focus more on the actions of the artist than on his product *per se*. The psychologist, in other words, may give more attention to what the artist did than to what he produced.

A psychological treatment of art can take various forms. A relatively familiar version of a psychological approach to art is the psychoanalytic one, whereby the analyst attempts to reconstruct the psyche of an artist through an examination of one or more of his works. The psychoanalytic approach focuses on the individual artist and tends to be retrospectively biographical. The work of art is employed as a kind of Alice's looking-glass through which one peers hoping to fathom the idiosyncratic motivations of one artist. Via a procedure itself more artistic than scientific, there is performed a highly inferential, if not creative, psychoanalysis-at-a-distance. That is not the kind of approach to be adopted in this essay.

Here, the interest is in the behaviour as revealed by the art and not in the personality as revealed by the behaviour. Rather than attempting, as does the psychoanalyst, to go *two* steps beyond the work of art, one need only go one in order to focus on behaviour. Furthermore, one need not be concerned, as is the psychoanalytically oriented psychologist, with the behaviour of a *particular* artist. An equally legitimate concern is with the behaviour of artists who lived (or live) in a certain place at a certain time.

Art as culturally-influenced behaviour: By focusing on the artistic products of the behaviours of human groups, it becomes apparent that art is not only an aspect of culture but also a product of culture. A conceptualization of art as a record of what human beings of a particular time and place have seen fit and been able to produce underscores that much of all artists' activity is culturally-influenced behaviour.

Hence, our formulation for art as seen from the perspective of cross-cultural psychology is, very simply, this: *Culture, which includes but is not limited to art products of the past, influences the behaviour of those who produce the art of the present and future.* Via this formulation we can see that there is art in culture and culture in art. The connecting link is behaviour.

Cultural conventions in artistic behaviour

Underlying this essay, then, is a conception of visual art as it is viewed from a cross-cultural, psychological perspective. Any work of art is considered the end-product of what some artist witnessed in the world around him and what he wished to say about it. Considered in this fashion, a work of art reflects something about the real world as it is transmitted through someone's visual sensory apparatus, modified by his motives, wishes, intentions and skills, all of which themselves are residues of earlier experiences that he has had. The complex behaviour involved in the production of a work of art comprises, therefore, a prototypic example of a *culturally-conditioned* behavioural disposition. This is so because the disposition is, in part at least, shared by many artists of a given time and place.

Each artist's culture contains many forces which serve to influence his behaviour as an artist. These influences are revealed in his choice of subjects about which he decides to attempt an artistic statement, in the medium in which he decides to make it, and in the techniques he employs for making it. Above all, culture reveals itself in the artistic conventions which characterize every artist's behaviour.

As is often the case with culturally-influenced behaviours, the influence of culture is not obvious, particularly to those very people whose behaviour is influenced. Thus, the fact that there is considerable culturally-conditioned conventionality in the production of works of art is seldom obvious to artists. Indeed, it is common for artists to think of themselves as iconoclasts, as defiers of convention, which of course they can be. However, as Herskovits once put it, even 'the political revolutionary does not refuse to cast his revolutionary songs in the modal structure and scale progressions of the culture he is in process of changing; his formations, if his organized forces are strong enough, will operate in terms of accepted patterns of military procedure. The one who rebels against the religious and moral system of his time will couch his appeals in the linguistic patterns of his people, use established affect symbols, and employ accepted esthetic standards in heightening the responses of his followers.' (Herskovits 1951, 153).

As an example of a cultural convention that is today employed in much of the world's visual art, consider the use of a flat, rectangular surface as the 'vessel' containing the art product. So much of Indo-European art has employed this convention, and for so long, that its conventionality is seldom remarked. But surely one could paint pictures on round or even irregular surfaces! Yet, the very concept of *picture* has until recently meant a recognizable representation of a segment of visual experience, bounded by a rectangular frame.

As a matter of fact, this particular artistic convention, especially the decision to represent a three-dimensional world on a two-dimensional surface, relates to some important theoretical issues which have inspired considerable research by cross-cultural psychologists. The research has revealed that the way in which men 'see' the world around them is to some degree culturally influenced. In other words, visual perception itself is culturally influenced. Therefore, the ways in which they behave when they produce their works of art are affected by culture since what they see and what they decide to do about what they see are culturally influenced. There is also good reason to believe that the works of art they produce serve to influence, in turn, the way they see the world. In the body of this essay, to which we now turn, we shall review some of the cross-cultural research and theory and try to relate it to the conventionality and other cultur-ally-influenced aspects of artistic behaviour.

CULTURE AND VISUAL PERCEPTION

Not surprisingly, throughout most of human history, it was widely believed that we see the world as it is. That is, after all, the simplest possible assumption. Philosophers (e.g., Plato, Locke and Berkeley) long ago pointed out the preva-lent human error of assuming that the world is as it appears to be. This assump-tion, which may be characterized as *phenomenal absolutism*, has been described as 'one ubiquitous and misleading attribute of naive conscious experience' (Segall, Campbell and Herskovits 1966, 5), for it requires that the viewing organism be considered a passive receiver of stimulation, seeing what he does simply because it is there.

Modern psychology is in essential agreement with the philosophers who challenged phenomenal absolutism and who recognized that the state of the viewing organism always interacts with his sensory input jointly to determine a perception. This view insists that a perception is not solely stimulus-determined. The viewer always brings something to his perception. Accordingly, this alterna-tive to the naive realism of the phenomenal absolutist may be characterized as *stimulus relativism*, for it leads to the insistence that every stimulus is judged, evaluated, and otherwise perceived by being compared, consciously or not, with the residues of previous sensory experiences.

GEORGES SEURAT *The Artist's
[Mot]her (Woman Sewing)*. Conté crayon
[on p]aper. Chapter 7

53   CANALETTO *Piazza San Marco and
the colonnade of the Procuratie Nuove* (detail).
Chapter 7

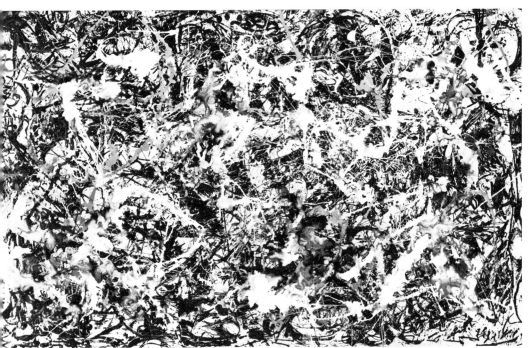

JACKSON POLLOCK *Convergence*. 1952. Chapter 7

55 MIROSLAV SUTEJ
Bombardment of the Optic Nerve 2
Chapter 7

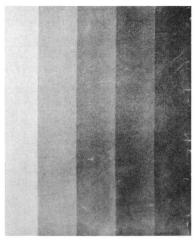

56 Mach-bands. The light and the dark areas
near the borders of the stripes vanish when the
remote side of each border is occluded. They
can be made to appear uniform if only one stripe
is exposed at any time. Chapter 7

57 'Moses Striking the Rock that Water may Flow' by a normal-sighted subject, visual type. Chapter 8

58 'Moses Striking the Rock that Water may Flow' by a normal-sighted subject, haptic type. Chapter 8

59 'Longing for Sight' by a congenitally blind subject, visual type. Chapter 8

60 'Inner Decay' by a congenitally blind subject, haptic type. Chapter 8

61 'Being Throttled' by a weak-sighted subject, 23 years of age, haptic type. Chapter 8

COLOUR PLATES I AND II >
Paintings by a patient in the Psychiatric Clinic of Lausanne University
Chapter 1

III

IV

The classical philosophical precursor of this contemporary psychological position may be found most tellingly expressed in the parable of the lukewarm water. It may be found in Locke (1690) and Berkeley (1713). As reproduced in Segall et al. (1966, 8–9), Berkeley's Philonous explains it to Hylas in this way:

PHILONOUS: Is it not an absurdity to think that the same thing should be at the same time both cold and warm?

HYLAS: It is.

PHILONOUS: Suppose now one of your hands hot, the other cold, and that they are both at once put into the same vessel of water in an intermediate state: will not the water seem cold to one hand, and warm to the other?

HYLAS: It will.

PHILONOUS: Ought we not therefore by your principles to conclude it is really both cold and warm at the same time? That is, according to your own concession, to believe an absurdity?

HYLAS: I confess it seems so.

Stimulus relativism underlies the theoretical position developed by Herskovits, Campbell and Segall in 1956 on the basis of which they predicted cross-cultural differences in visual perception. In summary form, their line of argument follows: Every human organism, in the process of accumulating experiences, changes. Each experience leaves its mark; each subsequent experience interacts with the residues of earlier ones, so that at any point in his life span, the individual can be thought of as possessing a set of behavioural dispositions (or habits) which are the joint product of all his experiences to date. (These experiences, of course, interact in very complex ways. Some are weighted more heavily than others. Earlier ones colour subsequent ones more than vice versa. But all experiences have an impact.) Therefore, whenever the individual is confronted with an external stimulus impinging on his sensory apparatus, the way in which that stimulus is perceived depends mightily on his experientially-established perceptual dispositions. Much more of the nervous system than the visual cortex is involved in a visual perception.

Since persons who live in a given place at a given time tend to share numerous experiences which are also labelled via a common language, they will tend to develop similar perceptual dispositions and, hence, the external world will appear pretty much the same to each of them. For such people, united as it were by a culture, there is a shared way of seeing the world. By the same token, another set of persons, living in a different place or at a different time, will have developed different perceptual dispositions so that, while they will agree with each other about the gross details of the external world, their view of it very likely would be different from that held by the other cultural group.

COLOUR PLATES

III *Painting by a young male chimpanzee, showing a subsidiary fan pattern motif. Chapter 2*

IV *Lopsided fan pattern painted by a chimpanzee. Chapter 2*

At first glance, this may not appear to be saying very much. It is common knowledge that people in different cultural settings possess different values, make different judgments, have characteristically different preferences, and so on. But Herskovits et al. applied this line of reasoning to some very fundamental visual-perceptual phenomena which many scholars, including at least one school of psychologists that specialized in the study of perception (viz., Gestalt psychology), had long thought to be immune from cultural conditioning. To Herskovits et al. it seemed reasonable to argue that even the apparent length of a straight line would vary from culture to culture, at least when the line appeared in certain contexts. Similarly they expected that the appearance of an angular juncture (particularly whether or not acute and obtuse angles might be seen as right angles) would also be subject to cultural influence.

Their arguments, and the research to which they led, were concerned with a class of visual stimuli which had long beguiled philosophers, psychologists and visual artists alike, although for somewhat different reasons. These stimuli are commonly referred to as 'geometric illusions' because, in the Western world at least, it has long been known that people generally perceive them in ways which do not accord with 'reality' as determined with the aid of standard measuring instruments.

Consider, for example, this figure, known to psychologists as the Sander Parallelogram.

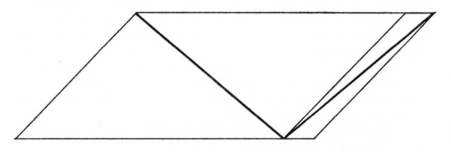

In the example shown here, the two heavy diagonal lines are objectively equal. To most viewers, however, the one on the left appears considerably longer. Since the one on the left is *not* longer, we must begin by rejecting phenomenal absolutism. For the world, at least this bit of it, is surely not as it appears. With what, then, should this naive realism be replaced?

The Gestalt psychological explanation was that the human nervous system (particularly the visual receptors and the visual cortex) is structured in such a way that the illusion becomes inevitable; it is a product of certain hypothetical neural forces. An implication of this 'nativistic' argument, which accords virtually no role to learning, is that the illusion must be universal; all humans, unless their nervous systems are significantly different,[1] should be equally susceptible to the illusion, and to others like it.

Leaning heavily on a more 'empiricistic' tradition in psychology (see, especially, Brunswik 1956), Segall et al. (1966) stated why it should be, on the contrary, that people in different cultures should vary markedly in their susceptibility to geometric illusions.

Our general theoretical position can perhaps best be epitomized by Brunswik's phrase 'ecological cue validity'. . . . It involves some general assumptions that Brunswik summarized as 'probabilistic functionalism'. It is hypothesized that the visual system is functional in general, although not in every specific utilization. The modes of operation are what they are because they are useful in the statistical average of utilizations.

When this is applied to optical illusions, it is hypothesized that the illusion taps a process that is in general functional, although it is misleading in the particular instance because of 'ecological un-representativeness'; that is, this type of situation is unlike the general run of situations to which the process is functionally adapted and adaptive. (Segall et al. 1966, 74.)

The view that optical illusions are products of the same processes that mediate normal visual achievements is . . . at least implicit in the bulk of older discussions of optical illusions. . . . A modern revival of these older empiricist perspective theories emphasizes the role of perceptual constancy . . . as . . . contributing to the optical illusions. . . . For example, Gregory (1962, 16) argues that the mechanism of constancy scaling (by which is meant the tendency to see things as they are despite marked changes in the retinal image of them) could produce distortion if it were misplaced, and that all the known illusions have features which commonly indicate depth by perspective. It is also clear in every case that the illusions go the right way; those parts of the figures which would normally be further away in 3-D space appear too large in the illusion figures. (Ibid. 76.)

Our theoretical system hypothesizes (1) *that the visual perceptual system uses numerous cues of low and probabilistic (but still positive) validity, and (2) that optical illusions demonstrate the function of normally useful cues but provide atypical visual performance settings.* (Ibid. 77.) (Italics in original.)

Applying this theoretical system to the Sander Parallelogram (shown above), on which the left diagonal is often judged longer than it really is, it was asserted, 'This bias is understandable if one perceives a nonorthogonal parallelogram drawn on a flat surface [which is what the Sander figure *is*] as the representation of a rectangular surface extended in space. Given such a tendency, it is clear that the represented *distance* covered by the left diagonal is greater than the represented distance covered by the right diagonal.' (Ibid. 84.) The 'tendency' referred to here is a visual inference habit which Segall et al. explicitly predicted would co-vary with culture. By direct extension of the ecological cue validity theory, they reasoned, '(3) *if human groups differ in their visual inference tendencies, it is because their visual environments differ.* . . .' (Ibid. 78.)

Applying this extension to the tendency to exaggerate the left diagonal in the Sander Parallelogram, it was predicted that this tendency would be more likely to be found in Western societies than in non-Western ones.

A tendency such as this constitutes a habit of inference that has great ecological validity – and great functional utility – in highly carpentered environments.

Western societies provide environments replete with rectangular objects; these objects, when projected on the retina, are represented by nonrectangular images. For people living in carpentered worlds, the tendency to interpret obtuse and acute angles in retinal images as deriving from rectangular objects is likely to be so pervasively reinforced that it becomes automatic and unconscious relatively early in life. For those living where manmade structures are a small portion of the visual environment and where such structures are constructed without benefit of carpenters' tools ... straight lines and precise right angles are a rarity. As a result, the inference habit of interpreting acute and obtuse angles as right angles extended in space would not be learned, at least not as well.' (Ibid. 84.)

The preceding hypothesis was dubbed 'the carpentered world hypothesis' and it provided the main basis for predicting cross-cultural differences in susceptibility to the Sander Parallelogram (as well as to two other figures that also involve line arrangements that could be interpreted as linear perspective cues. These two will not be discussed here for the discussion would be redundant.)

Yet another dominant ecological characteristic of Western environments that would similarly enhance susceptibility to the Sander and related figures, might also be suggested. This is simply the pervasive use in the West of symbols on paper to represent objects in space, particularly as in representational drawing which involves the deliberate effort to represent three-dimensional spatial arrays on two-dimensional surfaces. For children who grow up in a world full of such pictures, the result must be that they learn to interpret perspective drawings (and photographs) in ways that would have to enhance the tendency to interpret acute and obtuse angles as right angles. Hence, learning to interpret two-dimensional representational drawings should enhance illusions like the Sander Parallelogram.

Both of these two ecological conditions, carpenteredness and the tradition of drawing, should make Western peoples more susceptible to the Sander Parallelogram than non-Western peoples.

The cultural-differences predictions were tested in a cooperative data-collection effort by some fifteen anthropologists and psychologists in as many societies, some in Europe and the United States and most in Africa. Among the several prediction-sustaining findings was that European and American samples were indeed significantly more susceptible to the Sander Parallelogram than any non-Euro-American sample.[2] Thus, empirical support could be claimed for the two hypotheses – the 'carpentered world hypothesis' and the 'experience with two-dimensional representations of reality hypothesis' – and, by implica-the theory from which the hypotheses were derived. So it was concluded, 'that to a substantial extent we learn to perceive; that in spite of the phenomenally absolute character of our perceptions, they are determined by perceptual inference habits; and that various inference habits are differentially likely in differing societies.' (Segall et al. 1966, 214.)

Recently, there have been several follow-up studies and critiques. Stewart, working in Zambia, found the degree of susceptibility to three illusions within that single culture to increase as the degree of environmental carpenteredness increased. (Stewart 1973). There has been one serious challenge to the ecological validity interpretation in a suggestion by Pollack (1963a, b) that cultural differences in illusion susceptibility might better be explained by differences in racial pigmentation. Jahoda, working in Scotland and Malawi obtained some support for this rival hypothesis (Jahoda 1971) as did Berry, who used data he collected in Canada. Sierra Leone, Australia and New Guinea (Berry 1971). These few studies employed only the Müller-Lyer illusion and involved comparisons of societies that differed both ecologically and 'racially' (i.e. biologically). In an intra-cultural study done in the American urban Middle West, with three illusions applied to White and Negro schoolchildren, age was the only variable which related to illusion susceptibility. Skin colour did not. (Armstrong, Rubin, Stewart and Kuntner 1970).

So, further study is clearly desirable. Culture obviously influences visual perception, but precisely to what degree is still to be learned. Physiological differences, which tend to be confounded with culture, may also play a role, but even so, the main thrust of the argument still holds.[3] People in different cultures see things differently.

Now, what has all of this to do with visual art? Whereas the foregoing discussion was based on considerable empirical research and careful theorizing, what follows is speculative, designed to provoke some reflection and critical reaction among readers.

SOME IMPLICATIONS FOR ART FROM RESEARCH ON PERCEPTION

Art has a history, indeed many histories, at least one for every cultural context in which it has developed. Thus, contemporary Western art is a tentative achievement which occurred in a particular historico-cultural context. One of the major developments of its fairly recent past was the 'picture', a design on a flat, two-dimensional surface, usually bounded by a rectangular frame, intending to represent (and succeeding quite well) a three-dimensional world. This was accomplished after many preliminary moves in this direction, during the Renaissance by artists who set for themselves the task of mastering what we now know as the 'laws of linear perspective'. As was suggested earlier in this essay, there is much about this that is culturally conventional. Although it must be acknowledged that, once the decision is made to represent the world in perspective on a flat surface, there is only one proper way to do it (i.e., to reproduce the retinal image of the scene represented), the decision to do so is conventional.[4] In some cultures, artists made different decisions.

In much Oriental art (particularly Indian painting) for example, the prevalent tendency has been to produce flat, perspective-free pictures, most probably because such a technique accords with culturally sanctioned aesthetic tradition. It is possible that Indian artists long ago decided to present a view of the world as they knew it to be rather than as it appears from a particular vantage point. This decision, a convention of Indian art, is simply different from the one made by Western artists.

Artists in the West prior to the Renaissance either didn't decide to attempt to draw in perspective or, if they did, they couldn't overcome all the difficulties it entailed. It took a Leonardo to do it.[5]

Moreover, there has to be a little Leonardo in every artist who follows him. Everyone who accepts this post-Renaissance artistic convention must go through a learning process that involves suppressing his tendencies to draw on a flat surface the thing-as-he-knows-it-to-be. My first drawing of a table looked rather like this!

That this *should* be so follows quite directly from the cross-cultural research findings and the interpretation discussed here. For those of us who live in a world full of rectangular objects, it is an ecologically-valid inference habit to perceive these objects as composed of right angles, regardless of the non-rectangular retinal images which they most often project. This kind of 'perceptual constancy' in the face of visual variance is essential for competent functioning, for manipulation of objects in the real world, and for locomotion in it. Thus, although the table 'out there' projects lines meeting in acute and obtuse angles on the retina, we know those angles to be square – and it is a very useful thing indeed that we know it. The child who draws it so is, thus, more of a realist than the artist who follows in the da Vincian tradition.

Learning to 'write' in this post-Renaissance conventional 'language' is difficult, as we have just seen. So might be learning to 'read' it. Even though a picture when 'well-written' reproduces a retinal image of a real object, the object may not be obvious to a naive viewer of the picture. There is reason to believe that persons reared in cultures without this convention, who therefore lack experience with two-dimensional pictures or photographs, on viewing their first example of one do not immediately perceive its content. Until recently, anthropologists anecdotally reported failures of non-literate peoples to recognize photographs of loved ones.[6] More recently, some systematic research by Hudson (1960) showed that tendencies to read drawings three-dimensionally were related to school experience among both Black and White South Africans. His findings suggest that ability to read representational drawings is related to experiential familiarity with the representational convention of Western art.

The fact that many Western artists from time to time have vigorously rejected this (and other) conventions merely supports the general line of argument which has been presented here. These rebels have, in fact, underscored the conventionality of Western artistic traditions by departing, in one way or another, from practices which result in photograph-like reproductions. Cubism is only the single best-known example of such departures but it is particularly relevant to our present argument because it was a movement inspired in part by the discovery of art produced in another culture.

Up to this point our speculations about art related rather closely to what has been learned recently about visual inference habits from cross-cultural research with geometric illusions. I have attempted to show that just as visual perception is culturally influenced, so is visual art. Finally, I would like to suggest that art will always, in one way or another, reflect cultural influences. Although the artist is encouraged to present highly individualized interpretations of experience, he will, presumably, be constrained by the need to communicate his interpretation to some audience, however small, most likely composed of members of his own culture. Although my most recent visit to the Museum of Modern Art makes me doubt the generality of my last point, it must be valid in the long run. The artist with no audience may enjoy himself, but until his work occupies a meaningful place in other people's environment, it has no place in culture and, by my definition, it is thus no work of art.

Now, cultures change continuously, so what artists may say and how they may say it also change. Since the cultural influences impinging on artists (and these include, of course, the work of other artists) are constantly changing, we must expect art itself to change. Because we know that art is the product of culturally-influenced behaviours, can we predict trends in art on the basis of what we know about how culture is changing? Probably we can.

Since this century has seen an almost quantum leap in the frequency and profundity of contact between cultures, it is likely that artistic practices world-wide will become more uniform than ever before. It may thus come to pass that some culturally-unique arts will be found only in museums. There may soon be no new African art as such, only new art made by Africans. But increasing cultural uniformity and cross-cultural trait adoption *per se* are not necessarily debasing. Even the most conservative cultural purist would acknowledge the enrichment of European life stemming from adaptations by Frenchmen of Indo-Chinese and African creations, in the culinary as well as the graphic arts.

In any case, welcomed or not, increased world-wide cultural homogeneity is likely. In many domains, the process is already relatively far advanced. With regard to visual art, one area of possible change relates to certain *decorative-functional* art in respect of which cultures have long been known to differ. For instance, it is probably true that in the West, visual art products tended to be specially made addenda to environment, designed solely to decorate it. Few Westerners confused coffee pots with art objects.[7] In many non-Western cultures, by contrast, although a large variety of objects were designed and worked with great care so as to make them 'beautiful', those objects were designed primarily for some other function. Relatively few were designed merely to decorate.

If this is so, and if increasing cultural uniformity will have its effects on art, one that is clearly to be expected is that in the West our artists will come to produce an increasing number of everyday, materially useful objects. Our coffee pots may, after all, become works of art! And conversely, African houses will come to have pictures on their walls.

One could continue with additional examples. It could, for example, be predicted that visual art made by people who claim the title 'artist' will become increasingly abstract and non-representational, in order that their work be distinguished from what may be seen, with boring regularity, in the tabloids, in the cinemas and on the television screens. The 'picture' as we have known it for so long in the West may disappear from art, to be replaced by more ephemeral, dynamic visual experiences, as in light shows, for example. Whatever may come to be accepted as art, however, will still be what some men make for other men to comprehend. Both the making and the comprehension will for ever reflect the influence of culture on visual inference habits.

NOTES

1 On the basis of what we know about the nervous system, there is no reason to believe that anatomical or physiological differences are great enough to produce differences in illusion susceptibility. And, certainly, no one can predict the direction of differences in susceptibility on the basis of nervous system differences.

2 A convenient summary of results of the empirical studies may be found in Segall, Campbell and Herskovits, 1963, *Science* 39, 769–71.

3 Besides, as Segall et al. argued, 'It is no longer possible to explain . . . group differences . . . by attributing them to arbitrary genetic differences. Most manifest structural features and their related functional processes are determined by scores of genes. On these genes, each human population is heterozygous and differs from other populations only in relative allele or gene frequencies. These specific gene frequencies are maintained by selection pressures . . . which would result where different environments made different structures and processes optimal. In the case of the perceptual processes under study, this would require theories as to how ecological differences made different perceptual functions optimal.' (Segall et al. 1966, 78.)

4 'What is arbitrary is the decision to represent three dimensions in two. Once this useful arbitrary convention has been invented, the optimally efficient device is, no doubt, to imitate the retinal display, to produce a two-dimensional frontal display that generates a retinal display most comparable to that generated by the three-dimensional display that is the topic of the message. Leonardo da Vinci's success in anticipating the photograph indicates how nonarbitrary his principles were.' (Segall et al. 1966, 94.)

5 See Hochberg (1961) for a discussion of the role of artists since Leonardo in revealing the cues which facilitate depth perception. Here is an implication of art for psychology!

6 See, for example, Herskovits 1948, 381.

7 Even Andy Warhol, when he elevated a can of soup to an art object, did so by making one especially to be looked at; Warhol's can thereby lost its original function as a container.

Chapter Seven

Trompe l'œil to rompe l'œil: vision and art

R. A. WEALE

For the first fifteen or twenty thousand years of his recorded artistic life, man employed art as a language. This implies that it was a code used for the purpose of communication. Whether it was intended to be artistic in the first instance can hardly be established at this point in time. But it can be assumed that whoever made the Venus of Willendorf expected her to be seen as he saw her. If he wanted her to represent a fertility symbol then he had to endow her with the rotundity which would convey to the faithful that that was what she was. It follows that an artifact can only make sense if the beholder understands the visual grammar which the artist uses. Like all grammars of living languages, the visual grammar of painting, sculpture, architecture has undergone many changes: therein lies hope for the future.

Four basic visually grammatical stages can be discerned in the course of the last one thousand years. Like all categorization, this view contains arbitrary divisions. The question is: can we agree on them?

THINGS ARE WHAT THEY ARE

The artistic representation of light, colour, and space was not generally a problem in the Byzantine world and its derivatives. The artist had to tell a tale and this had to be understood. If people had been able to follow hieroglyphics he would have drawn or carved them as long as he got the message across. Of course, he had to presuppose a knowledge of his conventions; e.g. the largest figure in the apse of a basilica was the Pantocrator, the next size being reserved for His relations and apostles, and the size after that for mere saints. The characteristic features of a holy person or a sacred event (nothing else was depicted before the fourteenth century) had to conform to descriptions given in authentic sources. And the Pantocrator and others could not be shown in profile, which is, of course, easier to render than full-face, because the idea of venerability demanded a relation of the image to the beholder (Demus 1947). Three-quarter views are a compromise which permit contact and conversation between linked figures. Full-face figures can also establish contact across space when they face each other across the volume, rather than along the surface, of an apse. The rigour of this

Plate 36   concept is striking at Cefalù in Sicily, where mosaics of saints on walls perpendicular to the axis of the basilica show them in profile so that they may be enabled to face the beholder in the interior of the church. The centralization of the worshipper epitomizes the advantages of cross-in-square churches with a central cupola, for he may venerate literally the whole church.

We may safely assume that artists were aware of the desirability of realistic representation. Generally we see Byzantine figures on reproductions by well-meaning but misguided photographers before we see them in reality. They show them to us square-on, just as they show us Master Gislebert's magnificent carvings in the tympanum at Autun from an angle from which no earth-bound tourist can possibly see them. But in both cases we are being deceived. The long bodies of the Byzantine figures look less long when seen from underneath, just as we would see largely the wrap round the Judge's knees if we knelt on a cloud underneath Him after our hour had struck. It is because Sutherland's tapestry in Coventry Cathedral can be seen across the building rather than from underneath a tympanum as were its Romanesque prototypes, that his concept strikes some of us as questionable. Unlike the Renaissance artists who imitated, those of the Byzantine and Romanesque eras compensated for, visual effects: they knew reality and if the weaknesses of the human frame distorted it, they were at hand to render assistance and to restore the status quo. This may also explain the continued use of the peculiar almond-shaped frame – the mandorla – which

Plate 38   frequently surrounds Christ-in-Judgement (as in Lincoln), and also Nanni Bigio's
Plate 37   Virgin on the south porch of Florence Cathedral. The Egbert Codex in Trier shows one of the early attempts to render a circle perspectively: the artist presents it, not as an ellipse, but more like a half-open mouth. If Christ were to emerge through a circular opening in the clouds – none other would be perfect enough for Him to pass through – then the principle of compensation would demand that He appear in an ellipse with its major axis vertical: the two corners of the mandorla would reflect an unwillingness on the artist's part to forgo indicating a diameter.

This wish to render reality as it is and not as it seems to be appears also in
Plate 39   painting. Humphrey (1971) has stressed that Ugolino di Nerio's *Resurrection* – which heralds that of Domenico Veneziano and also that of Piera della Francesca – and some early oriental paintings show rectangular shapes, such as the grave or a couch, as rhomboids rather than trapeziums. In Ugolino's case the lid of the tomb, dislodged by the Risen Christ into an altogether different plane, is a precise match to the opening it covered. The artist was nevertheless compromised. No doubt he used a rhomboid rather than the more realistic rectangle to indicate that Christ was perpendicular to the plane of the opening.

The defiance of the human eye extended understandably to architecture both in Romanesque and in Gothic days and, as we shall see in a moment, even in the Renaissance. However, the reasons were different. The Gothic architect built for the eye, not of man, but of God. The type of triangulation taken over by Romanesque builders from the geometry for example of the Roman Pantheon appears in the round church still preserved in Cambridge. The proportions between its width and height, and those of the central octagon and the design

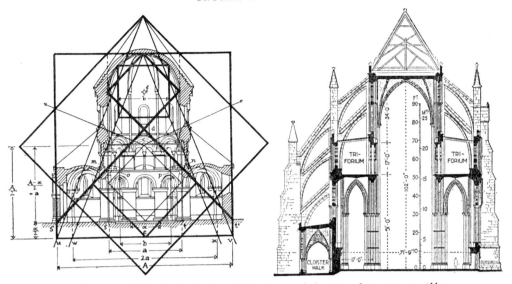

Fig. 1 *(Left) The round church, Cambridge; (Right) Sectional elevation of Westminster Abbey*

as a whole are mathematically rigorous. They make no concession to viewpoint, to perspective, to the background. It is interesting to observe that no such obvious pattern underlies the general plan of the basilica which is based on the Roman temporal judgment hall. No such pattern appears to underlie the first generation of England's Norman cathedrals either.

However, this is patently untrue of the fully-developed Gothic style. Lesser (1957) has drawn attention to the intricate combinations of $\sqrt{2}$ and $\sqrt{3}$ which lace not only the plan of Westminster Abbey, for example, but also its elevation. When we compare the height of the round church in Cambridge with that of *Fig. 1* London's Abbey then the inadequacy of the human eye for the purpose of the architect's plan becomes manifest. It is only by removing himself to such a distance that the façade may appear to him no larger than it would on the sheet of paper on which it was planned that the observer may discern the network of the inherent mathematical relations. And as for the plan? He would have to lift off the roof like Montesquieu's devil and hover on high to comprehend how stone followed pen.

This preoccupation with paper numbers extended into the Renaissance. The reason for this was Alberti. Architect of the façade of S. Maria Novella in Florence, of the Tempio Malatestiano in Rimini, of San Andrea in Mantua, self- *Plate 43* portraying medallist, and prolific writer – this universal genius was and is held by many to be a mathematician. No theorem or principle due to him appears to have reached us, and perhaps he is more appropriately described as a numerologist. Legion are the rules which he enunciates for the appropriate proportionate lengths, widths, and heights of walls, columns, buildings. As might be expected, the golden section is an important ingredient in his theorizing.

Although it is derivable from the almost magic pentagon (Bouleau 1963) there is no obvious visual correlate which it recalls. The visual field is projected by the corneae and lenses of our eyes on to our light-sensitive retinae; but unlike photographic emulsions, they are not uniformly sensitive all over their surface: it can be shown that the underlying patterns are concentric ellipses with their major axes horizontal. This is understandable when we recall that our ape-like ancestors had to scan the field for food or enemies because, unlike for example those of rabbits, their eyes and ours point forward. There is no known physiological reason why the golden, or indeed any other, section should be preferred above all others. However, the matter is settled once we insist that the ancients said that this is how we should build. While much emphasis has been laid on the fact that baroque sculpture makes vast concessions to the observer's point of view (Wittkower 1966) – as is only to be expected from the proselytism of the Counter-reformation – no such attention seems to me to have been given to the liberation of the eye from the shackles of numbers, as effected in architecture.

Plate 41 Just as the visual thrill of viewing Ghiberti's *Flagellation of Christ* on his first pair of doors in the Baptistery in Florence derives from the pendulating eye movements induced by the lashing whips, so do the kinetics of seventeenth-century baroque move our eyes physically, though not necessarily emotionally, after the long statics of the preceding centuries. God may indeed have created the integers, about which Alberti sings; but the human eye does not seem to use them. The joke is that the old masters, the cunning Greeks who inspired Alberti, knew enough about human vision to depart already in their Doric architecture from the rigours of simple proportion. Although there are many examples to support this, one must suffice. Where Renaissance columns (even unfluted ones)

Plate 40 are cylindrical, those of the Parthenon and of Paestum show entasis, i.e. a subtle bulging which insinuates the notion of strength. It is perfectly true that entasis would look horrible with arches: the appearance of strength is needed for an architrave, but can be dispensed with in connection with the all but levitating

Plate 42 elegance of, for example, Brunelleschi's San Spirito. The fact remains that, unlike Renaissance architects, the Greeks bent mathematical rigour in the interest of visual physiology.

THINGS ARE WHAT WE KNOW THEM TO BE

If the fifteenth century could not introduce realism into its architecture, it certainly opened the gates to it in its sculpture and its paintings. The ability to represent the three-dimensional world on two-dimensional surfaces in a manner which – dare I say it? – a camera might do it was learnt in fits and starts, and the lessons were being absorbed even two hundred years later by Rembrandt and Frans Hals. Many were the circumstances that led to success but from the visual point of view we can select three.

In the first place, the rendering of the human body had made vast strides in the preceding century, notably under the prolonged influence of Donatello

Plate 45 (1386–1466). He had introduced drama and pathos into sculpture before the excavation of the Laocöon could remind Rome that statues need not be static.

Secondly, the advance in the rendering of form provoked interest in light. While two types of light were recognized – the 'luce' and 'lume' of Lomazzo (1584) – to distinguish light shed by the source from that reflected by terrestrial objects, the Renaissance replaced the universe permeated by light with rays that are directed. Schöne (1953) believes that Signorelli's *Pan* (1491) contains the first piece of conclusive evidence that this lesson had been learnt, but Piero della Francesca's earlier *Victory of Constantine over the Emperor Maxentius* in Arezzo shows also good indications to this effect. The secret lay in shadows. The problem of the direction of shadows was beginning to be tackled also in the North (see Mair von Landshut's woodcut of the Holy Family, 1499), even though this was unaccompanied by an understanding of Brunelleschian perspective (see below). The time would come, as Velasquez and Hals and Constable were to show, when the rotation of the earth and the resultant changes in the directions and lengths of shadows could produce apparent inconsistencies which puzzle commentators to this day. The Renaissance, however, introduced order into the world of shadows. This was due to the fact that painting in the open air was not practised till the beginning of the seventeenth century: Claude Lorrain seems to have been amongst the first artists to let us know that he had done so.

Plate 46

Thirdly, there was the discovery of perspective with a single vanishing point. This is attributed to Brunelleschi (1415) and it is amusing to note that an architect is credited with having discovered it, while a sculptor, Donatello, was the first to use it (1421). However, Brunelleschi may have been anticipated by an unknown Sienese painter. There are two panels (D.L. 1967–1 bis) in the Louvre depicting *The Fall of the Rebel Angels*. They are ascribed to 1340–50 and one of them represents almost a textbook example of Brunelleschian perspective; a reservation one can make is that there seem to be two juxtaposed vanishing points rather than only one.

Plate 44

Fig. 2   *Draughtsman drawing a lute. Woodcut by Dürer*

These principles relating to form, light, and space came to be assimilated and refined by artists whose names are household names wherever men can read and use their eyes. And use of eyes is the key phrase for Renaissance painting. It was not the thing-in-itself that was being painted, but how it appeared to the beholder, for it is by looking that he knew. Small wonder that Dürer examined closely how the appearance of lutes and of nudes depended on the point of view. Small wonder that Uccello would exclaim in his conjugal bed what a marvellous thing perspective was, and that the more single-minded Leonardo would be amongst the first to draw from life.

Fig. 2

In the world of colour, too, the Renaissance made advances. This had been revolutionized by the discovery of oil paints, perhaps by Van Eyck, and the first oil paintings arrived in Italy between 1470 and 1480, in Urbino and Florence respectively. Now the theory of colour was still governed by Aristotle's ideas. Alberti followed him, saying that all colours represented mixtures of black and white. A hundred years later Lomazzo repeated this; for, although Leonardo had tried to break out of the classical yoke, little progress was possible in this respect till the workings of the eye were understood better than was true in the sixteenth century. Nevertheless, Leonardo studied what effect light reflected from one coloured object had on the apparent colour of another and, though he was no Newton, he realized that light, and therefore shadows, could be coloured in addition to objects.

Plates 47, 48

This is illustrated in the two versions of *The Virgin of the Rocks*, the earlier of which (1483) is in the Louvre, the later (1506?), perhaps not entirely by Leonardo's hand, in London's National Gallery. The tonalities of the two versions differ. The earlier contains more colour, the later is more subdued. Shearman (1962) attributes this to the Purkinje-shift. This is named after the man who observed that, whereas yellow-green is, in controlled experiments, the brightest colour in full daylight, at dusk this is no longer true; blue-green takes its place. In my view, the illumination in the later painting is ambiguous. It certainly does not give the impression of being the effect of moonlight in the sense in which Piero went a long way towards achieving this in *The Dream of Constantine* at Arezzo. An alternative explanation is that Leonardo, now 54 years of age, suffered from a marked yellowing of his crystalline lenses. This happens to all of us at some time or another as we age, and is equivalent to looking at the world through a yellowish filter. It is noteworthy that neither the *Bacchus*, nor the *Leda* nor *St John*, which Leonardo painted later in 'daylight' environments, are acutely colourful. It might be argued justifiably that the Louvre painting of St Anne, the Virgin, and Child is colouristically rich in tone, and therefore disproves the above suggestion. However, the principal 'diurnal' colour is the rich red of St Anne's skirt, and this would not be much affected by lenticular yellowing.

Michelangelo, Leonardo's sometime rival, rang out the Renaissance and rang in the Baroque. He developed a new sense of space, replacing the mathematical rhythm of Brunelleschi's legacy with the almost macrocosmic waves of integrated design. The staircase to the Laurentian Library in Florence is an example grasped by those who have seen it – it defies verbal description.

Plate 49

Architecturally of wider significance was his concept for the reconstruction of the Capitol, which was commissioned by Pope Paul III. This space is enclosed by three palaces: that of the Conservators, that of the Senators, and the Capitoline Museum. The two buildings flanking the older, central Senatorial Palace do so at acute angles of about 80°. This is incomprehensible till we realize that Michelangelo also re-sited the statue of Marcus Aurelius. Originally believed to represent the Emperor Constantine, it used to stand in front of the Lateran Palace and when Rienzi was crowned Tribune of the People the horse sneezed red and white wine. Now the Roman Emperor and philosopher rides towards Rome. The statue stands low and, as Hermann Grimm explains, gives the impression to anyone emerging from any of the three palaces that it is at ground level for two or three steps raise that of the palaces. This is the key to Michelangelo's visual intent. The flanking palaces slope inward to increase the apparent depth of the smallish square (as though it were a stage) when, following Marcus Aurelius, we view the spectacle of the Eternal City.

Bernini echoed this arrangement in front of St Peter's. At its side, the Scala Regia which leads off to the right is a masterly example of his understanding of perspectival effects – effects, to be sure, he employed on this staircase to overcome difficulties and mistakes which would have led a lesser man to pull down this approach to the Papal buildings. A gentle tapering of rows of pilasters, dramatic illumination which came to be imitated in the *trasparente* in the cathedral of Toledo and in the Nepomuk church in Munich, subtle changes in level, they all bear witness to Bernini's consummate control of the theatrical. At the top of the stairs there is the flamboyant statue of Constantine and this time there is no mistake.

But St Peter's Square – is there no mistake there? The mighty colonnades as it were embrace the pilgrim as he approaches his Mecca. He passes the central obelisk, the colonnades close in and then as he faces St Peter's, straight flanks run outwards to the corners of the edifice. The apparent distance of the façade is reduced. This trick, if trick it be, imposes a barrier between the beholder and the target in view. Could it be that, after an initial embrace, the Church would blow cold before ultimately swallowing the swaying pilgrim? Does it wish, in a sense almost of coquetry, to seem further than it is? Would it, in its desire to hold the faithful, would it wish to tease them?

Perhaps Bernini did not consider the eye. However, I doubt it. John Evelyn stresses his competence as a theatrical producer and it is not only the pilgrim one has to consider. Just as Marcus Aurelius rides over the Capitol, so the Pope looks over the Square. The embracing arms, thronging to bursting point, recede, and the distance between people and priest, which the Counter-reformation sought to increase in its combat with Protestantism, is enhanced if it is the flanks which close in front of the Pontiff just as they open out before the pilgrim. The Pope receives a sense of greater power.

THINGS ARE WHAT THEY APPEAR TO BE

As this brief chapter contains not a history of visual effects in art but only a

Plate 50

Plate 51

Plates 47, 48

selection of them, chiaroscuro, the drastic juxtaposition of light and dark, which followed almost logically from the discoveries of the Renaissance, will not be considered in detail. In the hands of Caravaggio it led to the portrayal of dramatic situations rather than dramatic actions, in those of Elsheimer to the development of nocturnes. Honthorst derived from it the idea of painting by candlelight, and, together with De La Tour, presented the world's galleries with problems of exhibiting their works which illuminating engineers, lacking the advice of art historians, cannot be expected to solve. This is also true of Rembrandt and his contemporaries who frequently painted in a light environment differing appreciably from the fluorescent *ersatz* for daylight with which their works are indiscriminately illuminated at the present time.

We stressed in connection with Leonardo's two renderings of *The Virgin of the Rocks* that our eyes respond to colours differently in daylight and at dusk, problems which are highlighted almost literally by the invention of chiaroscuro and its offshoots. It is, however, not only our sense of colour brightness that changes. Alterations can also be noticed in colour quality, in the perception of detail, of contrast, etc., and the first reasonably reliable information on these difficult problems was obtained only in the late eighteenth and the nineteenth century. Although Dürer and Leonardo had interested themselves in the properties of the eye, this was done for the sake of portraying realism. Aristotelian and Albertian claims that all colours could be considered as mixtures of black and white clearly were invalid. However, in the second half of the eighteenth century, a new approach to colour theory evolved (Weale 1957). The question was whether there was a minimum number of some basic colours which, mixed together in suitable proportions, enabled one to match any other colour: black and white could be ruled out as Newton had shown white to be a mixture of all spectral lights. Moses Harris, an artist and naturalist, was an art theorist who rejected Newton's notion of seven basic hues (Finley 1967). In his treatise, dedicated to Sir Joshua Reynolds and published about 1770, he claimed that 'all varieties of colour' can be formed from red, blue, and yellow, 'which three Grand or Principal Colours contain all hues and tints to be found in the different objects of nature'. He also saw that complementary colours, i.e. those which when mixed together produce white or grey, show great contrast, an observation which Delacroix was to exploit for example in *The Expulsion of Heliodorus* which he painted for S. Sulpice in Paris.

COLOUR PLATES

V *Children's activities with space may start with shapes that are very small, like matchboxes, and can be extended to shapes which can be climbed into and looked out of. Chapter 5*

VI *Children will paint on surfaces that are outside the normal concept of art. Chapter 5*

VII *The basic method of handling visual information is that of sorting. Chapter 5*

VIII *Time changes the appearance of materials. Chapter 5*

V

VI

VII

VIII

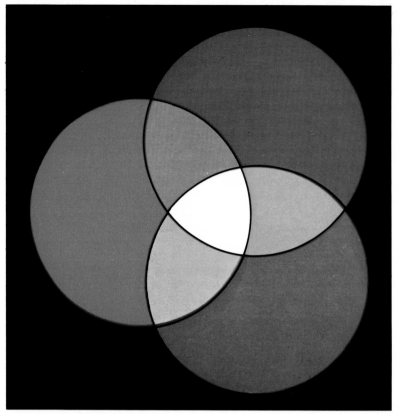

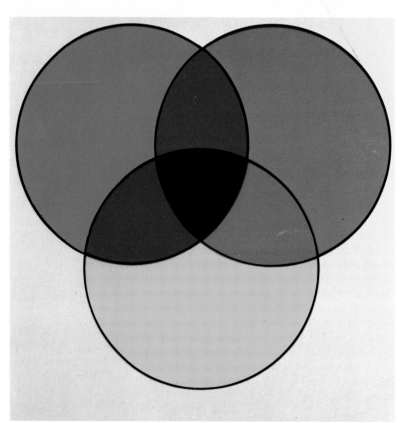

These and other considerations led Thomas Young, a physician and polymath of Welbeck Street, to put forward (1807) the trichromatic theory of colour vision according to which our sensations of colour are mediated by the relative stimulations of three independent retinal colour mechanisms. Although the theory was fully proved only recently, artists of the nineteenth century showed great interest in studies of the properties of the eye in general and colour theory in particular. Turner who became Professor of Perspective at the Royal Academy in 1807 accepted Moses Harris's red-yellow-blue scheme, and noted a matter of cardinal importance for our understanding of, among other things, the origins of Seurat's pointillism: white can be produced from a mixture of three colours only if this refers to coloured lights. If the mixture is obtained by mixing pig-   Plate IX
ment the result is mud. The difference is due to the distinction between additive   Plate X
and subtractive colour mixture. A coloured pigment owes its appearance to some parts of the daylight spectrum being absorbed more than others: e.g. red, yellow and green are heavily absorbed by a truly blue pigment, while blue and violet are reflected and so give it its appearance. Now if a blue pigment is mixed with another, say yellow, which reflects yellow but absorbs blue, some of the original blue is lost. Hence, in general, pigment mixture entails loss of light. Turner experimented with the trichromatic principle notably in two of his water-colours, namely *Shields in the River Tyne* and *Norham Castle on the River Tweed*. An echo is to be found also in the near-impressionistic *Fighting Temeraire* and *Steamer in a Snow Storm*. His sketches illustrating lectures on trichromatic principles hang in the Tate Gallery.

But whereas light *per se* was to Turner a matter of cosmic forces (Canaday 1959), to the impressionist followers of Delacroix it was an optical phenomenon. Its representation partly derived from the physiological fact that, at any one moment, the only area of the visual field which we see sharp is the one we are looking at. This covers in practice an angle no larger than that included by a 10p piece at a distance of 1 metre. The rest is fuzz. The reasons why the world appears distinct in general are (i) we know it to be so, and (ii) we move our eyes about so that the whole scene can, in time, be imaged on the central parts of our retinae where the visual 'grain' is at its finest. In particular, we do not, could not, normally see distant objects bounded by lines and sharp outlines, not because they are not confined by surfaces expressible in terms of orthodox geometry – they are – but because we lack the visual means. We have to go by appearances.

Without additional evidence, the eye cannot decide whether the fuzzy image it perceives in a brief interval of time is due to inadequate contours, i.e. impressionistic presentation, or to movement. The distance between Degas's and Renoir's impressionism to the depiction of movement (cf. Giacomo Balla's *La Bambina che corre sul balcone*, or Marcel Duchamp's *Nu descendant un escalier*,

COLOUR PLATES

IX   *Light mixture. Chapter 7*

X   *Pigment mixture. Chapter 7*

both painted in 1912) is therefore short. The philosophical problem of whether a painting can represent only one instant in time, which worried Lessing very greatly in connection with the Laocöon, is thrown overboard once the physiology of the eye is assimilated, and sinks without trace the moment cinematography gets under way.

If the Impressionists paid attention to science, Seurat made it his religion. Guided, as John Russell (1965) has shown in his splendid appraisal, by the teachings of Chevreul, he had absorbed all that was known about the visual process which was remotely relevant to his work. His impressionist leanings were made clear in his early carbon drawings. In these the carbon is not drawn across the fibrous paper, but as it were made to waft across it. It is all the more interesting that, in the painting with which he conquered Paris in 1886 overnight, namely *Un Dimanche d'été à l'île de la Grande Jatte*, he employed a principle whose
Plate 53 discovery the Swiss aesthete David Sutter attributes to Canaletto about a century earlier: it can in fact be traced to Carpaccio (1490–1523?). Canaletto favoured very precise delineations of his outlines, and achieved this by painting Mach-
Plate 56 bands, so named after their official discoverer (Mach 1865). These appear near a sharp border between two tones. If either of two adjacent fields is covered, the uncovered field will appear uniform. As soon as both fields are viewed, the bands – a dark one on the darker of the two fields and a light one on the lighter one – return. They are not in the field of view but the retina responds to borders in this peculiar manner because, unlike for instance a photographic film, neighbouring retinal areas can interact with each other. It is one thing for a photographic realist like Canaletto to paint what the retina really manages better on its own, and another for Seurat to do likewise. It is as though, aware of the physiological basis of Impressionism, he tried to retrieve the balance by adding the sharpening effect of the Mach bands.
Plate 52 Colouristically, Seurat continued where Delacroix had stopped. He made a determined effort to increase the luminosity of the painted picture by mixing colours not subtractively but additively. If the surface were to be built up of dots of the colours to be mixed, but viewed from a distance large enough for the eye to be unable to resolve the individual dots, then the light reflected by each of them would be 'mixed optically' on the retina. The originator of this idea seems to have been Chevreul, one-time director of the dyeing section of the factory producing Gobelin tapestries, but the principle is clearly seen even on older tapestries.

William Homer Innes (1964), who is (alas!) less conversant with colour theory than with Seurat's work, the underlying scientific principles of which he is purporting to be discussing, has described how the appearance of pointillist paintings changes with viewing distance. When we read in Lucretius that he had been aware of the disintegration of colours when objects are fragmented:

> *Quin etiam quanto in partes res quaeques minutas*
> *Distribitur magis, hoc magic est ut cernere possis*
> *Evanescere paulatim stinguique colorem;*

(Moreover the smaller the particles into which anything is divided, the more readily can you observe that the colour gradually fades and vanishes), then the loss of colour of pointillist paintings seen from a distance cannot surprise. But it surprised Seurat's contemporaries. We know now that our eyes see colours quite differently depending on whether they are presented in large or small areas, and that the above-mentioned interaction between retinal parts likewise varies with the extent of stimulation. Seurat's life work represents the most consistent attempt ever made to base artistic technique soundly on scientific principles (Weale 1971). The reason why he failed as a technician is that the information available to him was incomplete; the reason why he succeeded as an artist was that he did not depend solely on his technique.

THINGS AREN'T

When Raphael had died and Michelangelo had virtually given up painting, the artists of the mid-sixteenth century believed that the zenith of painting had been passed and that there was little they could do to advance the art. The sack of Rome in 1527, not to mention Martin Luther, did not conduce to an exactly rosy view of life. Mannerism was born. In some ways, modern art finds itself in an analogous position, aggravated if anything, by the development of photography. With visual problems solved, psychological difficulties solved, questions of space, light, colour, subject matter solved, no wonder that modern artists are driven to abstraction. From the point of view of theories of vision this represents really the most interesting facet so far.

Except for isolated cases, modern abstract art can no longer fulfil the object of art I mentioned by way of introduction. It cannot, does not wish to, speak. Its linguistic content is minimal, and the reasons are not far to seek. It does not employ a grammar: that is why we are presented with statements *ex cathedra* every time an abstract artist exhibits. The canvas may show detail or there may be plain areas too large to accommodate in a 'semi' even with a 'through' room. And this is anti-élitist art, for the people. The absence of a message is accentuated by incoherent, if verbal, designations like Larry Poons's 'Mary Queen of Scots' describing a very pleasant assembly of coloured dots, or by titles such as 'The cock has phoned is found'. The language, if any, is that of extra-terrestrial beings and we only learn to make 'sense' of some of the artifacts if a given artist is self-consistent over a period of time: Jackson Pollock furnishes a good example. Plate 54 His outpourings teach us to look for a rhythm, and if our eyes learn to follow his lines we derive aesthetic satisfaction.

However, during the last decade or so the question of aesthetics has been washed away in many instances. With Op art and Kinetic art we find artists demonstrably using patterns which experimental psychologists and visual physiologists had been using for decades in order to study the visual systems of man and brute. The visual system, be it noted: not what we see but how we do it. Artists no longer want to tell us anything – what is there left to say? – but wish us to experience our own reactions. If Frank Stella calls his square spiral in the Tate Gallery 'Hyena Stomp', then this is of no consequence for it rings no bell: but if we notice how the effect of the four colours he uses varies dramatically with viewing distance, then we can approach and recede and enjoy it like the changing patterns in a kaleidoscope. The effects are based on subtle phenomena of colour contrast, which are as yet unexplored, and it is safe to assume that Stella does not understand the why of his success any more than you or I do. Indeed, Bridget Riley, who with her 'Cerise, olive, turquoise, open disks 1970' merely elaborates what Chevreul had published more than a century earlier for didactic purposes to illustrate the nature of simultaneous contrast; Miss Riley, as I say, takes pride in not having studied the optical principles underlying her work. This in no way detracts from the inventiveness of her constructions, any more than does the fact that the 'Supernovae' of Vasarely relies, unbeknown to the artist, on an optical illusion discovered at least one hundred years ago, detract from his.

Plate 55 The object, then, is not to tell you anything over the phone but just to enable you to find out how you react when the phone rings. No one has stated this with more honesty than Sutej who, modifying a figure published in the scientific journal *Nature* in 1958, called his work 'Bombardment of the optic nerve'.

It is easy enough to show that this wave of geometrical paintings – many of which can, incidentally, be described by relatively simple mathematical equations – relies on well-understood properties of the human eye. These include our inability to keep our eyes still: the scintillation of Vasarely's 'Supernovae' would disappear if it were flashed before our eyes with exposures lasting less than one-tenth of a second. This is also true e.g. of Bridget Riley's 'Cataract 1970'. Other factors are the colour contrast reactions of our eyes, and the fact that all of us tend to confuse certain colour pairs when the coloured areas are small: calling yellow white or vice versa is the least striking but best known effect.

A parallel situation arises in truly kinetic art, i.e. when the object seen is made to move. Movement illusions have been described over many decades, and some go back to the Greeks. These new developments are new only because conventional artists are rushing in where scientists have been treading for years. It would not be right for us to debate to what extent their activities can be described as art. The cynic might be forgiven for observing that if a pattern appears in a book it is part of science, but if it is brushed on to a canvas it becomes art.

However, the story does not end here. The reason why art has flourished is because it utilized our sensations of light, space, and colour as a vehicle of language, and could do so with relative ease, for the appropriate system was well developed. We have no electric sense, so there can be no electric art. But this need not remain so for all time. To give an example: as yet we have only the barest understanding of how we see in depth. In fact, new sensations are being discovered by suitable laboratory techniques, and who is to say what the potential is in the non-pictorial world? Drugs apart, visually satisfying hallucinations may be produced one day with methods which do not involve undesirable side-effects. While it is unlikely that the variants of bombarding the optic nerve are inexhaustible, new materials and new techniques might, after all, score novel hits.

Chapter Eight

Defective vision and art

R. W. PICKFORD

Myopia, or 'short-sightedness', and astigmatism may have interesting effects on visual art, but it is clear that various degrees of blindness and defective colour vision will have more serious consequences for the artist. In studying blindness it is important to distinguish between congenital blindness, early blindness which is not congenital, and later blindness, and between partial and complete blindness. In studying colour vision defects there are several degrees and forms of red/green defective vision, yellow/blue defects, and also total colour blindness in which only shades of grey and black and white are seen. The difference between congenital and acquired colour vision defects is significant.

In every case no doubt the individual's peculiar temperament or personality plays a considerable part in his success in overcoming the influence of his defects and compensating for them. Little is known about this, but essentially it is a question of how far and in what ways the artistic gifts and abilities of the individual can manifest themselves in spite of his deficiencies of vision.

MYOPIA AND ASTIGMATISM

Trevor-Roper (1970) has shown that many of the Impressionist painters were myopic or 'short-sighted', and it seems definite that they exploited this form of sight in relation to their art. Monet was myopic and he was the first to cultivate myopic vision in painting. Renoir and Degas were also myopic, Segonzac probably so, and among later artists after the Impressionists Cézanne, Dufy, Derain, Braque, Vlaminck and Matisse are also believed to have had this form of vision. A survey of the masters and pupils at the École des Beaux-Arts in Paris showed that 48 per cent were myopes and 27 per cent hypermetropes (or long-sighted), whereas in the population at large the proportion is more like 1 to 3. It seems that the motivation of myopic sight, in which distant objects are not clearly focused and appear blurred although their blurred forms are clearly represented on the canvas, may have been important in the development of Impressionistic and later forms of art.

Astigmatism is very interesting, but much less easy to understand in relation to painting. As shown by Trevor-Roper (1970) the elongated figures of El Greco can be reduced to normal appearance by photographing them through a

—1 Dioptre astigmatic lens at an angle of 15° to the vertical axis, while the horizontally extended figure of *Henry VIII* by Holbein, and his horizontally elongated figure of *Christ in the Tomb*, may be brought to apparently normal proportions by photographing them through a —1 Dioptre astigmatic lens on a horizontal axis.

While these corrections suggest that El Greco and Holbein may have had nearly vertical and horizontal astigmatism of a marked degree respectively, it is still possible that their figures were vertically and horizontally distorted for expressive reasons. And it is not easy to see why, if they did have astigmatism, they should not have represented the figures in a way which would make them appear normal to us.

VISUAL AND HAPTIC PERCEPTION

The problems of the art of the blind and partial blind are tied up with other interesting problems of perception. It is generally assumed, and is almost certainly correct, that perception of external objects – and the person's own body is an external object in this sense – starts in the infant by touch and exploratory movements. Touch and movement preceded vision in the evolution of perception in the animal kingdom, and are of primary significance in ourselves. Vision develops later. Whether space perception in particular is built up by touch and movement in the first place, with its learned effects transferred to vision subsequently, or due to a congenital or nativistic capacity for the appreciation of space, is a difficult question. However, the mode of perception by touch and exploratory movements is known as 'haptic' perception, in contrast to 'visual' perception by sight, and especially binocular perception, which is very important for the full appreciation of space and certainly develops subsequently to haptic perception.

Haptic perception is essentially successive. The objects and parts of objects experienced by its means are apprehended one after the other, and as it were, added up to form a whole. This is true of distance as well as of relative size and area. In visual perception, especially in binocular vision, objects and their parts are presented together, and even if the eye explores a scene by successive movements to different points of fixation, the items perceived are experienced side-by-side or in their relative positions and sizes. This also applies to relative distances, with appropriate differences in the perceptual processes where solid or stereoscopic vision is concerned. The result is that visual perception leads to a map-like conception, or even to a conception of space and its contents like a solid map. Objects and their parts and relationships are established in perception and correspond within ascertainable limits to what we believe to be their true shapes and sizes. In haptic perception, however, there need be no such stabilization and the appearances of objects and their sizes and relationships may depend on the amount of interest they excite on a given occasion, the time and effort spent in exploring them, and so on. A haptic map might be like a map by an early mariner who gave the passage round Cape Horn far more space than the whole crossing of the Atlantic, because it was much more difficult and dangerous.

VISUAL AND HAPTIC ART

As a result of the discovery of haptic perception an interesting controversy arose in which Viktor Lowenfeld (1939) was the major proponent of the importance of this type of perception in the art of those with good vision as well as in that of the blind and partially blind, while Révész (1950) was the proponent of the view that art was non-existent on the tactile basis and was necessarily dependent on the accurately perceived relationships of objects and their parts in space. Among adults with normal vision haptic perception tends to persist in less than a quarter of their number, while more than a quarter are partly affected by it, and the remaining half are exclusively visual. This is also probably true to some extent of the partial blind, and blind and partially blind artists tend to fall back if they can on haptic perception.

Much primitive and child art is clearly dependent on haptic perception, and so is much modern art, and the realization of this has led to a greater understanding of primitive, child and modern art; for such understanding V. Lowenfeld and Cizek were largely responsible. Classical and romantic art of the photographic kind, however, has followed visual rather than haptic perception. V. Lowenfeld has argued that it is from the sources of haptic perception, based on the earliest exploration by the infant of its own and its mother's body and other objects, that the creative qualities of art arise, and he has explained the so-called sterility of photographic art in terms of the displacement of these inner creative impulses by the demand for accurate objective vision. This is the reason why so many young children are natural creative artists, while most of them tend to lose artistic creativity in their early teens when they become dominated by vision and the demands of accurate perception in everyday life.

Révész, however, who cannot have been a haptic perceiver himself, takes the view that haptic art is not real art, and stresses the importance of accurate visual perception. While agreeing with what Révész says about the very real aesthetic qualities of much visual art, most of us would probably agree with V. Lowenfeld about the aesthetic qualities of child, primitive and modern art, for which haptic perception is important. It is also probably true that the problem of assessing the quality of the art of the blind depends much on understanding its haptic aspects.

THE ART OF THE BLIND

Lowenfeld and Révész give numerous illustrations of the art of the blind and partially blind, early and late, in comparison with the work of normal and weaksighted persons of both visual and haptic types. For the purposes of the present chapter it will be sufficient to give five illustrations from V. Lowenfeld (1939). Two of these photographs illustrate the theme of 'Moses Striking the Rock so that the Water may Flow' by normal-sighted subjects. The former is by a visual type of person, the latter is by a haptic type. From these it is clear that while the visual artist presents the scene in at least relatively photographic proportions and relationships, the haptic artist makes a picture in which there is much more Plates 57, 58 distortion of the photographic shapes, and this is also a much more vivid and expressive work of art. The other plates show the contrast between haptic and

Plate 61
visual types in partially blind and blind subjects. *Being Throttled*, is by a weak-

Plate 59
sighted individual of haptic type, while *Longing for Sight* is by a congenitally blind person of visual type. Here again, the haptic artist has apparently disregarded photographic proportions and relationships altogether, while the visual artist, although blind, has attempted to conform to what he believes them

Plate 60
to be. Again the haptic work is much more emotionally expressive. *Inner Decay*, is by a congenitally blind subject of haptic type.

Révész (1950) has taken much trouble to investigate the facts about a number of well-known 'blind' sculptors. The first of these was the Tyrolese woodcarver, Kleinhans (1774–1853), who is said to have become blind at the age of four as a result of smallpox, and subsequently learned woodcarving and became famous for his crucifixes. Révész considers it most likely that Kleinhans never was completely blind but retained vision to a certain extent.

Another sculptor was Louis Vidal, (b. 1831, at Nîmes), who studied in Paris under Barye. He lost his sight as a result of an illness at 21 years of age, but regained it to some extent so that he was able to continue with his sculpture. Ultimately he lost his sight altogether. During the period of partial sight he was able to work well, but when his sight was completely lost his art declined in quality, according to Révész.

A third sculptor was Jacob Schmitt (b. 1891) of Mainz. He was trained as a silversmith but lost both his eyes in the 1914–18 War as a result of a gunshot injury. In 1915 he began to learn sculpture. Révész visited him and found that he used a tape measure and a yardstick in copying figures after handling them, and always worked from ideal proportions for the human figure. He was helpless without this synthetic construction and built up his objects out of separate and successive perceptions.

The fourth sculptor was Masuelli (b. 1899, at Nice). In the 1914–18 War he lost his sight from the effects of a shell splinter, but in 1932 he took up plastic modelling with success. Révész studied his technique very carefully and came to the conclusion that the methods he used were essentially visual not haptic, and says that in his view it is this that makes his works aesthetically good.

From these studies by Révész it appears that only one out of four blind sculptors had early loss of sight, and he may not have been totally blind; the other three became blind late, and vision almost certainly played a major part in their art.

Révész also considers four other blind sculptors, namely Giovanni Gonnelli (1603–64) who was a legendary person about whom little is accurately known; Hubert Mowdry (1865–1920), a talented sculptor who gave up his art when he lost his sight as a result of cataract in 1900; Georges Scapini (1893), and Filippo Bausola (1893) both of whom lost their sight in the 1914–18 War, and afterwards worked, according to Révész, at a level of handicraft rather than artistry. Révész therefore does not consider that there is any convincing evidence that artistic success in sculpture is compatible with absolute loss of sight or congenital blindness.

V. Lowenfeld, however, does seem to have had a number of gifted modellers who were congenitally blind, and others who, although not congenitally blind, used haptic techniques of artistic creation. It is almost certain that Révész would not have considered their works as falling within the boundaries of good art, and would probably have taken the same view of much primitive, child and modern art which is much admired today.

SOME EXPERIMENTS IN HAPTIC ART

Several illuminating experiments have been reported in relation to haptic perception and the art of the blind. Peddie (Pickford 1972, 59–60) studied 100 secondary school pupils who submitted drawings and paintings, which were graded as haptic or visual. A poetry completion test of 19 unfinished poems was also given, and each completed poem was rated for aesthetic qualities.

Peddie concludes from a statistical study of the results, that poetic ability could be dependent either on haptic or on visual tendencies, but at the same time, the haptic group were higher in aesthetic quality than the visual group.

Von Fieandt (1966) showed 14 clay models made by patients of the Vienna Institute for the Blind to about 80 University students and asked them to say what they thought each model might represent. Interpretations 'adequate to' or 'in agreement with' the original meaning were made. Also he showed photographs of some of the same works by the blind and some modern artistic productions to 285 University students. These were asked to say whether they obtained a certain impression of a feeling, reaction or mood from each, and to say what it was. Adequate interpretations of the sighted artists' works were given in about 40 per cent of the cases but of works of the blind in only about 14 per cent.

Von Fieandt (1966) also arranged for a group of six works, three by normal painters and three by blind artists, to be reproduced in a Finnish weekly magazine, and its readers were asked to judge the aesthetic value of the works. For 1,409 readers who responded the order was as follows: the two highest places, normal artists; two next places, works by the blind; the fifth place, Picasso's *Face*; and the sixth place, a work by a blind artist.

These experiments tend partly to support V. Lowenfeld's views of the significance of haptic perception in art but not to the exclusion of the importance of visual perception. The same general support was provided by an experiment by Stewart (Pickford 1972, 61–62), in which otherwise equivalent groups of 10 blind, 10 normal subjects of visual type, 10 of visual/haptic type and 10 of haptic type (blindfold), all rated 52 abstract models for 'overall æsthetic quality'. Stewart drew the conclusion that there are no significant differences in overall aesthetic judgment among blind and sighted subjects.

DEFECTIVE COLOUR VISION AND ART

Before it is possible to understand the effect of colour vision deficiencies in relation to painting and other arts it is necessary to know something about the nature of colour vision defects themselves. First there are major defects, which are great enough to interfere with a person's daily life and are occupational hazards, for instance where coloured signal lights are used. These defects would cause a person to fail on any competent colour vision test. They take the forms of red/green defects, yellow/blue defects and total colour blindness. The latter, which is very rare, probably of the frequency of one in 65,000, is an insensitivity to all differences of hue or colour so that only shades of grey and black and white are seen. Major yellow/blue defects are equally rare, and subjects who have yellow/blue blindness, or tritanopia, can see only two colours in the spectrum, red and green.

In contrast, major red/green defects are fairly frequent among men and boys, about 7 per cent or 8 per cent being affected in our community, although the frequency is much lower among Eastern peoples, negroes and Australian aborigines. Women and girls are much less affected, because the defects are sex-linked in heredity, and pass from mother to son without being more than very slightly detectable in the mother.

Major red/green defects fall into two groups, protan and deutan. In the protan group we have protanopia, in which only blue and yellow are seen in the spectrum, and the red end of the visible spectrum is cut off short; extreme protanomaly, in which there is much red/green confusion but these colours are seen to some extent, generally with an abnormal loss of red; and simple protanomaly, in which there is little or no red/green confusion, but an abnormal proportion of red is required to mix with green to match a standard yellow.

In the deutan group there are parallel deficiencies, but the red end of the spectrum is not shortened. These defects are deuteranopia, in which only yellow and blue are seen; extreme deuteranomaly, in which there is no confusion of red and green, but an abnormally large amount of green is required to mix with red to match a standard yellow.

Minor colour vision defects are not sufficiently great to be noticed in daily life except with the aid of sensitive tests, although in fine colour matching work they may cause difficulty.

They have generally been regarded as not sex-linked, but there is a possibility that some of them are, and in general they take the forms of deviations to the red, green, yellow or blue side in colour matching equations, or slight tendencies to confuse near shades or tones of red or green with yellow, or of yellow or blue with neutral grey. Minor defects are found in about 15 per cent of our population, but minor yellow/blue defects are more frequent in dark-skinned peoples.

Goethe (Pickford 1972, 99 and 103) was the first to recognize the possible effects of defective colour vision on painting, in 1810, and he described the colour vision of two young men who confused pink with the blue of the sky, called a rose 'blue', and confused green with dark orange and red with brown. We now know that these subjects must have been protanopes. Goethe made coloured illustrations to show how these defects would influence painting. He also discussed the colour vision of Uccello, whose colouring was in some ways unusual.

In 1872 the ophthalmologist Liebreich (Pickford 1972, 102–05) gave an account of the changes in Turner's paintings after 1830, suggesting that by the time he was 55 the lenses of his eyes had become rather dim, veiling lighted objects with a bluish mist.

Liebreich also discussed the art of Mulready. His paintings changed much after he was about 50, when there was a marked increase in blueness, which Liebreich attributed to the yellowing of the lenses of Mulready's eyes owing to ageing.

Angelucci (Pickford 1972, 104) had a collection of the paintings of six artists who had red/green colour vision defects. He considered that long experience would enable an artist to correct his faulty colour perception, but that most difficulty was found with green. He thought that red/green defectives should confine themselves to white, black, yellow and blue.

In 1933 Strebel (Pickford 1972, 104), an ophthalmologist of Lucerne, mentioned a certain German-Polish painter whose colour vision he had tested in 1916, and who was a red/green defective. He painted largely in loam-grey, sulphur-yellow and dark blue. Strebel also mentions El Greco, who was not only suspected of perpendicular astigmatism, which would account for the elongation of his figures, but also probably had a yellow/blue defect arising from increasing pigmentation of the transparent parts of his eyes owing to ageing.

Trevor-Roper (1970) suggested that Constable might have been protanomalous because, in spite of the predominant brown colour of his paintings, he said he never did admire autumnal tints but loved the freshness of spring. Constable was challenged by Sir George Beaumont, who asked, 'Do you not consider it very difficult to determine where to place your brown tree?' Constable replied, 'Not in the least, for I never put such a thing into a picture.' These observations are strongly suggestive that Constable had a colour vision defect, probably a red/green anomaly. Trevor-Roper also discusses many other cases and aspects of the problems.

RACIAL DIFFERENCE IN COLOUR VISION IN RELATION TO ART

The problem of the weakness in blue sensation found by W. H. R. Rivers in his studies of the colour vision of non-white people, and, in particular modern Egyptians, and the absence of a definite word for blue in many languages, was discussed by Myers (1935, Ch. I.) in relation to art. It has long been an intriguing question whether the absence of a definite word for blue or brown in the *Iliad*, for instance, shows that the Ancient Greeks had colour vision different from our own. There is no word for blue in the *Zendavesta* and the Norse *Edda*. The Uralis and Sholagas of Madras have a word for green which may also be used for brown and grey. They have no definite words for brown, violet or light grey, and the Todas of Madras and the Murray Islanders of the Torres Straits have no word of their own for blue. In Welsh '*glas*', which means green, may be used for blue, and in Scottish Gaelic '*gorm*', which means blue, may be used for the green of grass or the colour of a grey horse. '*Gormghlas*' means sea-green.

What is known about the differences in colour vision between various racial groups shows that blue/yellow vision is weaker among dark-skinned peoples than among Caucasian whites, as already mentioned, and that red/green major defective colour vision is found more frequently among Caucasian whites than among Indians, Chinese, Negroes or Australian aborigines, in that order. There are no corresponding differences in colour names for red and green hues. The evidence from colour names in a language is very weak evidence for racial differences of perception. Those who have no name for blue, except a word that may also be used for green or grey, may discriminate blue so little less efficiently than those who do have a name for blue that this could not account for the absence of the colour name.

The claim that the lack or indentity of certain colour names, especially concerning blue and green, in some languages, might be due to deficiencies in colour sensitivity among the people concerned, has been renewed in a very interesting and scholarly way by Bornstein (1973). He shows that the lack or indentities of naming in question occur very generally among peoples in a broad equatorial belt round the earth, and that in the same regions, approximately, the appropriate weaknesses of colour sensitivity also occur. The writer remains unconvinced, however, that there could be a causal connection between the very small average differences in sensitivity in question and the complete lack or identity of colour names. If the colour vision defects were large enough to cause general inability in a population to make a distinction between, say, blue and green, then it would be understandable that there need be only one word for both colours in their language, but this is not the case.

Myers points out that blue is frequently used by the Ancient Egyptians on their pottery, stone figures and in other ways. There is no connection between their insensitivity to blue and their use of the colour in an unexpected manner, or in strange colour schemes, which gave blue bulls, green men and so on. They must have been like modern artists, who make any object the colour they want for aesthetic reasons, so that we may have black milk coming from a blue cow, for instance, although their colour vision is normal.

In any case the differences reported by Rivers were average differences, and, among the people tested, some might be less sensitive than we are, but others might be more sensitive. In the same way, the increased frequency of red/green major defects in Caucasian whites has not resulted in any general change in their art with respect to primitive art, because at most only a percentage of men are affected and not many of these will have been artists.

In general, therefore, we must conclude that small average differences, or very infrequent but larger differences in colour vision sensitivity and defects could not be reflected in widespread differences in colour terminology or in the colours used in art. These colours, if peculiar, are more likely to be due to the prevalence of certain pigments accessible to the artists, as in the reds and browns of Australian aborigines' art. Modern artists use strange and unrealistic colours because they like them and not because they have defective colour vision.

SOME COLOUR VISION DEFECTIVE ARTISTS

Suggestions about the possible colour vision defects of artists like El Greco and

Constable are conjectural. Strebel knew and tested a red/green defective artist. The writer has met and tested several artists who had red/green defects. Full details of these studies are reported elsewhere (Pickford 1972, ch. 5).

A professional and successful artist, Mr Donald R. Purdy, of New Haven, Conn., U.S.A., was good enough to allow the writer to test his colour vision in detail and to photograph some of his paintings. He knew he had a colour vision defect, because he had been sent for tests by the U.S. Air Force when training as an engineer. In the tests conducted by the writer, with the help of the Medical Research Laboratory, U.S. Submarine Base, New London, he proved to be a simple deuteranomalous subject.

Mr Purdy discussed his art fully with the writer, and in its earliest phase he had proferred dull colours. Later there was a second phase of 'Barbizon' colouring, mainly in browns and greys. Then he learned to use brighter colours and developed a third phase of more colourful art, but always tended to avoid combining red and green in the same painting.

Another professional artist was fully tested by the writer, and proved to be a protanope. After completing his art training without this being detected, he came to suspect a peculiarity when he found that small dots and narrow strips of colour confused him, and considered that he had a different level of value for red from most people, which was quite true because he suffered from the shortening of the red end of the spectrum always found in protanopes. He gave up colour work altogether for 15 years, but not because of his colour defect. Later he took up painting in colour again, and used yellows, ochres, oranges, blues and black with very little red or green.

An Indian artist, an amateur of some ability, Mr P. A. Ray, also allowed the writer to test him fully, and proved to be protanomalous. He made many expressionistic pictures, using saturated reds, ochres, golden yellow and black very freely, but greens much less. Although his paintings rely on colour to a major extent, it is upon saturated colours that they depend.

COLOUR DEFECTIVE ART STUDENTS

The writer followed up his experience with colour defective artists by studying art students at four colleges where friends who were teachers kindly helped him to find colour vision defective students. These were at Croydon College of Art, Nottingham College of Education, Gray's School of Art, Aberdeen, and Glasgow School of Art. Nine defective men students were found with the Ishihara Test for Colour Blindness and then tested fully with the Pickford-Nicolson Anomaloscope, namely three at Croydon, two at Nottingham, two at Aberdeen and two at Glasgow, where one woman defective was also found. Their frequency and the relative frequency of types of defect did not differ in statistical significance from those for the population at large, and therefore it seemed that there was no tendency for self-selection according to type or degree of defect.

A similar result was arrived at in a more intensive survey of the colour vision of almost the whole intake of students in the Glasgow School of Art in two years, namely, 112 men and 111 women. Six of the men and one of the women were found to have defective colour vision, and their defects were of various kinds. Among these and the ten mentioned in the previous paragraph, 17 in all, four did not know of their defects previously, nine had been found by the school doctors at their secondary schools before they came to the Glasgow School of Art, one found his defect owing to errors in daily life and two theirs as a result of tests by friends after going to the School of Art, and one had his discovered by his art teacher.

In general, those with simple protanomaly or deuteranomaly do not have much difficulty. One deuteranomalous student was suspected by a consideration of the predominantly red/yellow/blue colouring of his paintings in an exhibition, and tests confirmed these suspicions. Those with extreme deuteranomaly or protanomaly have considerable red/green confusion, especially in respect of pastel shades, and may run into difficulties, such as making a face partly greenish, especially in the shadowed parts. Those with protanopia and deuteranopia have serious red/green confusion, and may make mistakes such as painting flames or the brown saddle of a bicycle green and wondering why people think it odd. All such students need help in handling colours, and, although artistic ability in general is not impaired by loss of colour vision, colour defective art students ought to learn what colour they are likely to confuse and how to avoid errors of colouring they do not intend.

In a survey of the colour vision of art students, excluding major defectives in the Glasgow School of Art, in comparison with that of ophthalmic optics students and chemistry students at Stow College, S. R. Cobb (1972) found that the art students were no better than the control groups in hue discrimination. It seems, therefore, that artistic ability does not depend on a high degree of colour discrimination, but on a special ability in the manipulation and integration of colours and forms in artistic work.

Therefore it is understandable that an artist or art student with a minor deviation of colour vision, in the sense that his hue discrimination is in certain ways slightly less efficient than that of most people, may do good artistic work if he discovers or learns how to avoid or compensate for the effects of his peculiarity. Similarly an artist or art student with a major form of colour vision defect, who is liable to make absolute confusions of such colours as rose and pale blue or green, or between red and black, may still do good artistic work if he avoids colours or colour combinations likely to lend themselves to errors for him and for other people with normal colour vision who look at his paintings.

Chapter Nine

The artist in the population statistics

PETER COX

Whatever occupation men and women may follow, the work of only a handful of individuals is so outstanding as to live on, in substance or by repute, to affect future generations. Among even such exceptional performers, life histories and other personal details remain known after their death for no more than a few. The criterion of survival for such records may well be largely a biographical one; the existence or absence of information may be determined as much by the degree of interest or peculiarity in the events of the lifetime, or the subject's ability to write a good letter, as by the quality of his work. The amount of information we have today about artists in the past must be strongly coloured by selective forces of this kind. What material exists is highly valuable in itself; but it cannot be relied upon to give a true representation of the life of artists as a whole, and certainly not to provide an accurate statistical measurement of their general social surroundings in earlier times. The men and women who figure in the art history books must have lived long enough and persevered sufficiently at their work to develop their skills, and so their longevity is superior to the average. Their children are recorded, in the main, only where they are notable; their marriages, liaisons and migrations solely where stormy or frequent; their illnesses but in isolated cases. Subject to variations associated with the intensity of artistic activity, the earlier the period of time the smaller the number of artists recorded. But the volume of painting and sculpting has probably increased over the centuries roughly in proportion to population size. The evidence is generally that man's artistic needs provide a steady demand – though the source and method of their satisfaction may change.

If those who were highly successful in their occupation, and whose work still has a meaning today, provide little data of value for a demographic measurement, how then is information obtained about the population in earlier times? Pointers are derived from parish registers and similar documents, when they possess the essential virtues of reliability coupled with a reasonable degree of comprehensiveness. These are the chronicles of the unsung heroes, mainly of the 17th and 18th centuries. For earlier periods still, information is scanty; but studies have been made of a select group – the Peerage – from which useful indications of mortality, fertility, marriage and other vital elements have been obtained. The membership of this group being largely independent of success in an occupation (except for the founder of each line) but determined instead by considerations of genealogy, it provides a viable standard of measurement, subject to the special qualification that the environmental conditions were in many respects greatly superior to the average for the generality of people. If equally complete records were available for artists, the environmental conditions might well be more representative, in some ways, of social conditions for everyone – although other circumstances would lead to doubts about the validity of such information as a general indicator: one would have to bear in mind any hazards of the occupation, the fact that it might tend to be pursued by those not strong enough for hard manual work, the mode of life of artists – by repute dissipated – and their poverty.

Once the point in history is reached at which census and vital registration data become available, then information is at hand not only for the famous but also for all those practising art, as a group, and indeed for the general population as well. From this stage onwards, therefore, we can measure statistically the numbers and proportions of artists, their distribution by sex and age, the areas in which they work, the status accorded to them in the population, the industries in which they were engaged; and we can acquire also perhaps some information about mortality, fertility and migration. It becomes possible to compare one country with another in these respects. The amount of detail and the degree of sophistication in the records increase with the passage of time, and the picture unfolds gradually, providing the greatest wealth of information for the most recent times.

In studying such data, it becomes important to find out just how the profession is classified in the official records, and to watch for changes of definition from time to time. Arlidge (1892) gives it as his opinion that 'under the name artists a very mixed body of workers is comprised' and he goes on to say that in France this appellation is bestowed on 'designers of dress, to hairdressers and wigmakers and persons engaged in employments of an ordinary business character, as well as to musicians of all sorts, public singers, ballet dancers, fencing masters, actors and actresses. . . .' This grouping certainly goes a good deal wider than the confines of pictorial art. A further point of importance is that the official statistics relate essentially to those who earn money, or attempt to do so, by their craft. It does not include amateurs, and professionals may well be outnumbered by those who practice only for their private amusement. Some interesting information is available about leisure pursuits in Britain today, and this shows that about 4 per cent of men quote 'crafts and hobbies' as their chief spare-time activity. The corresponding figure for women is much higher (17 per cent) but the excess appears to consist mainly of those who knit (*Social Trends*, 1971). Painters and sculptors no doubt constitute only a small proportion of these groups. A sample study conducted by the author among the pages of *Who's Who* suggests that about 2 per cent of its subjects are ready to confess to 'painting' as a special feature among their recreations (and presumably this is not intended to include household decoration, although one of the illustrious has made reference to painting of 'both kinds' as a personal activity). This proportion excludes those with such related pursuits as the collection of art objects, or a general interest in the arts, or photography. The proportion of amateur artists in the adult general population must surely be lower than 2 per cent, if only because of the more slender intellectual and financial resources of most people, relatively to those who figure in *Who's Who*; but even if (at a guess) it were no more than $\frac{1}{4}$ per cent for all British people aged 20–65 this would still mean that 80,000 indulge in some activity of visual art, a number about twice as large as that of the professionals today.

The statistics of artists may tell us little, or add nothing to other knowledge, about the population at large, but at least they can indicate something about the profession itself. What springs to many people's minds in this connection is mortality, in the expectation perhaps that it is unusually high (think of *La Bohème*) but it is conceivable that marriages and fertility may have special characteristics too: some would say too few marriages and too many children. The truth is, nevertheless, that the experience of artists in regard to most forms of population change and movement is not exceptional: the occupation as a whole is neither exposed to many particular health hazards nor prone to behave in a markedly unusual way socially. Arlidge (op. cit.) records that the number of artists' deaths noted by French authors is high but attributes this to people 'whose avocations are fraught with injurious consequences', and who are included with painters and sculptors in the rather too all-embracing official statistics of that country – acrobats for example. It is generally supposed that at least the practice of stonecarving involves some risk of dust in the lungs, with associated consequences, but Hunter (1955) records that marble and limestone are in fact quite harmless in this respect, and these are the most favoured materials for carving. Sculptors are said to suffer from temporary paralysis of the hands and painters to be in danger from lead in paints, while Michelangelo apparently had an attack of nystagmus after painting the Sistine Chapel ceiling (I.L.O. 1930) but these ailments must surely be temporary in character and unlikely to shorten life. Determined not to omit any scrap of information which might conceivably indicate special debility, the *Encyclopaedia* goes on to refer to the weakly constitution and nervous temperament of artists, and their tendency to suffer from tuberculosis and syphilis, and to the deleterious effects of their hard work, poor pay, drug-taking, and irregular meals. As a Parthian shot, the authors include as a relevant factor the misery they are caused by unfavourable criticism. In spite of all this, the *Encyclopaedia* has to confess that in general the working conditions of visual artists are less unfavourable than those for musicians, dancers and people who help in the making of films. True, official occupational mortality studies by the Registrar General in England and Wales have revealed a higher-than-normal incidence of wasting diseases (1921) and of nervous ailments (1931) but the numbers of recorded cases are small. In other respects, there are favourable factors. For mortality taken as a whole, normality is the rule (101 per cent of the standard in 1921).

Records of famous artists tend to emphasize their longevity. Those whose work is illustrated in colour by Hendy (1960), and whose years of birth and death are known, had an average lifetime of about 60 years, even in the 15th–17th centuries, which is much higher than the normal for that period. Only 10 per cent died before the age of 40. The ages at which some notable painters and sculptors died are:

Cézanne	67
Claude	82
Giotto	71
Leonardo	67
Michelangelo	89
Poussin	71
Raphael	37
Rembrandt	63
Rodin	77
Rubens	63
Turner	76
Watteau	37

The record of the lives of famous musical composers of the 16th–18th centuries is very similar, for instance:

J. S. Bach	65
Handel	74
Purcell	37
Rameau	81
D. Scarlatti	72

Although there are many very notable composers whose lives were short (Mozart, Chopin, Schubert, Schumann) these remain the exception, and to balance them are:

Fauré	79
Schoenberg	77
Verdi	88

In this connection, however, the remarks made in the first paragraph of this chapter must be borne in mind.

For the Peerage, Hollingsworth (1964) has calculated the expectation of life at birth to have been less than 40 years in the 16th century in Britain, and he arrived at a lower figure still for the 17th century. During the 18th and 19th centuries, there were rises, for men to 45 by 1800 and to over 55 by 1900, and correspondingly for women to 50 and then nearly 70. For the general population, the figures were only 40 (men) and 45 (women) even for those born as late as 1850.

If attention is centred on those who survived to the age of 30, however, the story is quite different. Such people, in the Peerage, lived until their mid-50s in the 16th and 17th centuries and to their mid-60s in the 18th, on the average. This information corresponds quite well with the experience of famous artists, who could hardly have achieved eminence if they had not first reached full biological maturity. Living British artists whose work is in the possession of the Tate Gallery have an average age of about 50 and hardly any of them are under 30. It is of interest to note that the ages at which each one's earliest painting in the collection was completed range from 20 to 60 with an average in the mid-30s; only about one-quarter of these works of art were created before the age of 30.

Artists' fertility has also been examined by the English Registrar General, and he found it to be about 70 per cent (1911) or 80 per cent (1921) of the general average. In 1911 they were among the least fertile 10 per cent of the population. The mortality of their children in infancy was also below normal. These indicators suggest that the social conditions of this profession corresponded to those of the upper classes. Indeed, the Registrar included them in his category II, which consists of professional and managerial people not quite at the top. He did so consciously, because he regarded the group as a mixture of high-class and low-class people, with this rating on the average.

The information given about artists in biographical dictionaries centres, quite properly, on their work. In the course of this, most of them travelled a good deal – certainly far more than the ordinary people of the day. Much of the travel was international in character, and so they may be said to have been 'migrants'. This in itself would seem likely to have constituted some special hazard to life, but there is little evidence that the practical effects were severe. As, however, the cause of death is hardly ever quoted in these sources of information, there is very little material for research. The same is true of the artists' family life.

The growth of the profession in the 19th and 20th centuries is illustrated by the Census statistics. The first Census of England and Wales at which the numbers of people were recorded in occupational groups, sufficiently well-defined to reveal useful information about artists, was that of 1841, when 3690 men and 278 women were attributed to the category 'Fine Arts'. Also counted were 262 sculptors (all men), 4461 men and 35 women engravers and 101 'herald painters', of whom 5 were female. Thus perhaps one-half of the artists were doing original work and the remainder were concerned with reproduction. The total population of working age was then about 9 millions and so those who were engaged in all these visual arts taken together represented about 1 per mille; this proportion is much the same as it was a hundred years later – though the artists' purposes have changed considerably.

In 1871, the following were counted, in round figures:

	Men	Women
Painter, artist	5000	1100
Sculptor	800	—
Engraver	4800	—
Photographer	4000	700
Others in fine art	100	100
	14700	1900

The total population had increased by nearly 50 per cent since 1841 and the number of painters had gone up in proportion; but the participation of women in this form of activity had clearly increased. Sculpture, up threefold, had grown in importance although still confined to men. The appearance on the scene of photography had curtailed growth in the number of engravers.

In 1881, some 60,000 artists were recorded in England and Wales. But these included – in the style attributed by Arlidge to France – actors, musicians and architects. (14,000 men and 11,000 women musicians, including music teachers, were enumerated and outnumbered visual artists by a large margin, especially for women). Consistency of definition, from one period to another, is an uncertain plant; it tends to wither in the force of new concepts, or practical convenience, in the Census volumes and it is always necessary to be watchful for changes. However, there is a sub-classification which shows a growth in the numbers of photographers in 1881, compared with 1871, and a rise for painters, but a further diminution among engravers. It seems that photography, so often quoted as the cause of radical changes in painting ethos, had not so far reacted unfavourably upon the numbers of practitioners of Fine Art. Women continued to penetrate the market increasingly, and for them 1880 painters and 16 sculptors were recorded. The proportion of all women at work who were engaged in the four pursuits had reached 0·10 per cent – the ratio for men was 0·18 per cent.

In other occupational groups, 1000 men and 100 women art dealers were counted, 2500 art students and 1500 'in the service of art'; also 5000 colour and oil-men and 200 manufacturers of paints and dyes.

The Census of 1891 adds little to our store of information, and is remarkable only, perhaps, in that it found 6 blind men among the visual artists. This is known because, for the first time, a question on 'infirmities' was included in this enumeration. But doubts about the accuracy of the results in general have caused it not to be repeated subsequently.

During the period 1891–1911, the numbers of painters and sculptors in Britain seem to have grown less rapidly than before and more slowly than the population. This may seem surprising, in the light of the intense artistic activity of the 1890s, but much of this was literary rather than visual. Perhaps by now the camera really was having an effect on the art world. But engravers, 5000 in number in 1911, had staged a comeback: the Registrar notes that there had been an 'increase in the number of photographic engravers, etchers, etc.' which made it difficult to separate artistic engravers from those engaged in more humdrum processes. Presumably the connection of art with advertising and other forms of communication, which is so powerful today, had already begun to be established by the turn of the century.

In modern times, visual art has become not only an occupation but also an industry, and in 1921 a flood of new censal information was released which tells us something of the manpower structure of the market. For instance, out of 8000 male painters, sculptors and engravers, only one-half were working on their own account. The rest were employers (500) or employees (3000). It is true that in Renaissance times great painters employed apprentices to fill in the lesser details of their work. But the scale of the modern operation smacks far more of the commercial. Even among women there were 50 employers and 2000 employees while 2500 were working on their own account. 500 persons of both sexes described themselves as 'retired' from this field, and their age-distribution suggests a fairly normal 'pension' age, although for women marriage and the rearing of a family is likely to have been the cause, in many cases, of the cessation of economic activity.

Gainfully-occupied artists are recorded as being at work in several industrial fields in 1921, notably in book production and advertising, as well as offering professional services. In addition, the Registrar shows that in England and Wales the Industry of Painting, Engraving and Sculpture found employment for nearly 11,000 people of whom only about 85 per cent were actually artists. Others were concerned with production, repair, maintenance, transport, commerce and the like, and there were 100 authors and even some domestic servants and general labourers in the category.

In the generally similar types of information collected in 1931, two new classes appear – managers and the unemployed: out of some 16,000 in the occupation artist, 600 were managers and 1,000 unemployed. A continuing trend towards commercialism, not to say industrialization, is underlined by these descriptions. It is also illustrated by two features not hitherto discussed here – namely the composition of the group by sub-occupations, giving a more specific description of the work, and the distribution of artists by region of residence. So far as the occupational breakdown is concerned, 40 sub-groups are quoted (without the corresponding numbers of practitioners) and they include such categories as:

Advertisement artist
Bank note engraver
Crest painter
Fashion artist
Fibre engraver
Lampshade artist
Medallist
Trade mark designer

as well as Miniature painter and Royal Academician. (But artists' models, repairers, art critics, art dealers and architects appear in quite separate groups.) The industrial classification incorporates such categories as chocolate-box painting, costume designing, artists' models and cartoon drawing.

The regional analysis shows quite a wide variation in activity between areas, the proportion of artists to all gainfully-occupied people being twice as high as the national average in London and the South-East – and below it everywhere else. The South-West has the highest proportion of artists outside the South-East; the fame of Cornwall as a centre may have much to do with this. Other regions with relatively high ratios are Lancashire and Cheshire, the West Midlands, South Wales and Scotland – probably in association with their big cities; the more rural parts show lower concentrations.

The 1951 Census of England and Wales is in some ways less informative about artists than the immediately-preceding enumerations. Art was now merged with

other industrial groups into a larger aggregate and cannot be separately identified. The occupation 'artist' still remained separate but it had suffered a change
in classification since 1931, by the inclusion of some stonemasons and the exclusion of some types of engraver. The total numbers of people recorded were
12,000 men and 4,500 women – little apparent advance on 1931. Nevertheless,
the fuller details then available of the industry groups in which artists are
engaged do much to compensate for the lack of news. Besides the expected
categories:

Ceramics and glass	700
Paper and printing	1900
Professional services	10000

which account for over three-quarters of the class, artists are found in no fewer
than 21 other industrial activities, notably chemicals, engineering, vehicle
manufacture, textiles, food, wood processing and retail trade. There are even
small numbers in the leather trade, in mining and quarrying and in agriculture –
one can only suppose in the preparation of advertisements, visual aids and the
like in these activities. If the Government could commission artists to depict the
Second World War, as it had done with notable effect, then presumably there
is no reason why farmers should not have an authorised record made of (say)
their dairying operations. It is often alleged that the artist of today has no patron,
but paints to please himself and in so doing tends to lose all contact with the man
in the street, but this can hardly be true of those who work in industry.

The proportion of occupied people who work as visual artists in some capacity
or other varies with age. It rises to its highest level late in life – perhaps because
retirement is less obligatory than in other jobs or because pensioners supplement
their income through art employment. At normal working ages, however, art
Fig. 1 is a young man's affair, in Britain at least. The graph shows that the proportion
occupied with art falls in middle life. Here there has been a change, because in
1911 the proportion was higher for people aged 50 than it was for people aged
20; since then the reversal has emerged gradually. The formation of such bodies
as the Design in Industry Association, the Council of Industrial Design and the
Society of Industrial Designers, and a large increase in the numbers of art schools
and polytechnics, have been associated with this development.

Difficulties associated with radical changes in classification affect also the
relation between the results of the 1961 Census, in which there is found a new
occupational group called 'painters, sculptors and related creative artists', and
its predecessors. The numbers in this group in England and Wales, namely
22,000 men and 12,500 women, represent more than a doubling from 1951.
Commenting on this change of classification, the Registrar General states that
the degree of subdivision in earlier census occupational groups was 'over-elabor-
ate', having regard to the quality of the answers given. In general, the new categorization introduced a number of changes of principle which precluded direct
comparisons with earlier data even for larger aggregates of occupational codes.
But a sample reclassification for men suggested that on the 1951 definition of
painters, sculptors and engravers there would have been recorded some 14,000

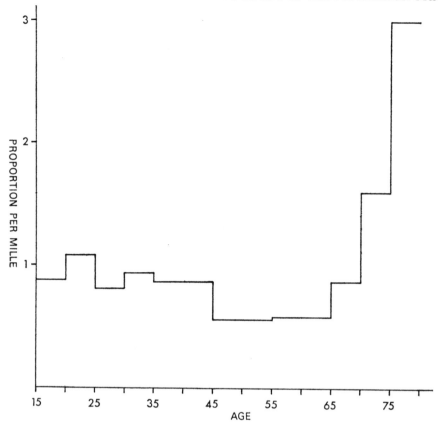

Fig. 1 *Graph showing proportions of male painters, sculptors and engravers (artists) to all occupied men in England and Wales, 1951*

in 1961 – an increase of nearly 20 per cent over 1951. About as many people as in 1951 were working on their own account but an increase in employers and managers from under 1000 to 3000 and a growth in the number of employees from 9000 to 25,000 resulted, very strikingly, from the new presentation. So clearly it is the commercial and industrial sides of art which had swelled the total. By 1966 there had been a rise to no less than 15,000 people in the number of the profession engaged in 'distribution' and an increase of 6000 in the 'miscellaneous' group. In the plans for the 1971 Census a new group appeared – the 'hospital (medical) artist': a profession within a profession?

It is of interest that the number of musicians, even when combined as they now are with stage managers, actors, and entertainers, came to only 27,000 in 1966 – well below the number of 'artists' – and this shows how the balance has changed since 1881, though music teachers are probably excluded now and this exclusion could affect the comparison materially.

One of the new features of the 1966 Census is the emergence of a considerable mass of new details about people who possess recognized technical qualifications.

In Britain, in the whole field of music, drama, art and design, the number so qualified was about 62,000. Such a number represents about 80 per cent of the work force in the occupation group of visual artists and musicians; but the comparison is not a valid one and the ratio is accordingly meaningless. Only 4000 artists and 6000 musicians have any appreciable academic qualifications; the remainder of the 62,000 artistically-qualified people are not practising in the field in which they were trained but instead are working in unrelated occupations or are retired. Only about 20 per cent of musicians and 10 per cent of visual artists are qualified: compare about 10 per cent for the population at large. Artists have in fact the lowest proportion of qualified practitioners of any professional group. Unlike other workers they are at least trained in their own subject: only a few have degrees in other disciplines. Moreover, one in ten have the best possible qualification, and this is above the national average. Even so, over half of them have a certificate or diploma judged by the Registrar General to be below ordinary degree level whereas, among all those 62,000 with qualifications in music, drama, art and design, more than two-thirds are up to that level. The general picture presented by these figures suggests a considerable mobility into and out of the art world.

The information about artists and their employment today has recently been enriched by the publication of a report on an official sample survey (H.M.S.O. 1972). The survey is in two parts. The first concerns the 4000 students who left Art Colleges in England and Wales in 1968; it relates the courses they had taken to the nature of their activities in the two years up to 1970. The second studied the 1800 employers (other than educational establishments) with which the responding students did work of an artistic nature. The rate of response in both parts of the enquiry was only about 60 per cent, which means that in the second stage the answers received represent only about 35 per cent of the maximum possible; thus there is room for error in the answers. Moreover, the group of employers approached could be expected to be representative neither of employers in general nor of employers of artists and designers in general. Nevertheless, the results should be of value as an aid to the planning of art education and in the search for employment by art graduates.

The courses taken by students may be grouped as follows; the statement shows the approximate percentage of people involved:

Fine Art	20%
Illustration & communication	40%
Textiles & dress	20%
Design of various kinds	20%
	100%

Men and women figured in the total in roughly equal numbers but the male sex predominated in the first two groups while the female accounted for most in the third category. In design work there was more of a balance.

It appears that nearly all the students had obtained some qualification or other. This does not seem to fit in well with the censal statistics, but there is inadequate information for a reconciliation.

About 50 per cent of the leavers had found steady employment of an artistic character. Of the residue most had done some art work but had also had other forms of employment. After two years, 1 in 5 were teaching art, 1 in 10 were continuing their education and 1 in 6 were doing work unrelated to art. About one half of the total had supplemented their earnings with freelance work, but total earnings were modest – most jobs bringing in only £9 – £15 a week.

The report suggests that the students distributed themselves fairly evenly between textiles, furniture and ceramics, printing and publishing, other manufacturing, transport and distribution, advertising, consultancy and other industries. It is difficult to align these results with the Census statistics, no doubt because of differences of definition and grouping. But the distribution of employed artists by sex and age is in more reasonable accord with the Census, although the establishments in which the students worked seem to have used a younger work force than the average; these establishments also appear to employ a higher proportion than the generality of those who had attended art courses.

Questions relating to business prospects for the near future elicited the answer that a further expansion in art work was expected.

Recent Census information for the United States of America is fuller than for Britain, in the sense that a wider variety of topics is covered. The number of artists in 1960 was just over 100,000, of whom about a third were women; but this includes teachers of art who, it would appear, may possibly be classed under the heading 'teachers' in some cases over here. In proportion to the work force as a whole, the American total is comparatively low, but this could well be due to differences of definition between the two countries.

Only 2 per cent of American artists are Negroes, which suggests some form of racial discrimination or difference, as they constitute 10 per cent of the population generally; but among other non-whites the proportion of artists is higher than the national average.

Where the U.S. statistics are particularly informative is in connection with the economic circumstances of the occupation, for instance in regard to hours worked and income earned. They also show the educational background. So it is possible to see how artists compare with other workers; are they lazy drop-outs, leading a bohemian life and subsisting on State Welfare? It would appear that this is very far from the truth. Their distribution by size of income is closely similar to that of the working population at large, and among men about one is six has $10,000 a year or more. Probably there is little really 'big money' earned, however. But 3 per cent of women artists also reach the $10,000 bracket, and this is above the national standard for their sex. Artists mostly work all the year round (90 per cent said that they were busy for at least 40 weeks out of the 52) and three-quarters of men put in 40 hours' work, or more, in a week. Six per cent of men claimed to work for at least 60 hours a week. Among women, however, the statistics show that about one-half are part-timers, and no doubt many combine painting with household duties.

The industries in which artists are engaged in the U.S.A. show the same extraordinary diversity as in Britain, and include such groups as oil wells, building construction and personal service. About one-quarter are concerned with education, which gives a good clue to the numbers who teach, although many no doubt combine this with doing original work of their own. The educational background of artists is superior to the average, and more than one-half of them have been to college.

In the hope that Paris, as the most famous centre of pictorial art culture in the world, would contribute some striking information to the Census statistics, an examination was made of recent volumes of French official data; but the result was disappointing. The proportion of workers classed as artists is quite unremarkable, in the country as a whole, and the amount of analysis devoted to this occupation is slighter than in Britain and the U.S.A. Perhaps this illustrates the thesis that the greater the heights reached by real culture the less attention is paid to such inessentials as economic analysis. Commercial art may very well have been relegated to the level of being grouped, without distinction, among ordinary desk work. There is evidence, still today, that in the French official mind 'the arts' are a natural group which embraces the theatre, the concert hall and the architects' studio as well as the painter's atelier – all that is independently creative, in fact.

To sum up, visual artists as they are measured in the statistics today exhibit few of the characteristics traditionally associated with painting. They mostly work steadily, earn good money and do not lack an industrial patron. They do not suffer from photography – many of them use the camera – or from a lack of discernment on the part of the public generally. They are numerous. The work of most of them is useful but ephemeral in character. Many change their jobs, but so does everyone these days. If those few who are destined to become famous are at present obscure, and poor, as may well prove to be so, then they are inevitably lost among the jostling mass of ordinary people of average capability who practise in this field. It looks as though this could have been true, to some extent, ever since records began to be collected early in the Victorian era – and probably it was so before that, too.

Chapter Ten

Psychology, culture and visual art

R. W. PICKFORD

This chapter is intended to give a short account of the point of view of the psychologist and of his approach to the problems of art. It is not intended as a substitute for the philosophical or other approaches, or to belittle them. The studies reported here in the psychology of art will include short sections on the psychology of perception in relation to art and of perceptual types among persons who make judgments of aesthetic preference. These sections will be followed by an account of experimental approaches to judgments of preference for pictures, cross-cultural studies, and a consideration of the psychology of personality in relation to aesthetic preferences. The chapter will conclude with a short summary of ideas about art as a branch of culture which is subject to the psychological influences underlying cultural change, development and decay.

THE NATURE OF PSYCHOLOGY

Psychology today is an experimental and empirical science of behaviour and conscious experiences in man and animals. From the point of view of art we are almost completely confined to man, although Morris has shown that there is good reason to believe that there is some degree of aesthetic experience among the higher apes. Indeed, some pictures by apes may be difficult to distinguish aesthetically from some by human artists (Morris 1962).

In the history of psychology there has been a very marked changeover from its subjective and introspective forms which were associated with philosophy, and which were the main aspects of psychology until approximately 100 years ago, to the experimental and purely objective or behaviouristic forms of the subject which have been derived from physiology since the middle of the last century. This change led first to the attempt to establish psychology as a purely objective and experimental science, called behaviourism, during the early part of this century, and then to its taking the present form as what is generally called a behavioural science.

Behaviourism was extremely radical and would have rejected every reference to conscious experience in the study of man or animals, as lacking in objectivity and being unreliable, unverifiable and not satisfying the requirements for the strictly quantitative treatment of a science. Most psychologists have felt the need to be less rigidly objective, because, to eliminate every reference to consciousness in a science of man is to reduce that study almost to inept proportions. If we want to study human activities and behaviour, but do not admit any reference to consciousness, we are not likely to be very illuminating.

Consequently psychology has been called a behavioural science, thus emphasizing the importance of objectivity in the observation, measurement and analysis of behaviour, but at the same time leaving room for consideration of the conscious and subjective aspects. Even the expression 'behavioural science' hardly leaves enough freedom to us in this way, because, especially in the study of art and aesthetics, neither appreciation, nor liking and disliking, nor, more technically, evaluation, can be identified, in our view, strictly with behaviour. Indeed, many people would say that the importance of behaviour is secondary in aesthetics, because no aesthetically significant behaviour could be conceived as occurring at all except as the outcome of conscious activities and experience.

While general experimental psychology tends to be concerned with the functions, capacities and abilities of the individual, in the directions of sensation, perception, intelligence and thinking, and of his behaviour potentialities as a single person, social psychology is concerned with the ways in which these are influenced by the presence of others. Of recent years social psychology has become a science of itself, and has a large field of observational and experimental studies to its credit. Social psychology also considers the effect of groups on each other, and of individuals on groups. Sociological psychology is more concerned with the large-scale phenomena of group life, and less with the individual and with group effects on him or his influence on groups. It is clear therefore that social and sociological psychology both have considerable relevance to the study of art and aesthetics. This will be seen as the final section of this chapter on the social psychology of cultural change.

PSYCHOLOGICAL APPROACHES TO ART

Some 100 years ago, Fechner attempted to establish experimental aesthetics as a psychological science (Fechner, 1876). He was a great pioneer of experimental psychology, who invented methods of studying subjective judgments and preferences quantitatively, and he may be called the father of experimental aesthetics. For 50 years or so after his work there was only a slight amount of interest in experimental aesthetics, but in the second 50 years there has been a rapidly growing spate of researches, and today the subject is an important branch of psychological science.

Fig. 1 An interesting problem first investigated by Fechner was that of the golden section. The upper drawing on the page opposite shows the golden section rectangle in which the short side bears the same relation to the long side as the long side does to the length of both sides together. This proportion, called the golden section, has played a considerable part at least in Western art, and is widely accepted as a preferred proportion. Figure 1 also shows the square-root-of-ten rectangle, which, it has been suggested, is preferred in American Indian

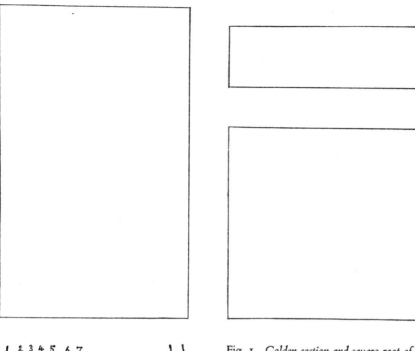

Fig. 1   *Golden section and square-root-of-ten rectangle and a square*

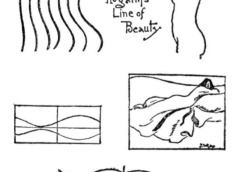

Fig. 2   *Hogarth's Line of Beauty. (After Poore)*

art, and a square, which is preferred to the golden section rectangle by blind subjects by touch. The preference for the golden section rectangle in Western art may be an effect of culture and tradition. The Japanese may prefer the square.

Another form of preference which is worth mention is called Hogarth's Line of Beauty. It is the middle one, number 4, of the series of seven curves shown at *Fig. 2* the top left of the smaller drawing; the other items show how this line of beauty enters into various aesthetic constructions, such as a woman's back, a double curve pattern, a reclining figure and a pair of lips. The liking for this shape may be a purely cultural preference, like that for the golden section.

Another outstanding contributor to psychological studies of art, Müller-Frienfels, as explained by Munro (1948), indicated that there were five essential ways in which psychology could contribute to aesthetics. The first was the experimental method by which, following Fechner, laboratory studies of the supposedly absolute or universal pleasantness or otherwise of forms, colours, rhythms and so on, could be established. This method has led to the study of individual differences in aesthetic experience on a wider scale outside the laboratory. The second was the use of questionnaires by which larger numbers of individuals could be studied than by laboratory experiments, and variations of this have been widely used. The third was the approach through the study of the individual as an inventive and creative artist. The comparison of different individuals was called the differential method. The fourth, or pathological, method was a special form of the third method dealing with individuals of abnormal personality. It finds its developments today in the study of the psychiatric aspects of art and of artists, and of what we now call psychiatric art, or the work of mental patients. The fifth was called the objective-analytical method. It was concerned with the investigation and comparison of works of art throughout their history, and among various peoples and cultures; it sought to understand the mental states that lay behind them in terms of cultural, political, economic and other aspects of life. Associated with this is the ethno-psychological method which considers art as the expression of collective rather than of individual creativity.

The approaches of psychology might, however, be summarized as taking four forms. Firstly, there is the application to works of art and to artists of psychological knowledge, gained in other ways, where it is appropriate. In the psychology of perception, for example, we find much that is relevant to art and illuminating in relation to it. Secondly, there is the invention of special techniques and experimental methods for dealing with aesthetic judgments and feelings. Fechner's great contribution lay in this direction. He showed how we can measure and compare the aesthetic preferences of different people, and concerning different objects, by special techniques called psychophysical methods, among which the method of paired comparisons is specially important. Thirdly, there are comparative and cross-cultural studies, which depend on the comparison of aesthetic preferences and judgments in different cultural and racial groups, by experimental techniques and descriptive analysis. Fourthly, we have the psycho-dynamic and clinical approaches. In these the works of art are understood through an examination of the motivations and conflicts in the lives of the artists. This links up, of course, with the approach through abnormal psychology and psychiatry.

PERCEPTION AND THE PSYCHOLOGY OF ART AND AESTHETICS

The most important aspects of the psychology of perception from the point of view of art and aesthetics, to be mentioned in a short chapter, are those of Gestalt psychology on the one hand and of perspective and binocular vision on the other.

As a study of the appearances of visual patterns and configurations, the contribution of Gestalt psychology remains paramount whatever may be said about the physiological basis of perception in other ways (Pickford 1972, 11–17). Gestalt psychology shows that the characteristic appearances of patterns of visual stimuli tend to follow four important laws or principles in their organization.

Fig. 3 *Figure and ground. The shape of the vase stands out against the background, but the background may stand out as two faces looking at each other, and these appearances tend to alternate*

The first law is that of 'figure and ground', according to which every experi-   *Fig. 3* ence in perception is essentially a form or figure seen against a background of other experiences. This applies throughout the visual arts, and also in music.

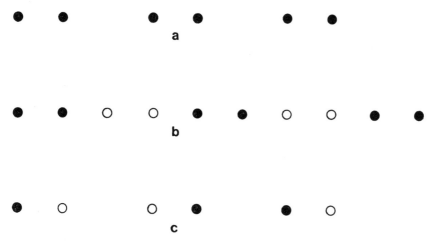

Fig. 4 *Differentiation and segregation I. In (a) the pairs of dots separated by space tend to be differentiated and to be segregated together. In (b), where the distances apart are equal, the pairs of black dots and of white dots are segregated. In (c) spatial segregation takes precedence*

The second is the law of 'differentiation' or 'segregation', according to which   *Fig. 4* patterns of stimulation organize themselves in perception into structures result-ing from their special perspectives. Thus, if a cross-shaped or ring-shaped pattern of large dots is included in a random pattern of small dots, it will stand out clearly   *Fig. 5* as a cross or ring in appearance.

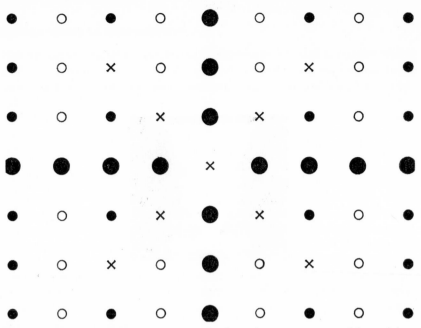

Fig. 5 *Differentiation and segregation II. In this figure there are two crosses of dots and the upright line patterns which are segregated by shape, size and appearance*

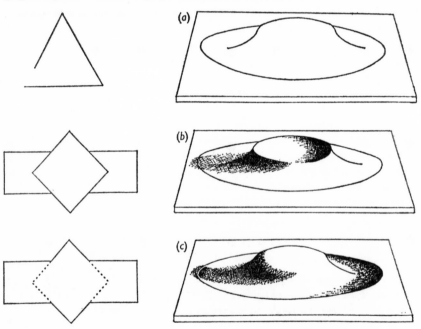

Fig. 6 *Closure and good Gestalt. The top triangle seems complete although there is a part missing. In the middle figure the rectangle is differentiated from the triangle, but seems complete behind it. In the bottom figure the square or diamond seems complete although parts of it are only represented by dots*

Fig. 7 *The effect of shadows. This shows two different effects of solidity (b) and (c) which may be produced by different shadowing on the same outline (a)*

The third Gestalt principle is that of 'closure', by which any partly obscured form or figure in perception tends to be experienced as if it were complete. *Fig. 6* A human figure, for instance, of which part is obscured, still looks like a whole person. The fourth principle is that of the 'good Gestalt', according to which a more strongly emphasized or more adequate pattern will take precedence in perception over psychologically weaker patterns. All these laws or principles can be shown readily to apply in normal art and music, and it is clear that the artist has traditionally worked with their help unwittingly.

The problems of depth perception, perspective, and binocular and stereo-scopic vision have figured very largely in psychological studies of visual art (Pickford 1972, 35–41). It is clear that apparent depth perception in pictures is essentially monocular, because pictures are generally flat and are viewed with two eyes as if they were one. In monocular vision the following factors are of first-class importance to produce the impression of depth in a flat picture: *Figs 7, 8* (1) shadows, which are of extreme importance in producing the impression of solidity; (2) overlapping of more distant objects by nearer ones; (3) decrease in precision of form and outline and in the representation of details, as distance increases; (4) changes of colour, usually towards less saturation, and greater blue-purple or grey coloration, with increasing distance; (5) strictly perspective changes of shape of a purely geometrical kind, based on the principle of recession of parallel lines to points in the distance, and upwards; and (6) the viewer's tendency automatically to vary and adjust the convergence or focus of his eyes for vision into the distance for far objects as represented, and the reverse for near objects. These changes of convergence and focusing are associated with differences of distance.

For actual solid objects themselves, such as architecture and sculptures, of course, the use of two eyes is extremely important. In this case the slight disparity of the optical images on the retinae, between the view as seen by one eye and as seen by the other, varies according to the distance of the object seen, and gives rise to the impression of distance and solidity in what is called stereoscopic vision. The actual use of two eyes for viewing flat pictures may even diminish the impression of distance for them, because then the two eyes are used in such a way that the appropriate disparity of the natural images does not exist. Some-

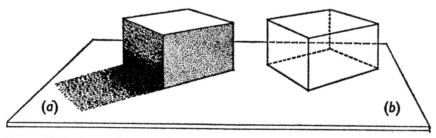

Fig. 8 *Shadowing, overlapping and transparency: (a) shows the impression of solidity produced by strong shadows; (b) shows how the impression of solidity may be produced by transparency without shadows. Both illustrate the effect of the solidity due to geometrical perspective*

Fig. 9 *Expanding perspective in a Mogul picture, c. 1585. In this illustration several objects are given perspective shapes expanding into the distance instead of contracting. (After Thouless)*

Fig. 10 *'That Strange Feeling', by Dosh. The deformation of the column seems to have been produced by the pressure of the man leaning against it, and gives a dynamic feeling to the picture. (From* Punch, *11 February 1970)*

times a flat picture has a greater appearance of depth when seen with one eye than with two.

Fig. 9   An example of the way in which geometrical perspective does not apply is worth mentioning. The left-hand drawing above shows a reversal of perspective in several places, the shapes of various objects shown actually increasing instead of diminishing with greater distance. This has been discussed by various writers, in particular by Thouless (1932), from whose article this illustration is taken, and by Pickford (Wyburn, Pickford and Hirst 1964, 230–31). This expanding perspective effect was certainly traditional in much Eastern art, was found frequently in Primitive art, and has been brought back into Modern art, as, for example in Van Gogh's famous *Yellow Chair.*

Fig. 10   Another important principle of perception is empathy, or feeling-into the picture, by which the impression of weight or force applied, for example, is conveyed by deformation in objects represented. An arm reaching out for something may be elongated towards it. In one of Goya's famous bullfight pictures the impression that a matador impaled on the animal's horns will be tossed over its back is vividly intensified by the representation of the vacant space where he will fall.

APPERCEPTIVE TYPES AND MOOD-TYPES

In the earlier part of this century Edward Bullough carried out a number of experiments on individuals' liking and disliking of colours and made observations of how they felt about these judgments (Bullough 1908). In one experiment 35 subjects viewed 70 different colours, one at a time, and reported on their liking for, or dislike of them and on what explanations they could give. As a result he divided their attitudes into the four well-known aspects or categories, namely, (1) the objective, by which colours were liked because they were saturated or bright, for instance, and disliked because they were dull, mixed or foggy; (2) the physiological, by which colours were pleasing because they seemed stimulating, soothing or warming, and displeasing because they seemed dazzling or disturbing in some other way; (3) the associative, by which colours were pleasing or otherwise because, for instance, they reminded the viewer of a certain person or place; and (4) the character aspect, according to which colours were liked because they seemed jovial, fearless or energetic, for example, and disliked because they seemed stubborn, treacherous or aggressive.

These apperceptive types were the outcome of the interaction between the personality qualities of the viewers, and the properties of the colours viewed by them. Other workers, especially Bradford (1913), confirmed Bullough's findings, while Myers (1914) showed that they applied in the appreciation of music.

Many other experimental studies have been made of the emotions and feeling-tones excited by colours, most of which have been reviewed by the writer (Pickford 1972, 91–95). For example, Marion Monroe (1925) showed that the apparent weight of a colour varied inversely with its brightness. Bullough also had shown that darker colours appeared heavier than lighter colours. Margaret St George (1930) studied responses to six colours and white, by groups of art and non-art students, and showed that art students had more objective and impersonal attitudes towards them. Lois Wexner (1954) showed that the following mood tones and colours tended to be related: exciting – red, yellow or black; secure – blue, brown or green; distressed – orange or black; tender – blue or green; protective – red or brown; despondent – black or brown; calm – blue or green; dignified – purple or black; cheerful – yellow or red; defiant – red, orange or black; powerful – black or red. Murray and Deabler (1957) gave a similar series of associations. Wright and Rainwater (1962) showed that there were six principal dimensions in the feelings excited by colours, namely, happiness (depending mainly on lightness), showiness (depending on saturation), forcefulness (depending on colour darkness), warmth (depending on hue, especially redness), elegance (saturation and hue, especially blueness), and calmness (depending on darkness or blueness).

Hogg (1969a and 1969b) showed that the influence of colours on his subjects could be classified in terms of four factors or dimensions, which were approximately as follows: (1) impact, (2) usualness, (3) pleasantness, and (4) warmth or excitingness. For pairs of colours he established a similar group of factors, namely, (1) active/passive, (2) pleasant/unpleasant, (3) warmth and lushness, and (4) usual/unusualness (Pickford 1972, 79–81 and 157–58).

Studies of this kind would certainly have to be carried very much further if any generally applicable principles of colour-affect were to be established in relation to, or independently of race or culture, and individual differences would always remain important.

EXPERIMENTS ON PREFERENCES FOR PICTURES

Burt (1939) and Valentine (1962) as reported together with studies mentioned later (Pickford, 1972 ch. 5) were among the first to carry out experimental work upon preferences for picture material. Valentine confirmed Bullough's classification of types of attitude or judgment, calling them the character, objective, subjective and associative types. Burt showed that there was an increasing degree of agreement between experts and children, adults in general, students, teachers and art school applicants, and with increasing age and sophistication in art. He also claimed a general capacity for artistic judgment, subsequently supported by others. Eysenck made factorial studies of aesthetic judgments of picture material, and he in particular claimed the existence of two factors or dimensions, the first being of a general kind, which he called 'good taste', and the second depending on the personality quality of the individual making the judgments and the nature of the art. Thus he claimed that introverted persons tended to prefer classical and quietly coloured pictures, while the extraverts preferred modern pictures of a colourful kind.

Pickford studied the aesthetic qualities in pictures, such as design, emotional expression, atmospheric effect and religious feeling. He came to the conclusion that there was a general factor or dimension of aesthetic quality, represented by form and emotional expression, and a secondary dimension of representational accuracy contrasted with atmospheric effect and symbolic expression. This was confirmed by others, both for music and poetry.

In a related but different kind of study Francès and Voillaume (1964) showed that in the appreciation of portraits of women, landscapes, portraits of children and flower pictures, all by well-known artists, the viewer was influenced in seven different ways. These were all positive and negative, or bipolar, in character. They were: (1) realism (lively versus banal); (2) originality (imaginative versus eccentric); (3) technique (mastery versus maladroitness); (4) qualities of the model or object (beauty versus ugliness); (5) lightness and colourfulness (harmony of colouring versus obscurity); (6) subjective impressionism (romantic versus stupid or gloomy). In children there was an increasingly close relationship with increasing age, between order of preference for the pictures and fidelity of representation. This connection between preference and fidelity was strong for skilled artisans, but less or even negative for students of philosophy or aesthetics. Many other studies have been carried out which there is no space to report here.

CROSS-CULTURAL COMPARISONS

Cross-cultural studies have been among the most interesting researches, but the difficulty of separating the possibility of racial from purely cultural differences has always been very great. The spread of Western cultural standards, habits and material equipment is so wide now, that the chances of finding tribes or groups who have in no degree been influenced by the West are diminishing rapidly. Even when such groups are found it is also difficult to apply Western methods and techniques of experimenting to them, and the results of experiments may be open to doubt.

Colour preferences have figured largely in cross-cultural studies, although often it is doubtful whether the experimental techniques used would pass muster today. Eysenck (1941b) nevertheless summarized the results of 16 studies of white peoples' preferences and 10 of non-whites'. These in comparison showed a surprising degree of conformity, whites giving the following order for six saturated colours; blue, red, green, violet, yellow and orange; while the order for non-whites was blue, red, green, violet, orange, yellow. Indeed the only difference in order of preference, that for orange and yellow, was very small in any case.

Much more adequate and elaborate studies have brought out the influence of differences of brightness and saturation in addition to hue. The most impressive of these have been by Child and his co-workers (Child 1969). Some similarities and some differences emerge, and certain writers tend to think that the uniformities of human physiological organization round the world tend to produce uniformities of aesthetic preference, while cultural diversities tend to superimpose differences. At the same time it is true that there are considerable physiological differences, and one need hardly mention stature, shape of features, skin colour and so on. There might equally be physiologically determined differences of aesthetic preference, partly blurred in many cases by cultural influences and standards.

Omitting for the sake of brevity many researches on cross-cultural preferences for designs and shapes, it will be useful to summarize the outcome of Child's work with his collaborators on picture material (Pickford 1972, 176–78). One of the most impressive studies was in respect of preferences for BaKwele ceremonial masks, 39 photographs of which were used with American art experts on the one hand and BaKwele tribesmen in the Congo on the other. The BaKwele judges were divided into three groups, namely carvers of masks, ceremonial leaders who used the masks, and others. The correlations with the U.S. experts were highest for the carvers, lower for the leaders and lowest for the other tribesmen. These differences were statistically significant. The degree of agreement among the BaKwele judges themselves was even higher.

A comparable study was made with Japanese potters on the one hand, and U.S. experts on the other, of preferences for carefully selected photographs of works of art. Other comparisons with them were made between U.S. art experts and U.S. high-school students, between U.S. art experts and Japanese experts in flower arrangement, the tea ceremony and other traditional arts, and between the U.S. experts and working-class residents of Puerto Rico.

In general, again, the cross-cultural agreements were greater between the U.S. art experts and those expert at any kind of art such as pottery, flower arrangement or village craft-work, than with those not concerned in or expert at any artistic activity. This is an important conclusion, because it accords with the possible view that there is a general basis for aesthetic judgments, as suggested by Eysenck (1940 and 1941a), but provided we choose as our judges those who have artistic ability or experience. High degrees of agreement would not necessarily be expected between a group of specialist judges and a population of mixed experts and non-experts, since the average aesthetic knowledge and ability of the general population would be much lower than that of the specialists. It is important that the agreement reported by Child did not depend on special skill at a particular branch of art, but was general, as, for instance, between U.S. judges of pictures and Japanese potters or flower-arrangement practitioners. Although, of course, there may well be a general capacity for aesthetic judgment or preference, it would certainly be variable in any community, and it would also be affected in its operation by the influence of secondary factors provided by opportunity, tradition and circumstances varying from one social setting to another.

PERSONALITY AND AESTHETIC PREFERENCES

Burt (1939) was the first to show a relationship between the temperamental qualities of introversion/extraversion, and stability/instability of personality, with aesthetic preferences. Using his Picture-Postcard Test of 80 postcards of pictures of various types of art, romantic, realistic, impressionistic and classical, both good and bad, he found that there was a strong tendency for unstable extraverts to prefer romantic, stable extraverts realistic, unstable introverts impressionistic and stable introverts classical art. Eysenck, as mentioned before, also showed a connection between introversion and liking for classical art, and between extraversion and liking for modern and colourful art (Pickford 1972, 218–33). Many other researches have shown that there is a connection between aasthetic preferences and certain types of temperament. For instance Knapp and Green found that there was a tendency for extraversion to be associated with preferences for geometrical-abstract paintings, and introversion with non-geometrical art.

Child, again, has made major contributions in this field, and his results may be summarized as follows: firstly, aesthetic judgment was related to amount of background knowledge of art; secondly, tolerance of complexity, and certain other attributes, such as intuition rather than sensation and perceptual skill rather than judgment, were also connected with aesthetic judgment, together with anxiety, love of comfort, verbal aptitude and liking for colours of lower brightness, for abstract designs and for Baroque rather than Classical art. Knapp (Knapp and Green 1960) showed that persons preferring realistic art were practical, worldly, uncomplicated and naive, while those preferring geometric pictures were intellectual, systematic, theoretical and inhibited, and those preferring expressionistic paintings were subjective, imaginative, impractical and sensitive.

These points indicate some of the most interesting results achieved, and other researches, summarized by the writer (Pickford 1972, 233–44) concern the colour preferences of abnormal subjects and psychiatric patients. First of all Katz (1931) showed that blue was preferred by the majority of such patients, while green was a distant second choice and red a close third. Warner (1949), in a more adequate experiment, showed that the colour preferences of psychiatric patients were very reliable, while male anxiety neurotics preferred green to yellow more than did females, who preferred lighter to darker colours more often than males, while males preferred saturated colours to a greater extent than did females. Robertson (1952), as a result of a different kind of research in which patients actually made coloured pictures, argued that the central influence at the root of all the peculiarities in the use of colour in painting by seriously disordered patients is actually a diminished feeling for colour or a weakened reactivity to it.

Another research in which patients actually made paintings of their own was carried out by Joan Stapleton (1953). She showed that the following uses of colour tend to indicate neurotic disturbance: monochromatic pictures, and the emphasis of purple, red and black; avoidance of yellow, orange and brown; dullness of paintings; colours used in unbalanced proportions; persistent overlay of one colour with another; and rigid and separate placement of colours. Red was associated with aggression, love and the need to be loved; blue with control and mother-centred emotions; purple with emotional conflict and sorrow; black with morbid states of fear, guilt and depression; green with control, joy and activity; yellow with joy and love with a sexual connotation; orange with sexuality and with adaptive behaviour; and brown was associated with controlled aggression.

Cerbus and Nichols (1963) made three scales each consisting of pictures representing the following artistic variables: achromatic/chromatic, concrete/abstract and objects/people. The first two variables did not yield results above choice expectation in relation to 63 verbal personality measures and ratings. The third variable showed that persons who prefer pictures showing people to those without people are more outgoing and friendly, more expansive, self-confident and happy, than those who prefer pictures showing objects rather than people.

PSYCHOLOGY AND CULTURAL CHANGE IN ART

Art is a branch of culture, and is subject to the laws and principles of cultural change which have been studied from a psychological standpoint by the writer (Pickford 1943), following the example of Bartlett (1923) in his work on psychology of primitive culture, and of Sayce (1933).

All cultural material and ceremonies which are transferred from one social setting to another either undergo constructive changes, as in the elaboration of Moorish elements into the well-known Spanish dance rhythms and Spanish music; or they tend to disappear, like the Persian aspects of Mogul painting; or they tend to remain unchanged for long periods of time, like the Byzantine aspects of Russian icons. These are usually changes which enable the new material to be assimilated into existing patterns of culture.

Group contact is very important in cultural change and many people have supposed, rightly or wrongly, that it is the essential condition of creative developments. For instance, Burkitt (1928) has described four geographical categories in which there are Bushmen cave paintings of somewhat different character. They are the Eastern group (Southern Rhodesia); the central group (Drakensberg, Kei River, Molteno and Basutoland); the Wilton group; and the Western group (South West Africa). The most advanced and complex paintings are found in the central group, and apparently it was only here that incoming Late Palaeolithic invaders met with Early and Mid-Palaeolithic inhabitants. The weakest and most conservative forms are found in the outer areas where there was no such racial blending.

Borrowing as an aspect of cultural transmission and change is very important. English ideas of landscape painting were borrowed by French artists who immediately preceded the Barbizon School, and led to this interesting new development, which in part was borrowed later by Scottish painters.

As a final point it must be said that leadership is extremely important, and that the most constructive leaders are those who fit in with, and express exceptionally well in some way, the latent tendencies of the group. If they did not do this their influence would not be accepted, and there are many examples of potential leaders whose creative influence was not felt fully until social changes had brought the groups of potential followers more into relationship with them.

These ideas have been put forward in a condensed and simplified way, but the reader will probably have little difficulty in finding additional examples for himself to illustrate them. For a fuller study and analysis of the psychology of cultural change in painting the reader is referred to the Monograph which has already been mentioned.

Chapter Eleven

The artist and education in art and design in the sixties and the seventies

JEAN CREEDY

The year 1973 may be seen as a critical one for the system of art and design education in Britain, a system which is without doubt still the best in the world; it began its first full cycle in 1961 and 1962 with Pre-Diploma/Foundation Courses leading in 1963 to the first courses for the new Diploma in Art and Design. Now, that system, which had been so fully and continuously debated, was subject to still further review and to consequent radical change. New regulations were proposed, new modes of entry established, involving new provisions and constraints, which could profoundly affect the nature and quality of art and design education at all levels in the future from secondary to post-graduate; and all arising out of the change from a diploma of nominal degree equivalence, to a new qualification; an Honours Degree of the Council for National Academic Awards (C.N.A.A.).

To understand it, so far as that is possible at close range, some recapitulation is necessary – back to the late fifties when the system of art examinations then conducted by the Ministry of Education, a system which subsisted for a hundred years, though in progressively enlightened forms, came up for radical reconsideration. Those deliberations led to a thorough reappraisal of art education as a whole – beyond secondary level, and from this there followed proposals for a new scheme and a new qualification. In setting up the advisory machinery which was duly to launch that new system, the Minister indicated a degree of support which had never previously existed: Art Education was now to be regarded as of the first importance.

It may be that no field of higher education has been subject to such critical self-appraisal, from the cool to the frenetic; to such turmoil, breakthrough and advance as that of art and design education in England, Wales and Ulster between 1960 and 1973. Such spectacular progress has been made possible not only by radical change in concepts and teaching modes, by progressive means of assessment and validation, but also by provision of a greatly enhanced range of resources in staffing, buildings, plant and materials to implement and support those developments.

In this revitalized situation distinguished practitioners in various areas of art and design, administrators, industrialists and academics in other fields, became involved and through them art education drew closer to the mainstream of art and design practice, to the enormous benefit of the students. That achievement is the hallmark of the sixties. It may be said that the sixties came closest to a recognition of the full cultural significance of Art and Design Education in recent times. Colleges were encouraged to forge links with industry in various ways with, as a result, a more realistic preparation for those young artists who would make their way subsequently in an industrial or commercial field.

A study of the early documents produced by the Coldstream and Summerson Councils on the question of the new Diploma in Art and Design, reveal a breadth of policy and an intention to afford considerable freedom to the colleges to devise creatively as far as possible their new provisions. Subsequently this resulted in a healthy, vigorous reappraisal not without considerable controversy at the time of the first quinquennial review of the new Dip.A.D. Unfortunately – or fortunately, as history alone can determine – these deliberations were overtaken in 1968 by the first student revolts which were initiated in the world of Art Education.

A remarkable feature of the new system established in the sixties was the concept of the Foundation Course. In its First Report the National Advisory Council (Coldstream) made two specific recommendations on entry requirements to the new diploma courses: that there should be a preparatory course of at least one year in an art school and, for the first time in art education, a general education requirement (five passes in G.C.E. at 'O' level with certain stipulations), provision being made for exceptional cases. The pre-diploma course was seen as necessary in order to enable candidates for entry to Dip.A.D. courses to achieve an acceptable standard. Unlike the then existing Intermediate Certificate in Art and Craft leading to the National Diploma in Art and Design, that notional standard of acceptability was not encapsulated in any intermediate form of qualification, nor had the new validating body, the National Council for Diplomas in Art and Design (Summerson), any responsibility for, or control over, what was to become an integral part of the system and a major commitment for the many schools of art throughout this country. In 1965 the Coldstream Council returned to this subject in an addendum to its First Report in order to clarify certain issues and most particularly to stress the diagnostic and foundation nature and the broad function of such preparatory study, as distinct from a largely pre-diploma role which the First Report had tended to indicate. This concept of the foundation element had been evident in the best practice in the colleges from the beginning and it was not challenged in the open-ended debates of student unrest in 1968 when almost everything else was called into question – especially the 'five O level' requirement and the segregation of vocational courses from diploma study.

In 1970 a major report was entitled 'The Structure of Art and Design Education in the Further Education Sector'. A joint committee of the Coldstream and Summerson Councils upheld the continuation of foundation training as an essential element of what should be for most students a four-year education in Art and Design – though with provision for an increased proportion of direct entry from sixth forms to diploma courses; more particularly to the newly proposed four-year 'sandwich' courses. With this was coupled the recommendation that some form of validation be devised for Foundation Courses. This, predictably, raised a storm of protest and the Secretary of State referred back for further consideration the whole question of 'preparation and entry'. By 1975, however, largely resulting from rapidly increasing financial stringency and economic measures, direct sixth-form entry is well established as an alternative route. The results will be seen as these generations qualify with the new C.N.A.A. Honours degree.

In February 1973 the National Council for Diplomas in Art and Design made the recommendation that the qualification for entry to Dip.A.D. Courses be five passes in the G.C.E. of which two be at 'A' level, or whatever equivalent might be determined and that the essential requirement of a Foundation Course be withdrawn unless it be established through some form of validation as such an 'equivalent'. The significance of these administrative recommendations at high level and their effect on the future of Art and Design can hardly be overemphasized at this point in time. Such considerations must form an essential part of any serious examination of what goes to make a 'successful' artist or designer of the future.

It may be worthwhile even to digress for a moment on the subject of qualifications. All debate on educational change tends to centre on such considerations; the Diploma of Higher Education (Dip.H.E.) is such an example, for no one yet really knows what is to be involved in educational terms after some three years of debate, experiment and some firm proposals. Art education is no exception; yet qualifications *per se*, have but little reference in the professional field of art and design, and for art teachers would appear to have practical significance mainly in secondary education. It is important, therefore, that the question of qualifications shall not assume overriding importance and that the genuine needs of Art and Design education be the real issue; related of course to rapidly changing social and economic requirements. These 'needs' as seen by artists themselves, by the real educationists, and for that matter by the more perceptive psychologists are central to this essay. Thus in the merger of the National Council for Diplomas in Art and Design (N.C.D.A.D.) with the Council for National Academic Awards (C.N.A.A.) through which the Diploma in Art and Design becomes an Honours Degree, the true educational advantages to be derived therefrom must be the prime consideration. There should be many such advantages if proper priorities are observed and the needs of Art and Design fully understood. The great danger of the new provisions of the seventies referred to above may be a false conformity (reflected in the new G.C.E. intake requirements for high level courses). The high individuality and personal strengths of the artist, the 'imbalance' of personality even, which has been of such historic significance may be lost in great measure, affecting art and design significantly from now on, especially in the degree and quality of creative output.

Another major innovation in curricular development concerning the education of the artist and designer in recent years has been the introduction of a systematic study of Art and Design History and other Complementary Studies to include relevant arts and sciences, sociology and even psychology; with business, management and marketing studies, when appropriate, particularly in the design areas. A great measure of freedom has been allowed in overall coverage and even educational policy in these fields which accords well with traditional flexibility over the years through many changing systems. This is some compensation for the loss of discipline in draughtsmanship for example and the many difficult Fine Art skills lost to recent generations of young artists. New mixed media combinations are constantly being devised and the sharp divisions between printmaking processes for example have largely disappeared with the development of new combined techniques. In the Fine Art area in particular, the replacement of the artifact by other forms such as the performance or 'happening' on the one hand or the conceptual notation on the other, make a significant re-direction in this field. The return of figurative interest and in many schools and colleges a determined effort to restore draughtsmanship, may be seen as an important revival.

An enormous impetus has in recent years been given to Screen Printing and the Fine Art print processes of etching, lithography, and silkscreen with the emergence of the 'three-dimensional print' as a major art form. There have been extensions into photo-lithography and photo-screen printing. Technical advances have been rapid and these new art forms widely promoted and acknowledged with immediate commercial application. Creative use of these methods by graphic designers has followed these advances. The claim to total independence in the philosophical sense in Fine Art thinking affects a comparatively small minority in the overall field of Art and Design.

In approaching the current situation, but two aspects of possible impending change are highlighted; there are of course many others. The Gann Committee has made its recommendations for the future of vocational courses; certain new four-year Dip.A.D. 'sandwich' courses are now established; the way is opening for a whole range of new course structures at Honours and ordinary or sub-Degree levels, through inter-disciplinary courses and courses with varying levels of involvement of Art and Design with other subjects by means of modular structures. Such developments, and especially the move for a rapid increase of direct entry from sixth forms, must clearly cause problems in the secondary field where art education objectives are in the main very properly different in kind. Most welcome is an increasing involvement of visual education in the teaching of other subjects, an expanding role for the artist and art historian also.

In the present context it is important to note that many major colleges of art have already taken their place in the new Polytechnic structures. By 1973 nineteen out of thirty-one Polytechnics had Faculties of Art and Design or the equivalent, most of them formerly autonomous Colleges of Art and Design. In appropriate locations a number of smaller Art colleges have in various ways become associated with other Higher Education institutions, some of them becoming established within developing colleges of Further Education. Others large and small are still, despite a major county reorganization, in a state of uncertainty regarding their future role, their degree of independence or autonomy and the type of liaison they will enjoy with other Higher Education institutions.

ERRATA

p. 168, lines 16/17:

For 'Screen Printing' *read* 'print-making'
For 'silkscreen' *read* 'screen-printing'

Forward-looking University Schools of Fine Art have fulfilled a different role in linking the academic and theoretical side of Art and Design with practical courses (usually of four years' duration) while others have promoted courses in the interrelated arts to include Art and Design or provided joint degree courses linking Art and Design with the History of Art, Literature, Sociology, for example. Research into Visual Perception continues, extending its influence via University Arts Faculties and Schools of Education. In 1974/5 new opportunities for in-service post-graduate study provide a major innovation, offering yet further inter-arts/science combinations of related studies.

In Schools of Experimental Psychology study of subliminal reaction and response in creative persons may be said to be in its infancy. Further findings in this field could significantly affect future cultural patterns.

Throughout the country, experimental Arts Centres take various shape, offering provisions to which it is hoped the long delayed implementation of the Russell Report may give further emphasis and encouragement; most significant perhaps are those which now offer progressive courses for adults in a range of related courses.

All these educational developments help to throw light not only on the function of Art and Design in the present social system but on closer investigation give indication of inner response, and the problems of the artist as he faces the outer world in a variety of developing roles. There is radical change in the education of professional artists at various levels; change also in a general educational policy which puts Art and Design on a completely new footing in the secondary schools. At other levels it will be seen that, as in the case of other disciplines in the full-time academic field, there is evolving a welcome diversity of courses with proposals to safeguard flexibility and movement between courses and disciplines. This is particularly important for artists and designers who may expect to make use of individual talents, interests and a wide range of differing motivation.

It is therefore a good moment to attempt some evaluation of the needs of the young artist and with this, a reassessment of some of the processes involved in the Visual Arts. We need to study what is required environmentally as well as considering those rights of a personal, even private nature, which enable artists to maintain the vital interest, buoyancy and unique motivation to allow them to carry through their own original experimental ideas; developing in many cases highly personal means of communication and in other instances, particularly where designers are concerned, acquiring the means whereby they are best able to achieve their objective through individual, group, or mass communication.

One of the first considerations in providing a fundamental basis for Art Education at the professional level, must be the proper diagnosis of artistic potential where the young Art and Design student is concerned. Hence the need to provide maximum opportunity for experience and trial in a variety of skills and associate disciplines. It is now widely acknowledged that the Foundation courses up and down the country have played a highly significant role, pointing the way even outside the sphere of Art and Design. In the general ambience of an Art and Design Faculty there should be ample opportunity for students to become involved with other disciplines according to their talents and inclinations, not only in making available source material, but also to extend opportunities for intellectual stimulation, increased awareness and general cultural activities·

The experience and observations of successful artists of the past throw much light on such needs. The study of writings, diaries, biographies, letters and manifestos is highly revealing in discovering requirements which are common to all individual artists as well as those that apply to types and social groups to which artists belong, some of which characterize the century or decade in which they live and work. Here there can be space only for this very brief reference to such findings with the intention of making more widely known some of the most crucial facts which govern creative output, its quality and its impact. This has now become the province of the art historian also.

To go first to the heart of the creative process, we must consider something in the nature of poetic experience and the type of thinking which does not conform usually with accepted thinking and precisely formulated concepts. The poetic and creative mind links and makes constant cross-references, providing valuable new insights rarely immediately acknowledged; the value of these cannot always be fully assessed in the same generation. Understanding of the function of the imagination would appear to have advanced very little since the great discovery of this force by the 19th-century literary critics and aesthetic writers. Inventiveness is perhaps the modern counterpart of imagination. Artists today appear to be showing signs however of straining rather less after inventiveness as an end in itself. Carrying an argument or visual concept to its extreme limit, as in the case of 'minimal art', of necessity gives way to a totally new direction.

Artists, because they are particularly sensitive to pressures, tendencies, new lines of thought, and are at the same time constantly reminded of old values and traditions, aware also of what must have been historic discoveries and innovations, have a wealth of related ideas amounting almost to a creative burden.

To move to another essential experience common among artists; it seems clear that the strength to resist what is normally imposed is almost a prerequisite of the successful artist personality. Many artists in the mainstream of development do not find themselves involved however with controversial issues, though almost always they are opening up new ground, exploring new inventive possibilities, working on the borderline of, or outside, what is generally accepted. The development of a strong personal motivation is vital, and associated with this is the simple need for a confidence to proceed – to complete a statement or a sequence of statements before concepts and ideas advance too fast, or too far for others to grasp the link. This is a delicate and difficult matter for the young artist and no less important for the mature and established one in the professional situation. It must be widely appreciated that the Fine Art student in common with the professional painter or sculptor still shows little concern over the degree to which he is understood or not understood by others. Many are 'traditional' only in that they obey their own dictates and work primarily for their own satisfaction. Externally imposed discipline and personal discipline, so often in conflict, play a vital part in that they affect dynamically the amount and quality of creative output.

Mercifully, educational policy and philosophy in the teaching of Art and Design is rarely tampered with from outside bodies, on principle. Yet practical and economic issues can provide a serious threat, as in the matter of staff/ student ratios which affect class numbers and alter the type of teaching that can be provided, moving away from the personal man-to-man discussion on the individual student's thinking and endeavour to a situation where less tutorial exchange is possible between professional and student. Perhaps the greatest value of art in any culture is the example it gives in the recognition of and value placed upon 'individuality'.

The great strength of the artist and creative designer lies in his power to select in a highly personal manner even when he shares a common belief or when his skill is used ostensibly to promote a doctrine or to further religious, social or political ends.

Skills in the historic sense change as fashions change, but always practical skills involving coordination of hand, eye and mind are essential in the development in the Visual Arts. It has long been appreciated that information is received by way of the senses. Where artists and designers are concerned, sensory perception is often highly developed in the natural course of events. There are greater rewards however resulting from encouragement at an early age particularly in the matter of visual and tactile awareness of form, spacial relationships, texture, tonality, colour and linear design. These aspects of visual education should be available to everyone, if only to promote greater understanding of the Arts. Such responsibility is being taken increasingly by the secondary schools. In Higher Education student artists are often found to have one or another of these awarenesses highly developed, with quite often a blind spot in one or more of the others; hence they gravitate all too early towards a specific field, for example sculpture, painting, or architecture, before they have had time and opportunity to develop in other directions, building up in the contemplative atmosphere of College or Faculty source experience and visual memories for future reference.

One of the vital, now historic, effects of the Bauhaus teaching has been to develop awareness of the link between man's spiritual and practical needs resulting in the bringing together of different media and in the bridging of previous boundaries between sculpture, painting and design. A new breadth of experience combined with flexibility on these lines is significantly one of the great values arising out of the diagnostic Foundation courses in Further Education now at some risk in the mid-seventies by reason of the new encouragement for direct entry to Diploma courses from the secondary schools, and particularly the comprehensives. It is not within the capacity of schools other than the exceptionally committed few to offer such extensive facilities, practical and theoretical, as has been possible in a large majority of Colleges of Art in recent years. Even here the difficulty of providing suitable workshop experience in a wide enough range of activities is still the major concern of most Foundation courses which attempt to be thoroughly diagnostic and preparatory in function. The cost of metal workshop accommodation and services with the necessary supporting skilled technical supervision has been difficult enough even where Foundation Colleges have specialist facilities to call upon.

A constant preoccupation with visual phenomena and the freedom to engage at will in this activity is yet another prerequisite for creative visual development. This need demands certain conditions of environment and way of life. It is also true that artistic sensibility and a related hypersensitivity make it particularly easy for artists to adapt all too readily where circumstances are adverse. Society has some responsibility in this matter. It may be said that Society loses many potentially valuable artists and designers, artist-thinkers and craftsmen for this reason before they have learned to value their unique capabilities and to consider the wide range of possible creative careers or niches open to them. In recent years a number of Fine Artists particularly in the three-dimensional area have emerged from the ranks of well disciplined but artistically frustrated craft disciplines and skilled workshop practitioners. As a result, it is widely recognized that Britain leads in the field of European Sculpture in the seventies. The flowering of electronic art forms also bears witness, e.g. to the opportunities offered through access to the technologies. New educational opportunities have largely brought about these advances with new structuring and the necessary expansion in thinking essential to creative art. The entirely self-educated artist of the past is now a rarity.

The current concern to remove barriers between courses and academic structures is of the greatest significance in Art and Design. Some academic disciplines made readily available to young people at sixth-form level and the general demand of overall curriculum work in secondary schools inhibit the kind of visual preoccupation referred to above. Much was learnt about the differences between artist thinking and artist ways of learning and about perceptual understanding in artists, by those first generations of art historians who came to teach in Colleges of Art. University academics have recorded the quality of art-student thinking processes as evidenced in the standard of Diploma written work and in particular the Dip.A.D. – where invaluable discoveries have been made often through perceptual means – by young artists and designers; later to be documented by careful guidance on the part of academics.

The conversion of existing Diploma courses into Honours Degree courses, with all that this entails in the pre-selection for entry to such courses by conformity with other Higher Education academic course entry regulations, are not likely to be seen by artists and designers themselves as having unquestionably rewarding educational significance in the broad spectrum of Art and Design Education; only experience will tell. The outcome of the first quinquennial review to be held under C.N.A.A. arrangements will, in this connection, be of particular interest.

Nor does the promise of development in technically based sub-degree level courses alone, fill the educational gap for creative artists, particularly should the Foundation courses as such be lost at post-secondary level. The final solution has to be found in the light of this generation's experience and subsequent protest. The answer must ultimately lie in a wide range of courses at both Honours and sub-Degree level, with a sustained well-ordered, progressive curriculum fully documented.

62 The Zwinger, Dresden. Wall pavilion. Austrian-style Baroque. Chapter 12

63 Norfolk House, St James's Square, London. Designed by Matthew Brettingham. Neo-classical. Chapter 12

64 Osterley House, Middlesex. The Etruscan Room. Chapter 12

65   TITIAN *The Assumption*. Chapter 12

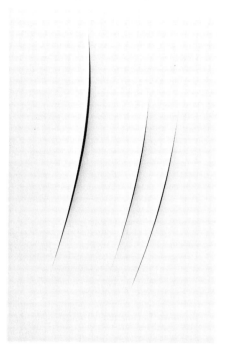

66   LUCIO FONTANA
Spatial Concept. 1960. Chapter 12

67   Advertisement from American Journal.
c. 1900. Chapter 12

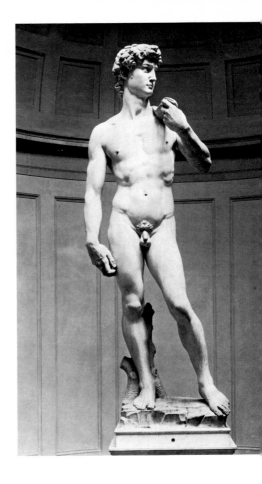

68 CIMABUE *Virgin and Child*. Chapter 12

69 MICHELANGELO *David*. Chapter 12

70 JEAN-LOUIS DAVID *The Oath of the Horatii*. Chapter 12

The artist more than most, is able to create his own personal environment and many are clearly increasingly concerned to influence their physical surroundings as part of an essential dedication. There is, however, a more profound significance in the year-by-year development of home or working environment in the case of the creative artist. Artists have, by tradition and privately, tended to bring together a highly personal selection of objects which appeal to the senses and to the imagination. Thus an intimate environment is created which in its turn gives back a constant flow of 'source material'; this will include inspiration and stimulus from other Arts. From childhood potentially creative visual artists acquire also a wealth of profoundly significant visual memories which are later constantly available for the making of those creative links already referred to.

Artists today are, generally speaking, more widely read and versed in the related Arts and Sciences than were their immediate forebears. In this respect the younger generation owes much to the forward-looking and progressive provisions of the Coldstream and Summerson Councils. The reports arising out of the work of the Summerson Committee in particular promoted a wide range of related studies, referred to as Complementary Studies, with History of Art and Design for Dip.A.D. Courses. Full-time courses in general involve a far greater measure of such studies today.

The comparatively recent move towards conceptual art forms takes into account new and changing methods of transmitting the more intellectual concepts by visual means; often by conscious, partly conscious, or unconscious use of visual symbols. The symbolism of literary artists, critics and academics in universities was fiercely resisted in the forties and fifties by some professional artists and teachers. Artists have since been found capable of taking Freudian and Jungian concepts in their stride, with a grasp of modern psychology at the instinctive or perceptual level which elicits some acknowledgement from scientific and literary academics.

In recent years artists have greatly benefited from a much closer direct link with technologists and from the opportunity through study, to cross the borders between the interrelated arts and related sciences.

This essay emphasizes throughout imminent change in the education of artists. The term 'flux' has been used frequently in connection with Art Education over the last decade. The fact is that the educational system to be set up for young artists and designers of the future reflects powerfully in its ultimate provisions, the struggles, the frustrations, the ideals and the needs of artists in a constantly changing role. The overall system with the final outcome of the Gann proposals for vocational courses taken into account does not, however, *inevitably* reflect *advance* in every respect. Artists and designers in their present educational situations, as in their daily lives, have much to lose in an uncertain future, particularly with the onset of real economic stringency.

In conclusion some reference should be made to overall representative bodies at administrative level. It is significant that when N.C.D.A.D. gave place to C.N.A.A. as the validating body for advanced courses in Art and Design, their excellent registration scheme, which had been of great service and which the C.N.A.A. did not feel able to sustain, has been kept going through the good offices of the Association of Art Institutions, whose reponsibility it now is. The annual conference of this body (the A.A.I.), bringing together as it does through its tripartite membership of Principals (to include Polytechnic Directors), Governor Representatives, Local Authority Representatives, bears witness over the years to a unity of purpose and provides a forum for vital issues of the day at all levels.

A related body, the Council for Higher Education in Art and Design (C.H.E.A.D.), is able to comment independently on issues of special relevance to the advanced sector, while the work of the National Standing Committee for Foundation Education in Art and Design (N.S.C.F.E.A.D.) demonstrates also the responsibility and effectual commitment of artist teachers up and down the country.

This is a moment for the greatest vigilance, not only on the part of those immediately concerned, but for any who claim genuine interest and understanding of the visual arts in society and its future overall cultural development.

Note: With regard to the second paragraph on page 167 above, up to the time of going to press the former Dip. A.D. requirements are as outlined below and the two 'A' level requirements have not as yet been enforced.

The requirements are:
(a) Five subjects at Ordinary level; or
(b) three subjects at Ordinary level and one other subject at Advanced level; or
(c) two subjects at Ordinary level and two other subjects at Advanced level; or
(d) three subjects at Advanced level provided there is evidence that other subjects have been studied.

Chapter Twelve

Art, morals and Western society

H. R. ROOKMAAKER

It is peculiar to man that he not only sees reality coloured by his presuppositions, or if you wish, his prejudices, but that he also always wants that reality to conform to the way he sees it, or would like to see it. The visual arts are born out of man's vision, they make visually explicit what man sees or likes to see in reality (Panofsky 1955; Segall 1966; Gombrich 1965), and in this manner they help man to visualize what he wants to realize in reality. As, for an example, painters in the seventeenth century had painted landscape in a certain way, as a beautiful Arcadia, a kind of dream of reality (Panofsky, 1955, 295; Dorival 1953), so in the eighteenth century people wanted to change the real world according to this vision, and began to make gardens and parks, even trying to make the landscape as such, *picturesque*, i.e. using pictures as their example (Price 1794; Stroud 1962; Hirschfeld 1780).

In this way – which is often indirect and more related to the way of life, manners and customs, than to morals as such – art has been important in shaping the face of society. 'Whether or not the pen is mightier than the sword, it is even more difficult to suggest that the artist's brush has ever wielded influence over the deeds and destiny of man . . . . But whilst art may not stimulate action, it can be prophetic in reflecting reactions to social and political events, which in their turn provoke action.' (*Art and Artists*, Ch. Spencer, 4.) Certainly politicians in the past have tried to use art as propaganda. Even if it is doubtful whether the course of events has been changed by Rubens's Medici cycle (van Simson 1965), the works of art made for the Medici in 15th-century Florence as part of their policy (Chastel 1959), or the works intended as propaganda for Louis XIV in France have certainly exalted these patrons and probably helped to strengthen their rule, and without any doubt still make their political achievements great in the eyes of men. The use of portraits of rulers to this end, begun by the Romans (or maybe even much earlier by the Egyptians), and revived at the end of the Middle Ages or the early Renaissance, is still with us today, even if it is not now a very strong tradition.

Revolutionary groups have often tried to put art to their use. This was true at the time of the French Revolution, and in our day we have seen the surrealist group of artists deliberately trying to change a mentality and encourage a total revolution in men's lives. In the thirties there was even a journal devoted to surrealism helping the revolution. Breton wrote, in the preface of Max Ernst's *La femme à cent têtes*, 'La surréalité sera fonction de notre volonté de dépaysement de tout.' (See also *Art and Artists*, 4, 38; Egberts 1970; Leith 1965).

In almost all periods of history, the relationship of art and morality was evident, as well as the importance of art in inducing man to look to higher values and loftier aims, to direct his will towards God. At least this was almost invariably set down in art theory or aesthetics as a norm. In medieval theories on art we find that art 'works' on four levels, the literal, the allegorical, the moral and the anagogical. By the anagogical the general tendency of the work, its impact if you wish, was meant (Assunto 1963), as illustrated in a short poem synthesizing these aesthetic notions:

> *Littera geste docet*
> *quod credas allegoria*
> *Moralis quid agas*
> *quo tendas anagogia.*

Since the Renaissance the idea has been prevalent that art has to be useful, i.e. didactic, and at the same time pleasing to the eye, or in short *utile dulci*. A moral didacticism was considered to be a necessary element of the arts (Boyd 1968). In a book on the ceiling paintings by Luca Giordano in the Florentine Palazzo Medici-Ricardi published by Francesca Riccardi Vernaccia in 1822 a very late example of this at that time traditionalistic approach to art can be found. He wrote (p. 2, in the introduction): 'It is a grandiose theme, which asks for no ordinary talent to execute. We need the poet, who knows how to combine it all cleverly into a whole that suggests the total idea without missing the aim of exalting and surprising the mind; we need the philosopher whose thinking ensures that the story will be moral, and under the veil of this the most sublime truth always be hidden; . . . we need the painter to attract the eye, to please (*dilletasse*) and to persuade.'

Art was commonly held to have an influence on men. A curious example of this can be found in the writings of Shaftesbury, who wrote reacting against the Rococo style: 'So that whilst we look on paintings with the same eye as we view commonly the rich stuffs and colour'd silks worn by our ladies, and admir'd in dress, equipage, or furniture, we must of necessity be effeminate in our Taste, and utterly set wrong as to all Judgment and Knowledge in the kind.' (Levey 1966.) Indeed Shaftesbury is asking for a more austere intellectual art as is seen in later Neoclassicism.

The change in the outlook on the cosmos inaugurated by people like Descartes, furthered in the eighteenth century in England by Locke and Hume and finding its apogee in Kant, afflicted the arts as well as aesthetics. The didactic element was very strongly accentuated (Boyd 1968). Tischbein said that the art of a museum like the Vatican was a great school for the spirit, where the people were taught to behave morally, and kings to govern wisely, while Schlegel called the artist 'the higher spiritual organ of humanity' (Kraus 1925, 47, 37). Never in history have men thought so much about morality or have they tried so hard to use art to induce morality. Art 'could show moral precepts in poetic and in artistically beautified examples, through which knowledge comes alive and dry truth is changed into a passionate and sensitive perception', wrote Mendelssohn in 1757 (Balet 1936, 298, 303).

It may seem to be, and probably is, an apparent contradiction when at the same time and by the same people art is put on a high pedestal and is said to be unconnected with real life. Those things are beautiful that are without purpose, and art 'has retained its freedom from the reality principle at the price of being ineffective in the reality', sums up Kant's aesthetics (Marcuse 1969, 143, 146). Yet Schiller wanted to educate mankind through the beautiful and through art starting from these theories (Schiller 1795). Indeed, the didactic character slowly gave way, and the new artistic aims became clearer – it was not through the subject matter but through the activity of making art, that art should contribute to, or even heal or change the world (Pelles 1963, 131). Art had become in fact a religion (Shroder 1961). In the words of Saul Bellow: 'A century ago when the clergy began to feel certain doubts, poets and novelists moved into the centre of the spiritual crisis and assumed spiritual obligations, . . . the cure of souls . . . .' (Miller 1967, 27.) Of course the painters followed suit.

If, then, art had become religion, the predicament is even stranger in that religion itself has now become completely superfluous and has moved away from reality, for it means that art has gained a lofty position without much meaning. This is one of the strange enigmas of our age – the artist as a prophet who nevertheless stands completely aside from the realities of life (see *The Artist as a Prophet* in Rookmaaker 1969). However I want to come back later to this situation and the influence of the visual arts in our day.

In the nineteenth century, out of the ideas of German idealism eventually grew the theory of *L'Art pour l'art* (Wilcox 1953). Perhaps the shortest way of conveying what it means is to quote Pater, who said: 'Of this wisdom, the poetic passion, the desire of beauty, the love of art for art's sake, has most; for art comes to you professing frankly to give nothing but the highest quality to your moments as they pass, and simply for those moment's sake.' (Williams 1960, 167.)

In the meantime other cross-currents were active. Pugin, Ruskin, Morris, who in some way or other saw a deep relationship between beauty in art and beauty in life, gave all their energies to redeem something of the ugliness of nineteenth-century society, not only in its art, but also in the social conditions that were at the root of it. They understood that in order to have more beauty in art as well as in life one had to change these social conditions (Williams 1960, 130 ff.).

It all comes down to the fact that if we had lived in the time before, let us say, the eighteenth century it would not have been difficult to write an essay on art, ethics and society as I now have been asked to do. Yet, even if the arts as a matter of course had moral implications and obligations, people did not in those days exalt the arts to a lofty plane together with religion, and would not have looked to the arts as a way of redeeming the moral ills of their day.

But has art any influence on society? Is there any relationship between art and the ideas on morality in the society in which and for which it is made? Are we looking in the right direction if we look at those works that hang in museum or gallery and are surrounded by an aura of loftiness and respectability (Rook-maaker 1969, 9), which are feverishly discussed by art critics; or should we rather look at the more popular arts such as posters or perhaps even the mass media? The influence of the mass media has been and still is the object of much discussion and investigation, often on a sociological plane (Brown 1969; Haselden 1968; Williams 1968; Klapper 1960; Berger 1972). Most of these studies come to the conclusion that not much of a conclusive nature can be said. I feel this to be inevitable, as the arts, in any form whatsoever, when they exert some influence – be it the influence of one group in society on another, or just the strengthening of some existing tendencies – do this within a fluid cultural situation in which differences may be felt but are never really measurable. Yet I feel that no human action ever can be of such a nature that it would have no influence. This would not only question or deny the sanity of anyone trying to do something in this world, politically, religiously, morally or otherwise, but it would make man as such meaningless, in the sense of the Japanese poem: 'He jumped in the water and he caused no ripples.' To me, it seems there will always be ripples, some bigger, some smaller, that together with other ripples eventually will cause waves or even storms. Indeed, I feell that art alone, in the past and in the present, never can alter the face of the world, or even its own position in the total complexity of a cultural situation. So, for example, the change in the position of the arts in the eighteenth century which I have mentioned earlier might also have been influenced by the growth of capitalism (see Berger 1972, 86 ff, 135 ff.), and certainly also by religious, philosophical and social situations and conditions (Rookmaaker, 1971; Rookmaaker 1969; Pawek 1963). Influences can only be exerted if they are strengthened by other tendencies, and not rendered ineffective by counteracting forces.

Therefore, to come to a halfway conclusion, I can agree with Klapper when he writes (of the mass media): '. . . [sociological generalizations] [are] inapplicable to certain broad areas of effect, such as the effect of the media upon each other, upon patterns of daily life, and upon cultural values as a whole. To be sure, we have spoken of cultural values as a mediating factor which in part determine media content, but certainly some sort of circular relationship must exist, and media content must in their turn affect cultural values.' (Klapper 1960, 251.)

Art historians as a whole have almost never studied the impact of the arts on their society (Mierendorff 1957, 23 ff.). If they have not restricted themselves exclusively to style analysis, determining influences of artists on artists, they have studied meaning in the visual arts (Panofsky 1955) even if then the history of ideas is often brought into focus. Sometimes they have studied art in relation to a changing religious climate (Meiss 1964), or, influenced by a Marxist idea of culture, to its social background (Antal 1948; Balet 1936). In this way they have shown that art belongs to the cultural scene as a whole, in which social and economic, scientific or even natural phenomena play their role and have their impact (see also Antal 1966).

After these introductory remarks I should like to try to give some idea of how the visual arts are related, if not directly to morals, then certainly to life-styles, manners and customs. I shall try to show that the arts mean something in giving a face to a culture, to a society; in giving it its own particular form.

The first question to ask is: what is art? The visual arts, in my opinion, must be located between two extremes: (1) the purely decorative, the beautiful arrangement of lines and colours that are artistically combined into a totality, and (2) pure visual communication as such, that we find in a more or less unadulterated form in maps, road signs, letters, icons and idols. Or, I can place the arts between two other extremes: on the one hand entertainment, the means whereby joy, a pleasurable mood or amusement is induced, often in a social setting; and on the other hand the loftiest elements in man's life, revealed in the depiction of his gods in cult images, or in depicting holy stories for education or edification. As examples of our first extreme we may think of banquet embellishments, Christmas decorations, or patterns or fabrics for dresses or ties, etc. Also on that plane, even if falling outside the (visual) Fine Arts proper, are the entertainment programmes or documentaries on television. Film and TV – and I shall return to these, as much thought and study has been given to their possible impact – have had a great influence, and it has been said, 'Television is and has been building American ideals and abstract principles through concrete imagery. The image has in fact become more effective and affective than actuality.' (Rudisill 1971, 346.) Here the context was the influence of another human activity, at least very much akin to the visual arts, if not a branch of it – I do not want to enter into that argument now – namely, photography, whose 'visual image offer[s] even stronger spiritual and aesthetic experience than did the perception of visual reality itself' (Rudisill 1971; see also Boorstin 1961; Pawek 1963). Maybe, as this lower end of the two extremes between which the Fine Arts are located has the stronger ties to daily life, it seems natural that it would have the stronger impact; if not in all ages, then certainly in our age in which Fine Art in its loftier expression is relegated to the museum as a kind of secularized temple.

If I approach the visual arts using this wide definition, placing them between the extremes of decoration or entertainment on the one hand and visual communication or the cult image on the other, we can perhaps be clearer in defining their influence.

Let us begin with ornament, decoration and the like. Undoubtedly we all experience much of their influence every day and in all kinds of social settings. The interior decoration of our house determines something of the atmosphere in which we live, and certainly affects us, as well as expressing something of our own character. But that is not all. If we enter a restaurant, the lights may be dim, but certainly the total impact on our mood – which may induce actions – is the result of the colour scheme of its interior, and maybe even of the paintings on the wall, the decorative mouldings, etc.; so even the Fine Arts in a narrower definition can play a role in our surroundings which are created artistically, with or without taste. The theosophists have even made a system out of the impact on man's psychological condition of colours and shapes – in The Hague a hospital has been built and painted inside in conformity with these presuppositions. There is no need to go into a lengthy discussion of the impact of our surroundings on ourselves, as they have become quite topical today with regard to new buildings and their effect on the people who work there, etc. But in past ages, too, people have been very aware of this. Of course I can instance the rich and lavish interiors, with gold, rich mouldings and so forth, of the great baroque churches and the grand palaces, designed to induce awe for the values the church stood for or for the monarch who was living there. I can also instance a refined interior design such as that with which Adam graced the mansion at Osterley Park: the decoration and the colour schemes of the various rooms is expressive of the differences in character, mood and setting needed for a study, a drawing room, a state room, or a bedroom. And certainly things like this have an influence on our lives, on the way we live, maybe even on the way we feel, think and act.

Plate 62

Plate 64

Naturally I am not implying that people could be changed completely just by their surroundings – even if instances come to mind where the effect upon them has been marked (*Time* 1975) – but rather that environments are designed with their function in mind and so may have an influence on the people who use them.

When considering the other side, the visual communication in a beautiful form, in statues, paintings, mosaics or frescoes, we should not look for extreme cases of a direct influence on man's thoughts or behaviour. An immediate conversion, a change in moral outlook, as a direct result simply of looking at a work of art, is I feel, asking for too much – it may be even too much in other contexts. But the repeated unobtrusive impact, or the visual image enhanced by other influences, such as speech, writing, music and living situations, may have its results in either a changed attitude or the strengthening of the outlook we already have. In this way the images around us, the propaganda made – on any level whatsoever – the presence of the icon or the idol, may work as a conservative element, confirming and building up the direction people have already taken. In a stable cultural situation art certainly works like this. Also – to take a negative example – for that same reason dictators, sensing that free art may have the power to challenge their status quo, have often tried to compel the arts to be conservative and unchanging (Mierendorff 1957, 57).

In a way, art can persuade without convincing. Convincing, winning an argument, converting somebody to a particular truth or insight is not what the visual arts can do – or only in extremely rare cases. Thoughts and ideas can be expressed more directly – and therefore convincingly – with words, and for that reason the Bible teaches Christians that the Gospel should be proclaimed by means of words, and propagated through hearing. As an example from the field of music, Bach's St Matthew Passion, even though words are used, is not a good evangelizing instrument; even so, the fact that people listen to it does at least remind them that Christianity is still there, and exists as a viable option. The same can be said of church art from the Renaissance and Baroque period; I don't think anybody ever became a Roman Catholic just by looking at or studying these pictures – even the most beautiful of them – but they remind us that Christianity still plays a role in Western culture, and in this way these ideas they convey are kept alive and are shown to have at least been of importance to people at some time in history.

Art persuades. It will seldom, I think, influence a person directly in the sense that he will begin to imitate the acts that are shown in a painting. But in the way it depicts, in its total impact, in the mentality that speaks through the choice of subject as well as style, in the manner of representation, in short, in the anagogical element as defined in medieval art theory, art has its influence. Similarly a way of life, morals, and insights are taught to children not so much by overt lessons, but rather by the values inherent in the parents' attitudes and social background.

Art, of course, is an expression of the insights and beliefs of the artist, the group or movement or subculture of which he is a member or exponent, and more widely of the culture in which he is working. In a way art is part of that culture, and the role the arts play, the things they are asked to do, are part of the cultural patterns. Art is therefore subject to the customs and ethical norms prevalent in society. For example, in our society ('streakers' apart!) people don't show themselves nude, but in the artist's studio this can be done, and 'nudes' are certainly a respectable part of our cultural heritage and artistic production; they range from the small bronze copy of the Venus of Milo standing on the mantelpiece to the nude sculptures in parks and decorating fountains, from book illustrations to the masterpieces in museums and galleries. These are almost always without pornographic intention or content, and exist without raising questions in our minds whether the people who own these things are willing to parade in the nude or are immoral. On the other hand some kinds of 'nudes' will be considered to be pornographic within the patterns of our culture – this may raise difficult legal problems, but there are no problems in practice, as those looking for pornography know very well how to discern it (Shrapnel 1972; Fryer 1972; Longford Report 1972).

Once again, the arts express the insights and beliefs of the culture in which they play their part. The Fine Arts make explicit and visible the manner in which people look at things, what and how they see; art reveals both directly and by implication what is considered to be relevant and important – and, by omission, what is not deemed worthy of being expressed or depicted. The total impact of art is its meaning, which reveals a mentality – the scope and nature of cultural, moral or social values. This implicitness and explicitness makes clear what kind of gods a culture, a society, reveres. For the old pagan world this might be obvious, as well as for the great Christian era. It is no less clear, just walking through such an exhibition as the great one on Neoclassicism held in 1972 in London (The Age of Classicism, 1972), that Christianity was losing its cultural force and influence simply by the absence there of Christian subject matter. These days it seems to us either that there is in a way a hole in our culture, engendered by a non-religious religion, or that slowly new gods are coming in, the gods of pleasure, money and sex. Of course, if we look at present-day 'high' Fine Art, the modern art of the museum, we still look into the hole just mentioned – sometimes quite literally, as in Fontana's 'The End of God' (XX siecle, 1965), a canvas merely with holes cut in it, or again his 'Spatial Concept'. If on the other hand we widen our definition of the visual arts, as we have done, we see the other gods just by looking at the posters or at the advertisements in our magazines: pictures of holiday resorts, promising leisure and the open possibility of

Plate 63

Plate 66

sex (often slightly veiled, but that's also part of our culture and its morals) . . . examples abound (Berger 1972).

A curious example of what I have in mind is reproduced here: it was an advertisement in an American paper around 1900. The design is based on Titian's
Plate 65 *Assunta*, the world-famous painting in the Frari Church in Venice. It has been
'secularized' by showing, instead of apostles gazing at the heavenbound Virgin,
Plate 67 fashionable women gazing at a 'heavenly' corset, a new 'god', standing for
beauty, fashion, pleasure and – in the added announcement that money could be made by acting as an agent selling these corsets – cash. Such an example is almost a symbol of the spirit of the age.

Art creates the symbols *of* and *for* a society, the things it stands for and thinks relevant, the values it cherishes, and its aims (Barbu 1971, 96). Such a symbol
was, in the time of the French Revolution, not only the *tricolore* but also David's
Plate 70 *Oath of the Horatii* or his *Marat*. For the Florence of the early 16th century it was
Plate 69 Michelangelo's *David* and for the Gothic period not only the symbol of the cross,
but also the 'Beau Dieu', the figure of Christ in the portal of the cathedral in
Plate 68 Amiens, or the large *Madonna* by Cimabue (Uffizi, Florence). For the 19th
Plate 73 century one may think of Ingres's *La Source* or Holman Hunt's *Light of the world*
or van Gogh's *Potato eaters*, or, maybe even more apt are the countless monuments of great men in almost all cities of the Western world – testifying to the prevalent hero-worship – or the Eiffel Tower in Paris. And for our own age we
may think not only of the $ sign or the ☮ symbol, but also of Andrew Wyeth's
Plate 76 popular *Christina* picture, Dali's *Cross of St John of the Cross*, Andy Warhol's
Plate 77 *Campbell Soup Cans* and the latest popular 'ad' for a certain brand of 'bra' or
beer (Berger 1972; Pawek 1963, 249 f.). We may like or dislike these symbols, we may stand for the values they proclaim or reject them, we may even think they are irrelevant; yet they are there, showing the face of our era, expressing its overt and its secret thoughts and intentions. It is particularly through these symbols that the impact of art as visual communication will be made and will exercise its persuasion; maybe even more so when these works or items are 'hidden persuaders' and not recognized as such (Packard 1961), than when we are conscious of their meaning and the mentality they encourage.

Art, as I have said, can be a conservative element in a society, just because it reinforces again and again certain values. But a society is never a closed unit. At the beginning of this chapter I quoted from a book of 1822 ideas that were coined during the Baroque period. In any period of history there may be a mainstream, but there are also always side currents, counter-currents, and secondary streams. In a way the term 'culture', used to designate a certain period, only means the common denominator of different subcultures. A society is a complex whole of trends, some more advanced and some more conservative or even retarded. Now it is precisely in this interplay that art can really be influential. Where art is only expressing the prevalent cultural values, those that make up the 'common denominator', it 'works' conservatively, but at those points where it differs, certainly where it does so with persuasive force through its high quality, it can have an influence in promoting new ideas – ideas that are probably already alive in a subculture or counter-current. As long as art just expresses professed values, it only strengthens these; when it is at variance it can help towards a change. Of course, it can never do so when it is too different, when the forms or the ideas it embodies are too remote to be understood.

We may assume that art can exert the strongest influence when its message differs in an almost conformist way. The more its message is put over in an accepted artistic language (style), the better these new ideas will be understood. An example of this is Manet's *Déjeuner sur l'herbe* – we could also have chosen his *Olympia*. When Manet exhibited this painting in the mid-sixties of the nineteenth century, showing a picnic with two nude girls and some clothed men, apparently all contemporaries and some even well known characters, he caused quite a dispute, even a scandal (Hamilton 1961). Yet his composition and the way in which he handled the paint were almost traditional: the composition of the group was derived from a print by Marc'Antonio after Raphael, and the conception of the scene was related to Giorgione's famous *Concert champêtre* in the Louvre. Just because the work did not deviate from the accepted ways of making a painting, the one point in which it did differ came out very strongly, and in this way it could influence morals. The painting meant more than just that 'there are people in this world who act like this' – which I suppose nobody in those days would have doubted – but in the total context it implied that it was right and acceptable, even worthy of being the subject of a major work of art, and as such actually commendable. The same is true of Manet's other 'scandalous' picture, the *Olympia*, which portrays a reclining prostitute in the traditional composition of a Titian *Venus* or *Danae*. The values that those older paintings stood for – allegories employed to express universals – were shown to be dead as for Manet there were no longer any universals (Rookmaaker 1971, 78; see also Rosenblum 1967). Of course, as we have said before, a work of art can never be influential in a vacuum, and its tendencies have to be reinforced through other cultural elements – in Manet's case we can think of Flaubert's *Madame Bovary*, one of the first works of art to be brought to court on the charge of obscenity. Here again, what offended his contemporaries was the matter-of-fact and – as the prosecution maintained – photographic and uncommitted way in which the adultery of the main character was described. Certainly these works, together with the quasi-respectability of the many nudes shown in the annual exhibitions of the official *Salon*, marked a step in the direction of today's permissiveness.

So my thesis could be said to be that art can exert influence if it differs in its message and mentality from the current views, provided the gap is not too wide and the works remain intelligible – with the added provision that other cultural factors are working in the same direction or at least not neutralizing it. And I would emphasize again that these things can never be proved by quantitative sociological investigation. So we see the arts influencing society in a certain direction, step by step: only after the initial new ideas or values are accepted can the next step be taken. A good example of this, probably familiar to everyone, is the trend towards nudity – a form of permissiveness initially confined to depictions and gradually becoming a social reality in the last two or three decades. It cannot come as a surprise to anyone that advertisements, which are so very influential in our day (Berger 1972), have played the key role. Already in

Plate 72

the forties we find advertisements of 'bra's' showing women in underwear, even if it was done with some degree of modesty, by using drawings rather than photographs; or, if photography was used, the images were in silhouette, or rendered vague. Advertisements are meant to attract attention, and if the current trends are favourable we find that in due course another step can be taken. Of course it is nearly always done in such a way that modesty is not offended: it is a question of playing on the very boundaries of modesty, and yet these boundaries seem to grow wider as people become accustomed to each new and slightly daring step. In the sixties we saw this evolution – or, if you wish, revolution – gaining momentum so that around 1970 almost total nudity was acceptable in respectable magazines (I am not speaking here about pornography). This trend ran parallel to what was acceptable and permitted to be shown in films. Only after 1970 when magazines like *Penthouse*, and later *Playboy*, even began to show frontal nudity including the pubic region, did these things slowly come into magazines with a more general circulation, and in some countries more widely than in others. But today on TV and in 'family magazines' these things are accepted. So we see a change in morals, in this case in the acceptance of female nudity – to be followed more slowly by the acceptance of male nudity. Each step is heralded in the press, as if everybody were asking: can people really accept this, or have we now reached the limit? Now, too, the sex act has been filmed and photographed more and more openly with the result that the borderline between the 'blue' movie and the 'art' or 'entertainment' film has become much narrower. All this was preceded by an increasing frankness in displaying sexual activities in the visual arts – witness the prints done by the Dutch artist Veldhoen around 1960. But today things can be shown which would have caused a gallery to be closed on charges of indecency not more than ten years ago. Take, for example, the couple in the act of intercourse shown in a very naturalistic sculpture by John de Andrea at the Kassel Dokumenta exhibition in summer 1972, seen by thousands, but not even reported in the press as a scandal – and the fuss caused by Manet's picture just over a century ago seems out of all proportion.

Plate 75

These changes in art have their impact in real life. If the sexual revolution is progressing more slowly, a change in morals is discernible which manifests a more positive acceptance of the sexual side of humanity on the one hand, and a great laxity in these matters on the other hand – the much discussed permissiveness. In the same context we see new customs coming in, and fashions that allow more of the body to be exposed. Even if see-through blouses and the like still have not become fashion in the widespread sense, yet great changes can be noted on the beaches. Beginning in the fifties with the almost total acceptance of the bikini the recent trend towards nudity (total or monokini) on the beaches is now quite strong, and in some places along the Mediterranean coast or in California already an accepted fact.

Apart from the mentality, inherent in visual communication, that certainly strengthened this trend, I think that the visual example itself has been very important. Particularly, I feel, photographs and films of nude girls – first considered daring, then later accepted – have been very influential. Twentieth-century man feels, rightly or wrongly, that photographs are showing reality as it is; so, in a way, people were just copying things that were thought to be the fashion somewhere, maybe in the social environment of the 'jet set'. To this influence of the visual example given by art I should like to apply the term 'naturalistic fallacy'.

To explain this further we must look back to the 18th century. Of course there were many nudes to be seen in the arts of the preceding Baroque period, but they were obviously not naturalistic: the male and female figures shown in these pictures were almost never real naked men or women, but rather allegorical figures, ancient gods, beings outside our daily life and existence. The arts of those days were using natural forms, but were only in a very few exceptions naturalistic, and just as seldom realistic – naturalism being a term related to style, realism to subject matter. When art was realistic, for example in Dutch genre pieces, nudes were almost never depicted, just because the pictures were realistic.

Now naturalism in some way begins to suggest realism; this means that when in the beginning of the second half of the 18th century there was a strong trend towards naturalism, people also began to look at seemingly naturalistic works of art from the past as though they were realistic. This is the naturalistic fallacy, and we sense it very strongly in the writings of Winckelmann, the great proponent of Neoclassicism. He was cautious enough to add that 'sensual beauty furnished the painter with all that nature could give; ideal beauty with the awful and sublime; from that he took the Humane, from this the Divine' (Eitner 1971, 9). Yet Winckelmann was, I feel, deceived by the classical sculptures he studied, many of which show nude figures. Why the Greeks and Romans made them is one of the problems of cultural and art history which we need not go into here. But if we see a collection of classical works of art, for example the Vatican Museum, or a collection of plaster casts like the one in Charlottenburg (see *The Age of Classicism*, 1972, no. 188, reprod. p. 44), it might give us the impression that we are entering a nudist camp; that is, if we commit the error of the naturalistic fallacy in thinking that these things were an every day social reality in the days these works were made. Winckelmann fell into this trap, and in his *Thoughts on the imitation of Greek works in painting and sculpture*, 1755, he discussed at length not only the beauty of the ancient Greek people, but how the artists could daily see them in the nude around them: 'The Gymnasia, where, sheltered by public modesty, the youth exercised themselves naked, were the schools of art. These the philosopher frequented, as well as the artist. Socrates . . . Phidias for the improvement of his art by their beauty. . . . Here beautiful nakedness appeared with such a liveliness of expression, such truth and variety of situations, such a noble air of the body, as it would be ridiculous to look for in any hired model of our academies. . . . Phryne went to bathe at the Eleusinian games, exposed to the eyes of all Greece, and rising from the water became the model of the Venus Anadyomene. . . . Then every solemnity, every festival, afforded the artist opportunity to familiarize himself with all the beauties of Nature . . . .' (Eitner 1971, 7, 8). Just as an aside I may mention that the story of Phryne, a kind of Christine Keeler of the fourth century BC, was never related

Plate 79

Plate 78

before the late Hellenistic period. Its authenticity is hard to determine (Pauly-Wissowa 1892, s.v. *Phryne* and s.v. *Nacktheit*), as is that of other stories that tend in this same direction. Here we see the naturalistic fallacy working in late antique times, when people were looking at those same classical sculptures. For Winckelmann of course these stories served to confirm him in asserting that same fallacy (cf. Balet 1936, 236, 424). People who, after reading these lines from Winckelmann, written with such an enthusiastic glow, looked at the antique sculptures, and then at the modern ones in the Neoclassical style (cf. the recent exhibition of Neoclassicism in London) must have come to the conclusion that nudity in daily life was something positive and desirable. In the great revolutionary period at the end of the 18th century not only do we see a 'mode à la grecque' which was in a way tending towards nudity, at least in showing the body quite freely, but we hear also of nude swimming, and in yet other ways of nudity entering daily life (see also *The Age of Classicism*, no. 84). But the tide was to turn, and Victorian prudery was soon on hand to drive this all out of sight. Very interesting is the painting by Vincent of 1789, showing the girls of Crotona who are asked to exhibit their beauties for the painter Zeuxis so that he may choose the most beautiful parts of their bodies in order to make a composite beauty. It shows already, in the midst of the revolutionary tendencies, a generally bashful and prudish attitude, quite different from the dream of Winckelmann (*The Age of Classicism*, no. 263). The reason for this lies probably in the fact that the moral tone of the time was very much a reaction against the complete permissiveness of the eighteenth-century French nobility. It was as a sort of 'underground' movement particularly in the artistic circles in France with their 'bohemian' morality and way of life that the tendencies towards nudity as a social reality evolved, at least in paintings and sculptures – we are thinking of Manet, and also Courbet, Corot, and of course the *Salon* painters. These tendencies were to emerge once again in our own age, when the naturalistic fallacy was even more likely to prevail since the works were either realistic or naturalistic or both.

Plate 80

So in all these developments art has had a strong influence; on morality maybe in an indirect way, but certainly on our way of life, our customs and fashions, on the way in which the new ideas and morals (which are also very much a result of the growing influence of the idea of the social contract (Rookmaaker 1969, 45) and Freudian theories) are rendered concrete and realized.

I should like to give here another example of the impact of the visual arts on life. I have already mentioned the influence of paintings on the conception of gardens and parks. Related to this is the acceptance of high mountain scenery. In the 17th century people did not like the Alps and similar mountainous regions. The average traveller passing through such scenery in a coach would close the curtains in order not to see these horrors. But in the early 18th century we find Shaftesbury – and he is in the front line of a new sensibility in this respect – writing 'The wilderness pleases . . . Even the rude rocks, the mossy caverns, the irregular unwrought grottoes and broken falls of water, with all the horrid graces of the wilderness itself as representing Nature more, will be the more engaging, and appear with a magnificence beyond the formal mockery of princely gardens.' (In the *Moralist*, 1709, quoted in Huth 1950.) In this line of development we see that in the 18th century artists gradually began to paint such scenery – painters such as Cozens, Wilson, Towne, Sandby and others. These things were accounted for in aesthetics as well, even if they were placed in a special category – that of the 'sublime' (Nicholson 1959; Price 1794). In the years around 1800 we see the first visitors coming to Switzerland to enjoy the great mountain scenery: among them were such writers and poets as Goethe, Shelley, Wordsworth, Coleridge, the painter Turner, and many lesser men. In the 19th century this movement grew into tourism, first for the rich, and gradually in our century, into mass tourism. In this case the visual arts – together with literature – has opened the eyes of men to beauties they were previously unable to see, or rather, made them see the beauty of the things they had previously regarded as horrors. Slowly, just in the depiction of these things, they lost their horror, even if the awe remained. And today the new attitude is always reinforced through the posters that try to lure us to the mountain resorts – posters in which their beauty is exalted and emphasized, beauty which even the most common man now understands, while the 'horrors' are never shown, so that man begins to forget them. And there the basic idea of modern tourism is laid bare: adventure without danger (Boorstin 1961, 86 ff.).

Plate 71

We may conclude then that art in many ways seduces man, even if it does not convince him. It is not the subject matter, nor the style as such, but the total impact of the work that drives the message home; in McLuhan's terminology, by means of cool communication. Art opens our eyes to certain values, to certain beauties, to certain realities, and in its totality communicates more a mentality, a way of life, a way of looking at things than specific and definable morals or norms or rules. There is quite a difference in the mentality behind Ingres's *La Source* and that behind a nude by Otto Dix, the German painter working in the twenties who also idealized his subject, but instead of idealizing towards a heightened and more perfect beauty did so in the negative direction, dragging the beauties down. The same happens in the other arts: Mozart's *Magic Flute* will have convinced only a few people of the truth of Freemasonry, but the mentality behind it is one that seeks for a higher life and stands for higher values and for refined culture, while for example Prokofiev's *Love of Three Oranges* of 1918 drags all those ideals down into absurdity, and leaves us with very few values to uphold. In art serious values and tendencies are given form in a playful way – they are *played* – but a man who takes his girl out to a performance of *Il Seraglio* by Mozart will certainly be taught a better way to woo her (certainly not to abduct her) than if he takes her out to a film like *The Graduate* or Antonioni's *L'Avventura* (1960). The latter has been described in the following terms: 'Antonioni's film is an adventure story, though not of the sort that movie-goers are accustomed to. "In a cosmos devoid of absolutes", it says, "the only thing that human beings have is themselves, faults and all." ' (Kauffmann 1972.)

Plates 73, 74

I deliberately took examples from our own time, as I should like to end with a look at modern art and its influence. I totally agree with the following statement: 'Whereas art objects once symbolized an ordered cosmos, they are now assemblages of parts that do not belong to an ordered totality. Indeed collages ironically juxtapose such incompatibles, as make-believe and actuality. Art then becomes testimony to our dissatisfaction with our environment and our drive to snatch order out of chaos.' (Kuntz 1967.)

Art, as I suggested in the beginning of this chapter, at least in theory became divorced from life in the 18th century, and became a kind of religion standing for deep values, but totally outside reality. My response was that probably real art, the art in contact with and growing out of social reality, has found its refuge in such 'minor' arts as posters and advertising, through which its influence, as I have tried to show, has been greatest. But that does not mean that the 'high' art, the art of the gallery and museum, has no influence. Just because the artist had become a kind of high priest of culture but with no real function in social reality, while the 'minor' arts were often of a very low standard indeed, people like Ruskin and others saw that society had to change. They saw that people tried to misuse the arts to give them status and respectability, and in an unusual lecture Ruskin angrily told wealthy would-be patrons that, if they were honest, the building they wanted should be 'built to you great Goddess of "Getting-On" . . . I can only at present suggest decorating its frieze with pendant purses, and making its pillars broad at the base, for the sticking of bills' (Williams 1960, 145). The artists and their nearest friends, the true critics, became rebels and martyrs – except when they accepted the role of makers of status symbols – and implacable opponents of the bourgeoisie (Pelles 1963, 121).

The protest movement became very strong at the beginning of our century. The modern movement, a kind of unorganized strong and influential group alongside other twentieth-century art movements (Rookmaaker 1973) is the embodiment of protest against the dilemma of modern man, who has been reduced by science and modern psychology to a kind of 'naked ape' without freedom. Faced with the seeming absurdity of life, they began to subvert those values that the bourgeois were professing to stand for, but for which they had no true foundation, no base, and which had therefore become empty gestures. A participant of the Dada movement wrote later, 'After the self-satisfied rationalism of the 19th century, an ebullience of invention, of exploration beyond the realm of the visible and rational in every domain of the mind – science, psychology, imagination – was gradually breaking down the human, social and intellectual values which up until then seemed so solid. All of us, young intellectuals of that period, were filled with a violent disgust at the old narrow security. . . .' (Alford 1952, 270.) The arts were showing, in their very being, that the old values were dead. They showed that 'man is dead' (Sypher 1962; Lewis 1965), and out of this despair these works seemed to cry 'please do something' (see 'Commitment in art' in Rookmaaker 1971). They have had a great influence in forming the mentality of at least a minority, but it is an ever-growing group of people in our times. In the sixties the volcano erupted, and to the astonished bourgeois – who never thought much about art and completely ignored modern art – a strong movement looking for a cultural revolution, and related to a political revolution, came into the limelight. Its mentality was maybe best summed up by Tuli Kupferberg in a famous article in the *International Times* (Kupferberg 1967): 'The artistic revolution: great subverter of the hollow

71   COZENS *The Valley of Sion*. Chapter 12

72   MANET *Le Déjeuner sur l'Herbe*. Chapter 12

73   INGRES *La Source*. Chapter 12

74   OTTO DIX *The Artist and his Model*. Chapter

75   JOHN DE ANDREA *Arden Anders
and Nora Murphy*. Chapter

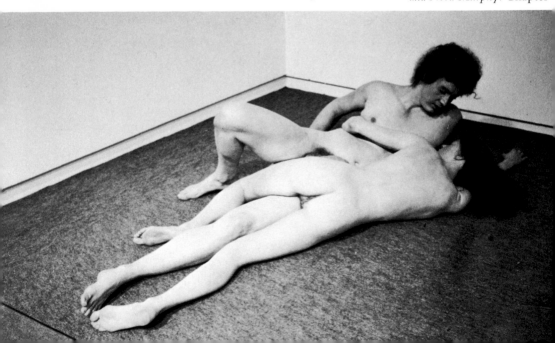

76 ANDREW WYETH *Christina's World*. Chapter 12

77 ANDY WARHOL *Soup Cans*. Chapter 12

78 H. D. C. MARTENS *The Antique Room of the Academy of Fine Arts at Charlottenburg.* Chapter 12

79 ZOFFANY *Charles Townley in his gallery.* Chapter 12

80 F. A. VINCENT *Zeuxis choosing his models from the most beautiful girls in Crotona.* Chapter 12

society. Mass your media – you are helpless before our skills. You don't know whether we are parodying you or you are parodying us any more. Beatles, Dylan, happenings, pop. Rock and Roll great continent. The Box will destroy you! Our bodies are opening. A thousand penises will bloom. Cunts too. We will force you to support us – to support the artists who are digging your dark grave. Join us before it is too late. Do not die! There is life enough for everyone! When the mode of the music changes the walls of the city shake.'

The revolution did succeed in many ways. The morals, way of life, fashion, attitudes, priorities and the general feeling of our times have changed. The students of today, the universities of today, the entertainment of our day, and even the political scene (Rookmaaker 1970) are totally different from those of ten years ago. Now the movement seems to have spent its energy, and at the time of writing it is relatively calm, but the fire is still smouldering. For the present what interests us most is that in all this the visual arts have played a very decisive role (Rookmaaker 1971). Again, not in a vacuum, but in conjunction with other cultural forces.

To make art is a responsible action. Even looking at it is a responsible action. Art may not seem to be very strong in its spiritual message, and its seduction can work very slowly. But the mentality inherent in it – a reflection of what moved the artist's mind and spirit – does touch us spiritually. Schiller instructed artists to 'Create for your contemporaries, but what they need, not what they praise' (von Schiller 1795, 57): indeed, there is no sense in creating empty beauties without meaning, but neither is there any sense in tearing down values that are worthwhile, or in going on to make almost pornographic things under the banner that in art everything goes. But I do agree with Ralph Pomeroy who wrote that 'Art is still basically for – protest is against' (*Art and Artists*, 1969, 62).

Bibliographical References

Chapter 1

ABERCROMBIE, L. 1926. *An Essay Towards a Theory of Art.* London.

ANON. 1961. Lysergic acid and psychotic art. *Spectrum* 9, 74–78.

ARNHEIM, R. 1966. *Towards a Psychology of Art.* London.

—— 1972. *Art and Visual Perception.* London.

BAHM, A. J. 1968. The aesthetics of organicism. *J. Aesthet. and Art Criticism* 26, 449–59.

—— 1972. Is a universal science of aesthetics possible? *J. Aesthet. and Art Criticism* 31, 3–7.

BALLO, G. 1969. *The Critical Eye. A New Approach to Art Appreciation.* London.

BARNETT, S. A. (Ed.) 1973. *Ethnology and Development.* London.

BARRON, F. 1963. *Creativity and Psychological Health.* New York.

BERGER, J. 1969. *Art and Revolution. Ernst Neizvestny and the Role of the Artist in the USSR.* Harmondsworth.

BRECQUE, M. LA. 1972. Photographic memory. *Leonardo* 5, 347–49.

BROOK, P. 1968. *The Empty Space.* Harmondsworth.

CARRITT, E. F. 1962. *The Theory of Beauty.* London.

CHAGUIBOFF, J. 1974. Can science lead to an understanding of beauty? *Leonardo* 7, 61–64.

CREEDY, J. (Ed.). 1970. *The Social Context of Art.* London.

Dartington Hall Trustees. 1946. *The Visual Arts.* Oxford.

EDWARDS, A. T. 1968. *Towards Tomorrow's Architecture. The Triple Approach.* London.

EHRENZWEIG, A. 1967. *The Hidden Order of Art. A Study in the Psychology of Artistic Imagination.* London.

FARR, M. 1966. *Design Management.* London.

FISCHER, E. 1964. *The Necessity of Art. A Marxist Approach.* Harmondsworth.

GETZELS, J. W. AND CSIKSZENTMIHALYI, M. 1967. Scientific creativity. *Science Journal* 3, 80–84.

GIMPEL, J. 1969. *The Cult of Art. Against Art and Artists.* London.

GOMBRICH, E. H. 1960. *Art and Illusion.* London.

HABER, R. N. (Ed.) 1970. *Contemporary Theory and Research in Visual Perception.* London.

HENDERSON, G. P. 1966. The concept of ugliness. *Brit. J. Aesthet.* 6, 219–29.

HODGE, G. P. 1969. El Greco: on ending the myth of distorted vision. *Abbottempo* 1, 10–15.

HOFSTADTER, A. 1973. The aesthetic impulse. *J. Aesthet. and Art Criticism* 32, 171–81.

HOLLISTER, L. E. AND HARTMAN, A. M. 1962. Mescaline, lysergic acid diethylamide and psilocybin: comparison of clinical syndromes, effects on color perception and biochemical measures. *Comprehensive Psychiatry* 3, 235–41.

JAKAB, I. 1968. *Psychiatry and Art.* Basel.

JELLY, O. 1963. *An Essay on Eyesight.* London.

LUCIE-SMITH, E. 1968. *Thinking About Art. Critical Essays.* London.

MOLNAR, F. 1974. Experimental aesthetics or the science of art. *Leonardo* 6, 23–26.

PHILLIPS, G. 1973. The social challenge to art in America. *Leonardo* 6, 219–25.

PICKFORD, R. W. 1967. *Studies in Psychiatric Art.* Springfield.

—— 1969. The psychology of ugliness. *Brit. J. Aesthet.* 9, 258–70.

—— 1970. Dream-work, art-work, and sublimation in relation to the psychology of art. *Brit. J. Aesthet.* 10, 275–83.

—— 1971. 'Stilwandel' (or radical change of style) in a normal artist. *Japanese Bulletin of Art Therapy* 3, 113–21.

—— 1972. *Psychology and Visual Aesthetics.* London.

PREUSSER, R. 1973. Relating art to science and technology: an educational experiment at the Massachusetts Institute of Technology (M.I.T.). *Leonardo* 6, 199–206.

RALEIGH, H. P. 1973. Film: the revival of aesthetic symbolism. *J. Aesthet. and Art Criticism* 32, 219–27.

READ, H. 1967. *Art and Alienation. The Role of the Artist in Society.* London.

ROOKMAAKER, H. R. 1970. *Modern Art and the Death of a Culture.* London.

ROTHSCHILD, L. 1972. Violence and caprice in recent art. *Leonardo* 5, 325–28.

SANDLE, D. 1967. The science of art. *Science Journal* 3, 80–85.

SCHMIDT, G., STECK, H., AND BADER, A. 1961. *Though This be Madness. A Study in Psychotic Art.* London.

SCHNEIDER, D. E. 1962. *The Psychoanalyst and the Artist.* New York.

SLATER, E. 1970. The problems of pathography, 209–15. *Acta Psychiatrica Scandinavica* 46, Suppl. 219. Studies dedicated to Erik Essen-Möller.

STEPHENSON, R. AND DEBRIX, J. R. 1970. *The Cinema as Art.* Harmondsworth.

STEVENI, M. 1968. *Art and Education.* London.

TOMLINSON, R. R. 1947. *Children as Artists.* Harmondsworth.

TREVOR-ROPER, P. 1970. *The World Through Blunted Sight.* London.

VALENTINE, C. W. 1962. *The Experimental Psychology of Beauty.* London.

VERNON, M. D. (Ed.) 1970. *Experiments in Visual Perception.* Harmondsworth.

WADDINGTON, C. H. 1969. *Behind Appearance. A Study of the Relations Between Painting and the Natural Sciences in this Century.* Edinburgh.

WEALE, R. A. 1968. *From Sight to Light.* Edinburgh.

WILLETT, J. 1967. *Art in a City.* London.

WILSON, F. A. 1963. *Art as Understanding.* London.

WOLLHEIM, R. 1968. *Art and Its Objects.* Harmondsworth.

Chapter 2

DEVALOIS, R. L. AND JACOBS, G. H. 1968. Primate colour vision. *Science* 162, 533.

GOJA, H. 1959. Zeichen Versuche mit Menschenaffen. *Z. Tierpsychol.* 16, 369–73.

GRETHER, W. 1940. Chimpanzee colour vision: 2. Colour mixture proportions. *J. Comp. Psychol.* 29, 179–86.

HUMPHREY, N. 1971. Colour and Brightness Preferences in Monkeys. *Nature* 229, 615–17.

—— 1973. Interest and Pleasure: Two determinants of a monkey's visual preference. *Perception* 1, 395–416.

—— 1974. The illusion of beauty. *Perception* 2, 429–39.

KELLOGG, W. N. AND KELLOGG L. A. 1933. *The Ape and the Child.* New York.

KÖHLER, W. 1925. *The Mentality of Apes.* New York.

KORTLANDT, A. 1959. Unpublished report quoted by Morris, 1962.

LAWICK-GOODALL, J. VAN. 1971. *In the Shadow of Man.* London.

—— 1973. Personal communication.

MORRIS, D. 1958. *The Story of Congo.* London.

—— 1962. *The Biology of Art.* London.

MUNTZ, W. R. A. 1962. Effectiveness of different colours of light in releasing the phototactic behaviour of frogs, and a possible function of the retinal projection to the Diencephalon. *J. Neurophysiol.* 25, 712–20.

RENSCH. B. 1957. Ästhetische Faktoren bei Farb- und Formbevorzugungen von Affen. *Z. Tierpsychol.* 14, 71–99.

—— 1958. Die Wirksamkeit ästhetischer Faktoren bei Wirbeltieren. *Z. Tierpsychol.* 15, 447–61.

SCHILLER, P. 1951. Figural preferences in the drawings of a chimpanzee. *J. Comp. Physiol. Psychol.* 44, 101–11.

Chapter 3

ADAMS, L. 1949. *Primitive Art.* Harmondsworth.

ALCOCK, J. 1972. The evolution of the use of tools by feeding animals. *Evolution* 26, 464–73.

BANNATYNE, A. 1966. The aetiology of dyslexia. Unpublished MS.

BARROW, T. T. 1956. Human figures in wood and ivory from Western Polynesia. *Man* 56, 165–68.

BODMER, W. F. 1972. Race and IQ: the genetic background, 83–113. In K. Richardson and D. Spears (Eds), *Race, Culture and Intelligence.* Harmondsworth.

BOHANNAN, P. 1956. Beauty and scarification amongst the Tiv. *Man* 56, 117–21.

—— 1961. Artist and critic in an African society, 85–94. In Marian W. Smith (Ed.) *The Artist in Tribal Society.* London.

CAMPS-FABRER, H. 1970. *Les Bijoux de Grande Kabylie.* Mem. XII. Centre de Recherches Anthropologiques Préhistoriques et Ethnographiques (Algérie). Arts et Métiers Graphiques. Paris.

CLAERHOUT, A. G. H. *et al.* 1965. The concept of primitive applied to art. *Current Anthrop.* 6, 432–38.

FARIS, J. C. 1973. *Nuba Personal Art.* London

FISCHER, J. L. 1961. Art styles as cultural cognitive maps. *Amer. Anthrop.* 63, 79–93.

FLEMING, A. 1972. Vision and design: approaches to ceremonial monument typology. *Man* 7, 57–73.

FORGE, J. A. W. 1965. Art and society in the Sepik. *Proc. Roy. Anthrop. Inst.*, 23–31.

FRASER, D. 1962. *Primitive Art*. London.

HALL, V. C. 1962. *Namatjira of the Aranda*. London.

HASELBERGER, H. 1961. Methods of studying ethnological art. *Current Anthrop.* 2, 351–84.

KOPPERS, W. 1950. The 'sketch book' of an Aurignacian artist. *Man* 50, 85–86.

KROEBER, A. L. 1963. *Style and Civilizations*. Berkeley.

MARSHACK, A. 1972. Cognitive aspects of Upper Palaeolithic engraving. *Current Anthrop.* 13, 445–77.

McCARTHY, F. D. AND MACINTOSH, N. W. G. 1962. The archaeology of Mootwingee, Western New South Wales. *Records of the Australian Museum* 25, 249–98.

MEGAW, J. V. S. 1970. Cheshire cat and Mickey Mouse: analysis, interpretation and the art of the La Tène Iron Age. *Proc. Prehist. Soc.* 36, 261–76.

MELDGAARD, J. 1959. *Eskimo Sculpture*. London.

MENDELSSOHN, K. 1974. *The Riddle of the Pyramids*. London.

MOLNAR, F. 1974. Experimental aesthetics or the science of art. *Leonardo* 7, 23–26.

MORRIS, D. 1961. Primate aesthetics. *Natural History* 70, 22–29.

—— 1966. *The Biology of Art*. London.

MURRAY, K. 1948. Ibo headdresses combining human and animal features. *Man* 48, 1–2.

NEWTON, E. 1967. *European Painting and Sculpture*. Harmondsworth.

OTTEN, C. M. (Ed.). 1971. *Anthropology and Art. Readings in Cross-Cultural Aesthetics*. New York.

PETERSON, 1972. Totemism yesterday: sentiment and local organisation among the Australian Aborigines. *Man* 7, 12–32.

POST, R. H. 1965. Notes on relaxed selection in man. *Anthrop. Anz.* 29, 186–95.

PRICE, R. 1970. Saramaka woodcarving: the development of an Afroamerican art. *Man* 5, 363–78.

RENSCH, B. 1972. *Homo Sapiens: from Man to Demigod*. London.

RIESER, D. 1972. *Art and Science*. London.

SALAMAN, R. N. 1939. Deformities and mutilations of the face as depicted in the Chimu pottery of Peru. *J. Roy. Anthrop. Inst.* 69, 109–22.

SANDLE, D. 1967. The science of art. *Science J.* 3, 80–85.

SCHILLER, P. H. 1951. Figural preferences in the drawings of a chimpanzee. *J. Comp. Physiol. Psychol.* 44, 101–11.

SHORTESS, G. K. 1974. Some physiological limitations on aesthetic experience in the visual arts. *Leonardo* 7, 57–59.

SIMMONS, D. C. 1957. The depiction of gangosa on Efik-Ibibio masks. *Man* 57, 17–20.

UCKO, P. J. AND ANDRÉE ROSENFELD. 1967. *Palaeolithic Cave Art*. London.

WILLCOX, A. R. 1963. *The Rock Art of South Africa*. London.

WILLETT, F. 1971. *African Art*. London.

WILSON, F. A. 1963. *Art as Understanding*. London.

WINGERT, P. S. 1954. Anatomical interpretations in African masks. *Man* 54, 69–71.

WOLFE, A. W. 1955. Art and the supernatural in the Ubangi district. *Man* 55, 65–67.

—— 1969. Social structural bases of art. *Current Anthrop.* 10, 3–44.

YUTANG, LIN, 1967. *The Chinese Theory of Art*. London.

YOUNG, J. Z. 1971. *An Introduction to the Study of Man*. Oxford.

Chapter 4

AMES, L. B., LEARNED, J., METRAUX, R. AND WALKER, R. 1953. Development of perception in the young child as observed in responses to the Rorschach Test blots. *J. Genet. Psychol.* 82, 183–204.

ARNHEIM, R. 1956. *Art and Visual Perception*. London.

BABSKA, Z. 1965. The formation of the conception of identity of visual characteristics of objects seen successively. *Monog. Soc. Res. Child Devel.* 30, No. 2, 112–24.

BERLYNE, D. E. 1970. Children's reasoning and thinking. In P. H. Mussen (Ed.), *Carmichael's Manual of Child Psychology*, 3rd ed. New York.

BERRY, J. W. 1966. Temne and Eskimo perceptual skills. *Internat. J. Psychol.* 1, 207–29.

BRUNER, J. S. 1966. On cognitive growth. In J. S. Bruner, R. R. Olver and P. M.

Greenfield (Eds), *Studies in Cognitive Growth*. New York.

BRYANT, P. E. 1966. Perception and memory of the orientation of visually presented lines by children. *Nature* 224, 1331–32.

CONRAD, R. 1971. The chronology of the development of covert speech in children. *Devel. Psychol.* 5, 398–405.

COUSINS, D. AND ABRANAVEL, E. 1971. Some findings relevant to the hypothesis that topological spatial features are differentiated prior to Euclidean features during growth. *Brit. J. Psychol.* 62, 475–79.

DEREGOWSKI, J. B. 1971. Responses mediating pictorial recognition. *J. Soc. Psychol.* 84, 27–33.

DI LEO, J. H. 1971. *Young Children and their Drawings*. London.

DRAGUNS, J. G. AND MULTARI, G. 1961. Recognition of perceptually ambiguous stimuli in grade school children. *Child Devel.* 32, 541–50.

ELKIND, D., KOEGLER, R. R. AND GO, E. 1964. Studies in perceptual development, II. Part-whole perception. *Child Devel.* 35, 81–90.

ELKIND, D. AND WEISS, J. 1967. Studies in perceptual development, III. Perceptual exploration. *Child Devel.* 38, 553–61.

GARDNER, R. W. AND MORIARTY, A. 1968. *Personality Development at Preadolescence.* Seattle.

GHENT, L. 1956. Perception of overlapping and embedded figures by children of different ages. *Amer. J. Psychol.* 69, 575–87.

GHENT, L. AND BERNSTEIN, L. 1961. Influence of the orientation of geometric forms on their recognition by children. *Percept. Motor Skills* 12, 95–101.

GIBSON, E. J. 1969. *Principles of Perceptual Learning and Development.* New York.

—— 1970. The ontogeny of reading. *Amer. Psychol.* 25, 136–43.

GIBSON, E. J., GIBSON, J. J., PICK, A. D. AND OSSER, H. 1962. A developmental study of the discrimination of letter-like forms. *J. Comp. Physiol. Psychol.* 55, 897–906.

GILGUS, J. S. AND HOCHBERG, J. 1970. Age differences in sequential form recognition. *Psychonom. Sci.* 21, 211–12.

GOODNOW, J. J. 1969. Problems in research on culture and thought. In D. Elkind and J. H. Flavell (Eds), *Studies in Cognitive Development*. Oxford.

GOTTSCHALK, J., BRYDEN, M. P. AND RABINOVITCH, M. S. 1964. Spatial organization of children's responses to a pictorial display. *Child Devel.* 35, 811–15.

GREENBERG, J. W. 1972. Synthesis and analysis of visually perceived forms by young children. *Percept. Motor Skills* 34, 735–41.

HESS, R. D. AND SHIPMAN, V. C. 1965. Early experience and the socialization of cognitive modes in children. *Child Devel.* 36, 869–86.

HOCHBERG, J. AND BROOKS, V. 1962. Pictorial recognition as an unlearned ability. *Amer. J. Psychol.* 75, 624–28.

HOLLENBERG, C. K. 1970. Functions of visual imagery in the learning and concept formation of children. *Child Devel.* 41, 1003–15.

HOLMES, A. C. 1963. A study of understanding of visual symbols in Kenya. *Overseas Visual Aids Centre*, No. 10.

HUDSON, W. 1960. Pictorial depth perception in sub-cultural groups in Africa. *J. Soc. Psychol.* 52, 183–208.

KAGAN, J. 1966. Developmental studies in reflection and analysis. In A. H. Kidd and J. L. Rivoire (Eds), *Perceptual Development in Children*. New York.

KAGAN, J. AND KOGAN, N. 1970. Individual variation in cognitive processes. In P. H. Mussen (Ed.), *Carmichael's Manual of Child Psychology*, 3rd ed. New York.

KAGAN, J. *et al.* 1964. Information processing in the child: significance of analytic and reflective attitudes. *Psychol. Monog.* 78, No. 1.

KATZ, J. M. 1971. Reflection – impulsivity and colour – form sorting. *Child Devel.* 42, 745–54.

KATZ, P. A., KARP, B. AND YALISOVE, D. 1970. Verbal mediation of children's perception. *J. Exp. Psychol.* 85, 349–55.

KEIR, G. 1970. The use of pictures as an aid to reading. *Reading* 4, 5–11.

KILBRIDE, P. L., ROBBINS, M. C. AND FREEMAN, R. B. 1968. Pictorial depth perception and education among Baganda school children. *Percept. Motor Skills* 26, 1116–18.

LAURENDEAU, M. AND PINARD, A. 1970. *The Development of the Concept of Space in the Child*. New York.

LEWIS, M., WILSON, C. D. AND BAUMEL, M. 1971. Attention distribution in the 24-

month-old child. *Child Devel.* 42, 429–38.

LIUBLINSKAYA, A. A. 1957. The development of children's speech and thought. In B. Simon (Ed.), *Psychology in the Soviet Union*. London.

LLOYD, B. B. 1972. *Perception and Cognition: A Cross-Cultural Perspective*. Harmondsworth.

LOVELL, K. 1959. A follow-up study of some aspects of the work of Piaget and Inhelder on the child's conception of space. *Brit. J. Educ. Psychol.* 29, 104–17.

MACCOBY, E. E. AND BEE, H. L. 1965. Some speculations concerning the lag between perceiving and performing. *Child Devel.* 36, 367–77.

MACKWORTH, N. H. AND BRUNER, J. S. 1970. How adults and children search and recognize pictures. *Human Devel.* 13, 149–70.

MALONE, C. A. 1966. Safety first. *Amer. J. Orthopsychiat.* 36, 3–12.

O'BRYAN, K. G. AND BOERSMA, F. J. 1971. Eye movements, perceptual activity, and conservation development. *J. Exp. Child Psychol.* 12, 157–69.

ODOM, R. D., McINTYRE, C. W. AND NEALE, G. S. 1971. The influence of cognitive style on perceptual learning. *Child Devel.* 42, 883–91.

OLIM, E. G. 1970. Maternal language styles and children's cognitive behavior. *J. Spec. Educ.* 4, 53–68.

OLVER, R. R. AND HORNSBY, J. R. 1966. On equivalence. In J. S. BRUNER, R. R. Olver and P. M. Greenfield (Eds), *Studies in Cognitive Growth*. New York.

OWEN, D. H. 1971. Developmental generality of a form recognition strategy. *J. Exp. Child Psychol.* 11, 194–205.

PEDERSON, F. A. AND WENDER, P. H. 1968. Early social correlates of cognitive functioning in six-year-old boys. *Child Devel.* 39, 185–93.

PIAGET, J. 1952. *The Origins of Intelligence in Children*. New York.

—— 1955. *The Child's Construction of Reality*. London.

—— 1969. *The Mechanisms of Perception*. London.

PIAGET, J. AND INHELDER, B. 1956. *The Child's Conception of Space*. London.

POTTER, M. C. 1966. On perceptual recognition. In J. S. Bruner, R. R. Olver and P. M. Greenfield (Eds), *Studies in Cogni-*

tive Growth. New York.

PRICE-WILLIAMS, D. R., GORDON, W. AND RAMIREZ, W. 1969. Skill and conservation: a study of pottery-making children. *Devel. Psychol.* 1, 769.

REED, S. K. AND ANGARAN, A. J. 1972. Structural models and embedded-figure difficulty for normal and retarded children. *Percept. Motor Skills* 35, 155–64.

ROBINSON, J. O. 1972. *The Psychology of Visual Illusion*. London.

RUDEL, R. G. AND TEUBER, H.-L. 1963. Discrimination of direction of line in children. *J. Comp. Physiol. Psychol.* 56, 892–98.

SANTOSTEFANO, S. AND PALEY, E. 1964 Development of cognitive controls in children. *Child Devel.* 35, 939–49.

SATTERLEY, D. J. AND BRIMER, M. A. 1971. Cognitive styles and school learning. *Brit. J. Educ. Psychol.* 41, 294–303.

SPITZ, H. H. AND BORLAND, M. D. 1971. Redundancy in line drawings of familiar objects. *Cognitive Psychol.* 2, 196–205.

TERMAN, L. M. AND MERRILL, M. A. 1937. *Measuring Intelligence*. London.

TRIESCHMANN, R. B. 1968. Undifferentiated handedness and perceptual development in children with reading problems. *Percept. Motor Skills* 27, 1123–34.

VERNON, M. D. 1940. The relation of cognition and phantasy in children. *Brit. J. Psychol.* 30, 273–94.

VURPILLOT, E. 1963. *L'Organisation Perceptive: Son Rôle dans l'Evolution des Illusions Optico-Géométriques*. Paris.

—— 1969. Contribution à l'étude de la différenciation perceptive chez l'enfant d'âge préscolaire. *Année Psychol.* 69, 37–54.

WISE, J. H. 1968. Stick copying of designs by pre-school and young school-age children. *Percept. Motor Skills* 27, 1159–68.

WITKIN, H. A. *et al.* 1962. *Psychological Differentiation*. New York.

WOHLWILL, J. F. AND WIENER, M. 1964. Discrimination of form orientation in young children. *Child Devel.* 35, 1113–25.

YANDO, R. M. AND KAGAN, J. 1970. The effect of task complexity on reflection-impulsivity. *Cognitive Psychol.* 1, 192–200.

YENDOVITSKAYA, T. V. *et al.* 1971. Development of sensation and perception. In A. V. Zaporozhets and D. B. Elkonin (Eds),

The Psychology of Preschool Children. Cambridge, Mass.

Chapter 5

GIBBS, EVELYN. 1934. *Child Art.* London.
KEPES GYORGY. 1965. *Education of Vision.* London.
LOWENFELD, VIKTOR. 1964. *Creative and Mental Growth.* London and New York.
McFEE, JUNE KING. 1970. *Preparation for Art.* Belmont, Cal.
MOHOLY-NAGY, LÁSZLÓ. 1947. *Vision in Motion.* Chicago.
PICKERING, D. AND J. M. 1974. *Pre-School Activities.* London.
PICKERING, J. M. 1971. *Visual Education in the Primary School.* London and New York.
READ, SIR HERBERT. 1945. *Education Through Art.* London.
RICHARDSON, MARION. 1948. *Art and the Child.* London.
VIOLA, WILHELM. 1942. *Child Art.* London.

Chapter 6

ARMSTRONG, R. E., RUBIN, E., STEWART M. AND KUNTNER, L. 1970. Susceptibility to the Müller-Lyer, Sander Parallelogram and Ames Distorted Room illusions as a function of age, sex and retinal pigmentation among urban Midwestern children. Unpublished monograph, Northwestern University.
BERKELEY, G. 1713. *Three dialogues between Hylas and Philonous.* London. Reprint edition, Chicago, 1927, 18.
BERRY, J. W. 1971. Müller-Lyer susceptibility: Culture, ecology or race. *International Journal of Psychology* 6, 193–97.
BRUNSWIK, E. 1956. *Perception and the representative design of psychological experiments.* Berkeley.
GREGORY, R. L. 1962. How the eyes deceive. *The Listener* 68, 15–16.
HERSKOVITS, M. J. 1948. *Man and his works.* New York.
—— 1951. On cultural and psychological reality. In J. H. Rohrer and M. Sherif (Eds), *Social psychology at the crossroads.* New York, 145–63.
HERSKOVITS, M. J., CAMPBELL, D. T. AND SEGALL, M. H. 1956. *Materials for a cross-cultural study of perception.* Evanston, Illinois: Program of African Studies, Northwestern University. Revised edition by M. H. Segall and D. T. Campbell, Indianapolis, 1969.
HOCHBERG, J. E. 1961. Visual world and visual field: perception, sensation and pictorial observation. Mimeographed.
HUDSON, W. 1960. Pictorial depth perception in sub-cultural groups in Africa. *Journal of Social Psychology* 52, 183–208.
JAHODA, G. 1971. Retinal pigmentation, illusion susceptibility, and space perception. *International Journal of Psychology* 6, 199–208.
LOCKE, J. 1690. *An essay concerning human understanding.* London.
Plato. *The Republic.* Trans. W. H. F. Rouse, *The great dialogues of Plato.* New York. 1956.
POLLACK, R. H. 1963. Contour detectability threshold as a function of chronological age. *Perceptual and Motor Skills* 17, 411–17.
—— 1963. Comments on 'Cultural differences in the perception of geometric illusions.' Personal communication to Donald T. Campbell, November 18, 1963.
SEGALL, M. H., CAMPBELL, D. T. AND HERSKOVITS, M. J. 1963. Cultural differences in the perception of geometric illusions. *Science* 139, 769–71.
—— 1966. *The influence of culture on visual perception.* Indianapolis.
STEWART, V. M. 1973. Tests of the 'carpentered environment' hypothesis by race and environment in America and Zambia. *International Journal of Psychology* 8, 83–94.

Chapter 7

ALBERTI, L. B. 1540. *De Pictura.* Basel.
BOULEAU, C. 1963. *The Painter's Secret Geometry.* London.
CANADAY, J. 1959. *Mainstreams of Modern Art.* New York.
DEMUS, O. 1947. *Byzantine Mosaic Decoration.* London.
FINLEY, G. E. 1967. *An Early Experiment with Colour Theory.* J. Warburg and Courtauld Inst. 30, 357–66.
GRIMM, H. *Leben Michelangelos.* Wien-Leipzig.
HUMPHREY, N. K. 1971. Contrast Illusions in Perspective. *Nature* 232, 91–93.
INNES, W. H. 1964. Seurat and the Science of Painting. Cambridge, Mass.

LESSER, G. 1957. *Gothic Cathedrals and Sacred Geometry*. London.

LOMAZZO, G. P. 1584. *Trattato dell'Arte della Pittura Scultura ed Architettura*. ed. 1844, Saverio del Monte.

MACH, E. 1866. Über den physiologischen Effect räumlich vertheilter Lichtreize. *S.-B. Akad. Wiss. Wien, math.-nat. Kl.* 54, Part 1, 131–46.

RUSSELL, J. 1965. *Seurat*. London.

SCHÖNE, W. 1953. *Über das Licht in der Malerei*, Berlin.

SHEARMAN, J. 1962. Leonardo's Colour and Chiaroscuro. *Zeits. f. Kunstgesch.* 25, 13–47.

WEALE, R. A. 1957. Trichromatic Ideas in the Seventeenth and Eighteenth Centuries. *Nature* 179, 648–51.

—— 1971. The Death of Pointillism. *The Listener* 85, No. 2188, 273–74.

WITTKOWER, R. 1966. *Bernini*. London.

YOUNG, T. 1807. *A Course of Lectures on Natural Philosophy and the Mechanical Arts*. 1, 439–40. London.

Chapter 8

BORNSTEIN, MARC, H. 1973. Color vision and color naming: a psychological hypothesis of cultural difference. *Psychol. Bull.* 80, 257–83.

COBB, S. R. 1972. A Study of the Normal Colour Vision of Art Students. *J. Biosoc. Sci.* 4, 153–59.

FIEANDT, KAI VON 1966. *The World of Perception*. Homewood, Ill.

LOWENFELD, VIKTOR, 1952. *The Nature of Creative Activity*, 2nd ed. London.

MYERS, C. S. 1925. *An Introduction to Experimental Psychology*, 3rd ed. Cambridge.

PICKFORD, R. W. 1972. *Psychology and Visual Aesthetics*. London.

RÉVÉSZ, G. 1950. *Psychology and Art of the Blind*. London.

TREVOR-ROPER, P. D. 1970. *The World Through Blunted Sight*. London.

Chapter 9

ARLIDGE, J. T. 1892. *The Hygiene, Diseases and Mortality of Occupations*. London.

HENDY, PHILIP 1960. *The National Gallery*. London.

HOLLINGSWORTH, T. H. 1964. The Demography of the British Peerage. Supplement to *Population Studies*, XVIII No. 2; Population Investigation Committee. London.

HUNTER, D. 1955. *Diseases of Occupations*. London.

H.M.S.O. 1971. *The Employment of Art College Leavers*. London.

—— 1971. *Social Trends*, 65, 170. London.

International Labour Office 1930. *Occupation and Health: an Encyclopaedia of Hygiene, Pathology and Social Welfare*. Geneva.

U.S. Bureau of the Census 1964. *Characteristics of Professional Workers*. Vol. ref. PC(2)7E. U.S. Department of Commerce, Washington.

Note: The British Census statistics mentioned in the text are published by H.M. Stationery Office on behalf of the Registrar General for England and Wales. Data on Occupations and Industries are given in those volumes which include these words in their titles, but for the 1966 Census the relevant information is given in the parts entitled 'Economic Activity'. Particulars of artists' mortality and fertility have been drawn from the Decennial Supplements: in 1911 from the volume 'Fertility of Marriage', in 1921 from 'Occupational Mortality, Fertility & Infant Mortality', and in 1931 from the 'Occupational Mortality' volume.

Chapter 10

BARTLETT, F. C. 1923. *Psychology and Primitive Culture*. Cambridge.

BRADFORD, E. J. G. 1913. A Note on the Relation and Aesthetic Value of the Perceptive Types in Color Appreciation. *Amer. J. Psychol.* 24, 546–54.

BULLOUGH, E. 1908. The 'Perceptive Problem' in the Aesthetic Appreciation of Single Colours. *Brit. J. Psychol.* 2, (1906–08), 406–63.

BURKITT, M. C. 1928. *South Africa's Past in Stone and Paint*. Cambridge.

BURT, C. 1939. Factorial Analysis of Emotional Traits. II. *Character and Personality* 7, 285–99.

CERBUS, G. AND NICHOLS, R. C. 1963. Personality Correlates of Picture Preferences. *J. Abnormal and Social Psychol.* 64, 73–78.

CHILD, I. L. 1969. Esthetics. Ch. 28 in

Handbook of Social Psychology, Eds G. Lindzey and E. Aronson. Reading, Mass.

EYSENCK, H. J. 1940. The General Factor in Aesthetic Judgements. *Brit. J. Psychol.* 31, 94–102.

—— 1941a. 'Type'-Factors in Aesthetic Judgements. *Brit. J. Psychol.* 31, 262–70.

—— 1941b. A Critical and Experimental Study of Colour Preferences, *Amer. J. Psychol.* 54, 385–94.

FECHNER, G. T. 1876. *Vorschule der Aesthetik*, Leipzig.

FRANCÈS, R. AND VOILLAUME, H. 1964. Une Composante du Jugement Pictural: La Fidelité de la Representation. *Rev. Psychol. Française* 9, 241–56.

HOGG, J. 1969a. A Principal Components Analysis of Semantic Differential Judgements of Single Colors and Color Pairs. *J. Gen. Psychol.* 80, 129–40.

—— 1969b. The Prediction of Semantic Differential Ratings of Color Combinations. *J. Gen. Psychol.* 80, 141–52.

KATZ, S. E. 1931. Color Preference in the Insane. *J. Abnor. and Soc. Psychol.* 26, 203–11.

KNAPP, R. H. AND GREEN, S. M. 1960. Preferences for Styles of Abstract Art and their Personality Correlates. *J. Projective Techniques* 24, 396–402.

MONROE, MARION. 1925. The Apparent Weight of Color and Correlated Phenomena. *Amer. J. Psychol.* 36, 192–206.

MORRIS, DESMOND, 1962. *The Biology of Art: A Study of the Picture Making Behaviour of the Great Apes and its Relationship to Human Art.* London.

MURRAY, D. C. AND DEABLER, H. L. 1957. Colors and Mood-Tones. *J. Appl. Psychol.* 41, 279–83.

MUNRO, T. 1948. Methods in the Psychology of Art. *J. Aesthet. and Art Criticism* 6, 225–35.

MYERS, C. S. 1914. A Study of the Individual Differences in Attitudes towards Tones. *Brit. J. Psychol.* 7, 68–111.

PICKFORD, R. W. 1943. The Psychology of Cultural Change in Painting. *Brit. J. Psychol. Monogr. Suppt.* 26.

—— 1972. *Psychology and Visual Aesthetics*, London.

ROBERTSON, J. P. S. 1952. The Use of Colour in the Paintings of Psychotics. *J. Ment. Sci.* 98, 174–94.

ST GEORGE, MARGARET W. 1938. Color Preferences of College Students with Reference to Chromatic Pull, Learning and Association. *Amer. J. Psychol.* 51, 714–16.

SAYCE, R. W. 1933. *Primitive Arts and Crafts.* Cambridge.

STAPLETON, JOAN H. 1953. A Study of the Significance of Colour and Form in Neurotic Patients' Free Paintings and Drawings. M. A. Thesis, University of Bristol (Unpublished).

THOULESS, R. H. 1932. A Racial Difference in Perception. *J. Soc. Psychol.* 4, 330–39.

VALENTINE, C. W. 1962. *The Experimental Psychology of Beauty.* London.

WARNER, S. J. 1949. The Color Preferences of Psychiatric Groups. *Psychol. Monogr.* 301.

WEXNER, L. B. 1954. The Degree to which Colors (Hues) are Associated with Mood Tones. *J. Appl. Psychol.* 6, 432–35.

WRIGHT, B. AND RAINWATER, L. 1962. The Meanings of Color. *J. Genet. Psychol.* 67, 89–99.

WYBURN, G. M., PICKFORD, R. W. AND HIRST, R. J. 1964. *Human Senses and Perception.* Edinburgh and Toronto.

Chapter 11

MONDRIAN, P. 1945. *Plastic Art and Pure Art.* Wittenbourn Schultz.

Report of the National Advisory Committee on Art Examinations. 1957. H.M.S.O.

Circular 340. 1958. Min. of Ed.

First Report of the National Advisory Council on Art Education. 1960. H.M.S.O.

Second Report of the National Advisory Council on Art Education. (Vocational Courses in Colleges of Art and Design). 1962. H.M.S.O.

First and Second Reports of the National Council for Diplomas in Art and Design. Followed by Memoranda 1–3. 1964 and 1970. Pub. N.C.D.A.D.

A Policy for the Arts. 1965. H.M.S.O.

Addendum to the First Report of the N.A.C.A.E. (Pre-Diploma Studies). 1965. H.M.S.O.

A Plan for Polytechnics and other Colleges. 1966. H.M.S.O.

NAYLOR, G. 1968. *The Bauhaus*. London.

Official Report of the First International Conference (London 1965) on the Professional Training of the Artist. 1968. V.L. Printing, London. for U.N.E.S.C.O.

Administrative Memorandum 6/69, Circular No. 7/71, and Administrative Memorandum 12/72. 1969, 1971 and 1972. Dept. of Ed. & Science.

CREEDY, J. (Ed.). 1970. *The Social Context of Art*. London.

The Employment of Art School Leavers (Survey). 1970. H.M.S.O.

Joint Report of the N.S.A.E. and N.C.D.A.D. (The structure of Art and Design Education in the Further Education Sector). 1970. H.M.S.O.

BLACK, M. 1971. Design Education in Great Britain. *Nature*, Vol. 231.

Coombe Lodge Further Education Staff College Publications:
(a) *Art and Design in the Polytechnics*. 1971. F.E. Staff College.
(b) *Development in Art Education*. 1974. F.E. Staff College.

Education: A Framework for Expansion. 1972. H.M.S.O.

Vocational Courses in Art and Design. 1974 H.M.S.O.

Chapter 12

The Age of Classicism, 1972 exhib. cat. London.

ALFORD J. 1952. The prophet and the playboy, Dada was not a farce. *College Art Journal* 11, 269 ff.

ANTAL, F. 1948. *Florentine Painting and its Social Background*. London.

—— 1966. Remarks on the methods of art history, in *Classicism and Romanticism and other Studies*. London, 175 f.

Art and Artists IV, 5, August 1969, special no.: Art and Revolution.

ASSUNTO, R. 1963. *Die Theorie des Schönen im Mittelalter*. Cologne.

BALET, L. 1936. *Die Verbürgerlichung der deutschen Kunst, Literatur und Musik im 18. Jahrhundert*. Leiden.

BARBU, Z., 1971. *Society, Culture and Personality*. Oxford.

BEEBE, M. 1964. *Ivory towers and sacred founts, the artist as hero in fiction from Goethe to Joyce*. New York.

BERGER, J. 1972. *Ways of seeing*. Harmondsworth.

BOORSTIN, D. J. 1962. *The Image or, What happened to the American dream*. London.

BOYD, J. D. 1968. *The function of mimesis and its decline*, Cambridge, Mass.

BOYD, review of, S. L. BARTSKY, 1969/70, in *J. of Aesthet. and Art Criticism* 28, 109–10.

BROWN, J. A. C. 1969. *Techniques of Persuasion*. Harmondsworth.

CASSOU, J. 1970. *Art and Confrontation: France and the Arts in an Age of Change*, (tr. from French). London.

CHASTEL, A. 1959. *Art et humanisme en Florence au temps de Laurent le Magnifique*, Paris.

DORIVAL, B. 1953. Expression littéraire et l'expression picturale du sentiment de la nature au XVIIe siècle français. *Revue de l'art* III, 44 ff.

EGBERTS, D. D. 1970. *Social radicalism and the arts, Western Europe, a cultural history from the French revolution to 1968*. New York.

EITNER, L. 1971. *Neo-classicism and Romanticism I, Sources and documents in the history of art*. London.

FOOT, P. 1970. *Morality and Art*. Oxford.

FRYER, P. 1972. The death of censorship. *Times Literary Supplement*, Feb. 18, 195.

GOMBRICH, E. H. 1965. Expression and communication, in *Meditation on a Hobby Horse*. London, 56 ff.

HAMILTON, G. H. 1961. *Manet and his critics*. New Haven Conn.

HASELDEN, K. 1968. *Morality and the mass media*. Nashville Tenn.

HIRSCHFELD, C. C. L. 1780. *Théorie de l'art des jardins*, (tr. from German). Leipzig.

HUTH, H. 1950. The American and nature. *J. of Aesthet. and Art Criticism* 13, 101 ff.

HUYGHE, R. AND RUDEL, J. 1971. *L'art et le monde moderne*. Paris.

KAUFFMANN, S. 1972. Michelangelo Antonioni's L'Avventura. *Horizon* XIV, No. 4, 49 ff.

KLAPPER, J. T. 1960. *The effects of mass communication*. Glencoe, Ill.

KRAUS, R. 1925. *Das Künstlerideal des Klassizismus und der Romantik*. Reutlingen.

KUNTZ, P. G. 1969/70. Review of A. Stokes, Reflections on the nude (1967), in *J. Aesthet. and Art Criticism* 28, 103 ff.

KUPFERBERG, TULI, 1967. When the mode of the music changes, the walls of the city shake. *International Times*, Feb/March.

LEITH, J. A. 1965. *The idea of art as propaganda in France 1750–1799.* Toronto.

LEVEY, M. 1966. *Rococo to Revolution.* London. Quotation on p. 121.

LEWIS, C. S. 1965. Abolition of Man, in *Riddell Memorial Lectures*, Durham, 2nd ed. London.

Longford Report. 1972. *Pornography* London.

MARCUSE, H. 1969. *Eros and Civilization,* 3rd ed. London.

McMULLEN, R. *Art, Affluence and Alienation.* New York.

MEISS, M. 1964. *Painting in Florence and Siena after the black death,* 2nd ed. New York.

MIERENDORFF, M. AND TOST, H. 1957. *Einführung in die Kunstsoziologie.* Cologne.

MILLER, J. E. AND HERRING, P. D. (Eds) 1967. *The Arts and the Public.* Chicago and London (1968).

MORGAN, D. N. 1967/8. Must art tell the truth? *J. Aesthet. and Art Criticism* 26, 17 ff.

NICHOLSON, M. H. 1959. *Mountain gloom and mountain glory, the development of the aesthetic of the infinite.* Ithaca N.Y.

PACKARD, VANCE 1961. *The Hidden Persuaders,* 16th ed. New York.

PANOFSKY, E. 1955. *Meaning in the visual arts.* Garden City N.J.

PAULY-WISSOWA, 1892 ff. *Realencyclopädie der class. Altertumswissenschaft.*

PAWEK, K. 1963. *Das optische Zeitalter.* Olten.

PELLES, G. 1962. The Image of the Artist. *J. Aesthet. and Art Criticism* 21, 119 ff.

—— 1963. *Art, Artists and Society, painting in England and France 1750–1850.* Englewood Cliffs, N.J.

PRICE, U. 1794. *Essays on the Picturesque as compared with the sublime and the beautiful, and on the use of studying pictures for the purpose of improving real landscape.* London.

RALEIGH, H. P. 1969. Value and artistic alternative, speculations on choice in modern art. *J. Aesthet. and Art Criticism* 27, 293.

READ, H. 1947. *Art and Society.* London.

—— 1958. *Education Through Art.* London.

ROOKMAAKER, H. R. 1969. *Art and the Public Today,* 2nd ed. L'Abri, Huémoz-sur-Ollon, Switzerland.

—— (Ed.) 1970. Nota: cultuur en kunst, *Anti-Revolutionaire Staatkunde* XL, 489 ff.

—— 1971. *Modern Art and the death of a culture,* 2nd ed. London.

—— 1972. *Gauguin and 19th century art theory,* 2nd ed. Amsterdam.

—— 1973. Modern Art and Gnosticism. *Jahrbuch für Aesthetik und allgemeine Kunstwissenschaft* XVIII, 162–74.

ROSENBLUM, R. 1967. *Transformation in late 18th century art.* Princeton.

RUDISILL, R. 1971. *Mirror image, the influence of the daguerreotype in American society.* Albuquerque.

RUDISILL, review of, by C. CHIARENZA, 1972, in *Art Journal* XXXI, 344 f.

VON SCHILLER, F. 1947 (orig. 1795) *Über die aesthetische Erziehung des Menschen.* Herford.

SEGALL, M. H. 1966. *The influence of culture on visual perception.* Indianapolis.

SHRAPNEL, N. 1972. The porn market. *Times Literary Supplement,* Feb. 11, 159.

SHRODER, M. Z. 1961. *Icarus, the Image of the Artist in French Romanticism.* Cambridge, Mass.

SIMSON, O. VON, 1965. Rubens' Maria de Medici cycle. *L'oeil* 125, 3 ff.

STROUD, D. 1962. *H. Repton.* London.

SYPHER, W. 1962. *Loss of Self in modern literature and art.* New York.

Time. 1975, April 7. The mural message (on the impact of public murals in East Los Angeles).

WILCOX, J. 1953. The beginnings of L'art pour l'art. *J. Aesthet. and Art Criticism* 11, 360 ff.

—— 1953. Le genèse de la théorie de l'art pour l'art en France. *Revue d'Esthétique* VI, 1 ff.

WILLIAMS, R. 1960. *Culture and Society 1780–1950.* London.

—— 1968. *Communications,* 2nd ed. London.

Sources of Illustrations and Acknowledgments

Colour Plates

I Collection Pasteur Ch. Gaillard. II Collection Dr A. Bader. III Collection Donald Harker, London. IV Private Collection, Los Angeles. V–VIII Photos J. M. Pickering.

Monochrome Plates

2. Völkerkundemuseum der Universität Zürich. 3. Collection Miss Mary Moore. 4, 5, 6. Courtesy the Trustees of the British Museum (Natural History), London. Photos D. Brothwell. 7. Photo Michael Lyster. Courtesy of Desmond Morris. 8. Desmond Morris: *The Biology of Art*, Methuen & Co., 1962. 9. Photo R. Edwards. 10. V. C. Hall: *Namatjira and the Aranda*, Angus & Robertson, 1962. 12. Courtesy the Trustees of the British Museum (Natural History), London. 13. Musée de l'Homme, Paris. 14. Archaeological Institute of the Czech Academy of Sciences, Prague. Photo J. Kleibl. 15. Photo Douglas Mazonowicz. 16. Photo Archives Photographiques, Paris. 17. Cyprus Museum, Nicosia. 18. Archaeological Museum, Teheran. Photo Josephine Powell. 19. Amman Museum. Photo courtesy British School of Archaeology, Jerusalem. 20. Photo Peter Clayton. 21. Courtesy the Trustees of the British Museum, London. 22. Directorate General of Antiquities, Iraq. 23. Cairo Museum. Photo Griffith Institute, Ashmolean Museum, Oxford. 24, 25. Courtesy the Trustees of the British Museum, London. 26. Field Museum of Natural History, Chicago. Photo Werner Forman. 27. Courtesy the Trustees of the British Museum, London. 29. Courtesy the Metropolitan Museum of Art, New York; Munsey Fund, 1924. 30. Freer Gallery of Art, Washington, DC. 31–35. Photos J. M. Pickering. 36. Mansell Collection. 37. Stadtbibliothek, Trier. Photo Marburg. 38. Mansell Collection. 39. National Gallery, London. 40. Photo Walter Drayer. 41. Photo Brogi. 42. Photo Alinari. 43. Photo Anderson. 44. Louvre, Paris. 45. Victoria and Albert Museum, London. 46. Formerly Kaiser Friedrich Museum, Berlin (destroyed). 47. National Gallery, London. 48. Louvre, Paris. Photo Giraudon. 49. Photo Mansell-Alinari. 50. National Gallery, London. 51. Nantes Museum. Photo Royal Academy of Arts, London. 52. Metropolitan Museum of Art, New York; Purchase, 1955. Joseph Pulitzer Bequest. 53. National Gallery, London. 54. Albright-Knox Art Gallery, Buffalo. 57, 58, 59, 60, 61. V. Lowenfeld: *The Nature of Creative Activity*, London, 1939. 62. Photo Deutsche Fotothek, Dresden. 63. Photo © B. T. Batsford. 64. Photo A. F. Kersting. 65. Photo Mansell-Anderson. 68. Photo Mansell Collection. 69. Photo Alinari. 70. Louvre, Paris. Photo Bulloz. 71. City Museum & Art Gallery, Birmingham. 72. Louvre, Paris. Photo Archives Photographiques. 73. Louvre, Paris. Photo Bulloz. 74. Private Collection. Photo Staatsgalerie, Stuttgart. 75. O. K. Harris Gallery, New York. Photo Edward Lucie-Smith. 76. Museum of Modern Art, New York. 77. Photo Frank J. Thomas. 78. Thorwaldsens Museum, Copenhagen. 79. Burnley Borough Council, Towneley Hall Art Gallery and Museums. 80. Louvre, Paris.

For permission to reproduce line illustrations we wish to thank the undermentioned:

CHAPTER 1: Fig. 1 *Science Journal*
CHAPTER 2: Figs 1, 2, 8–11, 16–18, 22, 23 Desmond Morris and Methuen & Co., London; Figs 3–7, 12–15, 19–21 P. Schiller and *J. Comp. Physiol Psychol.*
CHAPTER 3: Fig. 2 Dolf Riesser and Van Nostrand Reinhold Co., New York and Studio Vista, London.
CHAPTER 4: Fig. 1 D. Cousins & A. J. Angaran and *Brit. J. of Psychol.*; Fig. 2 S. K. Reed & A. J. Angaran and *Perceptual & Motor Skills*; Fig. 4 W. Hudson and *J. Soc. Psychol.*; Fig. 5 J. H. Di Leo and Constable & Co., London; Fig. 6 R. Arnheim and Faber & Faber, London; Fig. 7 E. Vurpillot and *Année Psychologique*; Fig. 8 K. G. O'Bryan & F. J. Boersma and *J. Exp. Psychol.*
CHAPTER 10: Fig. 1 R. W. Pickford and Hutchinson Publishing Group, London; Fig. 2 R. H. Poore and Baker & Taylor, New York and Batsford, London; Figs 3–8 G. M. Wyburn, R. W. Pickford & R. J. Hirst and Oliver & Boyd, Edinburgh and University Press, Toronto; Fig. 9 R. H. Thouless and *J. Soc. Psychol.*

Index

Numerals in italic refer to plate numbers

General

aesthetics 12, 13, 18, 37, 39, 49, 52, 133, 162; primate 39, 40, 42, 93; experimental 152–4, 160
Altamira 47, *15*
America 111, 161
Amerindians 52, 61, *26*
Antonioni 191
apes 18–31, 38–40, 42. *See also* primates
apperceptive types 159–60
art criticism 11–12, 13, 17, 177, 192
artistic profession, classified 140–1; growth of 143–8
astigmatism 129–30
Australia 52, 111; aborigines 52, 136, *10*
australopithecines 41

BaKwele 161
Baroque art 118, 120, 162, 184, 189, *62*
basketry 49
Batelela tribe *28*
behaviour 151; art as 98–100
Belgian Congo 52
Benin 51, *25*
biology and art 17, 31, 41, 45, 49, 62, 141–3; and variation 44–50
blindness 129, 130–3, 144, 153
body ornamentation 46, 50, 51; paint 46, 47, *9*
bone artifacts 48
brain 13, 39, 44
Bushmen *2*; cave paintings 164
Byzantine art 115, 116

Cambridge, Round Church 116, 117
Capitol, Rome 121
cave art 18, 42, 44, 47–9, 164, *15, 16*
Cefalú Cathedral 116, *36*
child art 15, 18, 31, 67, 70, 71, 131, 133
children, visual perception in 64–87, 92–7, *V–VIII, 31–5*; individual differences 76–86; visual education for 88–97
chimpanzee 19, 20–31, 38–40, *III, IV*; Alpha 20, 23, 24, 26, 27, 29, 30, 31, 39; Bella 30, 31, *7*; Congo 20, 21, 22, 23, 25, 26, 27, 28, 30, 31, 38, *8*; Gua 20; Joni 21, 22; Jonny 30
Chimu 61
China 62, *29, 30*
Churuga 48
cinema 17, 188, 191
clan designs 52

classical art 162
clothing 61
colour 93, 95, 96, 120, 122, 125, 126, 127, 128, 159–60, 163, 171; dislike of 159; preference 32, 37, 38, 45, 161, 162, 163; use by chimpanzees 30
colour blindness 19, 49, 133–8
colour vision 19, 49; defective 129, 133–8; racial differences in 135–6
composition 39, 40
computer art 13
conceptualization 74–6
Counter-reformation 121
Coventry Cathedral 116
crafts 49
creativity 90, 164, 170–1; in primates 19–30; in primitive societies 49; in children 93, 94
Cubism 112
culture, and art 12, 41, 44, 45, 49, 62, 76, 98–114, 151–64, 171, 192, 185–6
curriculum, development in art 92, 93–4

Dada movement 192
definition, of visual art 10–17, 183
design 168–9, 171; clan 52; clothing 61, 62
distance 69, 130
drama 17, 49
drugs 10, 13
dry paintings 53

education, art 15, 17, 88–97, 165–78
Efik-Ibibio masks 61
Egbert Codex 116, *37*
Egypt 11, 50, 52; pyramids 50; tombs 52; use of colour 136
electron microscopy 13, *4–6*
embedded figures test 85, 86
empathy 158
environment, and art 17, 41–63
Eskimo art 52, 85
'ethnographic' art 61
ethology 14. *See also* behaviour
Expressionist painters 88, 89
evolution, and art 41–63, 130

fashion 61, 197
fertility, in artists 139, 141, 143
figures, multiple 26; Byzantine 116; human 21, 70; ivory 52; matching 66; single 23; tracing 67
figurines 50, 52, *13*

Fine Art(s) 10, 168, 170, 183, 185
Florence 117, 118; Baptistery *41*; Cathedral 116, *38*; Laurentian Library 120; San Spirito *42*; S. Maria Novella 117
folk art 10, 42
form 118, 119; perception of 65–71
forms, complex 67

gelede dancers 52
Gestalt psychology 90, 91, 92, 108, 154, 155, 156, 157
Goethe 134
Gothic art 116, 117
great apes 20, 21
Greece 62, 128, *24*

Hadza 51
Haida 52
hallucination 10, 128
haptic art 131–3, *58*, *60*, *61*
Hogarth's Line 153
Homo erectus 46, 47
Homo sapiens 47, 48

Ibo 52
icons, Russian 163
illness, in artists 139, 141
illusions, visual 68, 111
imagery 74–6
Impressionists 125, 126–7, 129
Indo-European art 100
industry, and art 166

Japan 62, 153, 161, 162
jewellery, folk 52

Kinetic art 127
Kwakiutl 52

Laocöon 118
Lascaux 47, *16*
light 92, 93, 95, 96, 119–20, 122, 125, 128, *32*, *33*
longevity, in artists 139
Los Millares 48

Mach-bands 126, *56*
Makapansgat 41
Maori 11, *1*
Mannerism 127
marriage, in artists 139, 141
masks, Efik-Ibibio 61; BaKwele 161
Medici 179, 180
mental abilities 44; abnormality 14, 18
modern art 131, 133, 136, 158
Mogul painting 163
monkeys 32–8, 39; New World 19; Old World 19

morality, and art 14, 179–97
mortality, in artists 139, 141, 143
motivation, in chimpanzees 30, 38
Müller-Lyer illusion 68, 111
myopia 129

Navaho 61, *11*
Neoclassicism 180, 185, 189, 190, *63*
New Guinea 111; decorated houses 52
Nepomuk church, Munich 121
neurophysiology, and art 10, 12, 45
Niaux 48
Nuba art 51
nudity 187–90

Op art 127
Oppel illusion 68
Oriental art 111, 158
ostrich shell 11, *2*

Paestum 118, *40*
painting, European 62, 63; Indian 111; impressionist 125, 126–7
Palaeolithic 42, 47, 49, 50, 164, *12*; Upper 44, 48, 49, *13*, *14*
Pantheon 116
Pantocrator 115
Parthenon 118
perception, visual 13, 14, 18–40, 49, 100–14, 130–3, 154–60, 169, 171, 177; primate 18–40; depth 157; in children 64–87, 92–7, *31–5*; egocentric 64; haptic 130–3
perceptual activity 65, 74, 76–87, 92–7
Persian art 163
personality 162, 177
perspective 119, 157, 158
Peru 61
photography 17
Pleistocene 46, 47, 62
Polynesia 52
Population statistics, and art 139–50
pottery 49, 161, 162
primates 18–40, 47; visual preferences 32–8, 39
'Primitive' art 10, 42, 50, 131, 133, 158
prosimians 19
psychiatry 13, 163
psychiatric art 13, 154, 163, *I, II*
psychoanalysis 89, 98, 99
psychological testing 11
psychology, and art 13, 127, 151–64, 177; cross-cultural 76, 98–114, 161–2; social 152
psychopathological art 13, 14
Puerto Rico 161
Purkinje-shift 120

racial differences, in colour vision 135–6; among artists 149
red ochre 47
religious art 49
Renaissance 111, 112, 116, 117, 118, 119, 120, 122, 144, 179, 180, 184
revolution 14, 45, 192–3
Revolution, French 179–80
rock art 42
Rococo art 180
Romanesque art 116
Rome 62, 118

San Andrea, Mantua 117, *43*
Sander Parallelogram 108, 109, 110
scarification 51, 52
schizophrenia 14
science, and art 12, 13, 17
Scotland 111, 164
scribbling 70
shape 95, 96; copying shapes 67, 70, 71
Sierra Leone 111
society, in relation to arts 14, 15, 43, 44, 45, 49, 50–62; Western 179–97
space 92, 93, 95, 120–1, 128, 171
students 137–8, 166, 170, 197; courses for 148–9, 168–9, 171–8
sunbursts 71
Surinam 61
surrealism 179–80

tapestry 116, 126
tattooing 42

technology, and art 177
teeth, chipping 52
television 17, 188
Tempio Malatestiano, Rimini 117
terminology, in art 42
time, art in relation to 43, 62
Tiv, body decoration 51
Tlingit sculptors 52
Toledo Cathedral 121
tools 46, 48, 49
tomb paintings 49
trichomats 18, 122
Trier 116
trompe l'oeil 115–28
Tsimshian sculptors 52
Tutankhamun *23*

Ur *21*, *22*

variety, style and society 50
Venus of Milo 185
Venus of Willendorf 115
verbalization 74–6
visual attention 71–4
visual preferences 152–3, 160, 161, 162–3; in animals 32–40
vision, binocular 19, 130, 157; colour 19, 49, 133–8; ambient 71; defective 49, 129–38; stereoscopic 130, 157; monocular 157
visuo-spatial ability 47, 93

Westminster Abbey 117
wood-carving 61

Artists

Adam, R. 184, *64*
Alberti 118, *43*

Balla, G. 125
Bausola, F. 132
Bernini 121
Bigio, N. 116, *38*
Braque 129
Brunelleschi 118, 119, 120, *42*

Canaletto 126, *53*
Caravaggio 122
Carpaccio 126
Cézanne 129
Claude 142
Cimabue 186, *68*
Constable 119, 135, 137
Corot 190

Courbet 190
Cozens 191, *71*

Dali, S. 186
David, J.-L. 186, *70*
De Andrea, J. 188, *75*
Degas 125, 129
Delacroix 122, 125, 126
De La Tour 122, *51*
Derain 129
Dix, O. 191, *74*
Donatello 118, 119, *45*
Duchamp, M. 125
Dufy 129
Dürer 119, 120, 122

Elsheimer 122, *50*
El Greco 129, 130, 135, 136

Ernst, M. 180

Fontana, L. 185, *66*

Gentili 11
Ghiberti 118, *41*
Giorgione 187
Giotto 62, 142
Gislebert, M. 116
Gonelli, G. 132
Goya 158

Hals, F. 118, 119
Harris, M. 122, 125
Holbein 130
Honthorst 122
Hunt, H. 186

Ingres 186, 191

Kandinsky 11
Kleinhans 132
Knight, L. 16
Kokoschka, O. 16

Landshut, M. von 119
Leonardo da Vinci 112, 120, 122, *47, 48*
Lomazzo, G. P. 119, 120
Lowry, L. S. 16

Manet 187, *72*
Martens, H. D. C. *78*
Master of the Rebel Angels *44*
Masuelli 132
Matisse 129
Michelangelo 121, 127, 141, 186, *49, 69*
Monet 129
Moore, H. 11, 16, *3*
Mulready, W. 135
Munnings, A. 16

Namatjira, A. 45, *10*
Nerio, U. di 116, *39*
Newton 122
Nicholson, B. 16

Pasmore, V. 16

Pevsner, A. 16
Picasso 11, 133
Piero della Francesca 116, 119, 120
Pollock, J. 127, *54*
Poons, L. 127
Poussin 142

Raphael 127, 187
Rembrandt 118, 122
Renoir 44, 125, 129
Reynolds 122
Richier, G. 16
Riley, B. 128
Rodin 142
Rubens 142, 179

Sandby, P. 191
Scapini, G. 132
Schmitt, J. 132
Scott, P. 16
Segonzac 129
Seurat 125, 126, 127, *52*
Signorelli 119, *46*
Stella, F. 127, 128
Sutej, M. 128, *55*
Sutherland 116

Titian 44, 186, 187, *65*
Towne, F. 191
Turner 125, 134–5, 191

Uccello 120, 134

Van Gogh 11, 158, 186
Vasarely 128
Vasari *49*
Velasquez 119
Veldhoen 188
Vidal, L. 132
Vincent, F. A. 190, *80*

Warhol, A. 186, *77*
Wilson, R. 191
Wyeth, A. 186, *76*

Zoffany *79*